D1507829

DISPLACED

or

How I got from Budapest to Berkeley
In a Roundabout Way

—

My Emigration Chronicles—1942 to 1961

by

GEORGE KAPUS

DISPLACED

or

How I got from Budapest to Berkeley
In a Roundabout Way

—

My Emigration Chronicles—1942 to 1961

by

GEORGE KAPUS

Alive Book Publishing

Displaced
Copyright © 2017 by George Kapus

All rights reserved.
No part of this book may be reproduced or transmitted in any
form or by any means without written permission from the
publisher and author.

Additional copies may be ordered from the publisher for
educational, business, promotional or premium use.
For information, contact ALIVE Book Publishing at:
alivebookpublishing.com, or call (925) 837-7303.

Book Design by Alex Johnson

ISBN 13
978-1-63132-043-9

ISBN 10
1-63132-043-24

Library of Congress Control Number: 2017960050

Library of Congress Cataloging-in-Publication Data
is available upon request.

First Edition

Published in the United States of America
by ALIVE Book Publishing and ALIVE Publishing Group,
imprints of Advanced Publishing LLC
3200 A Danville Blvd., Suite 204, Alamo, California 94507
alivebookpublishing.com

PRINTED IN THE UNITED STATES OF AMERICA

10 9 8 7 6 5 4 3 2 1

This book is dedicated to my father, George Kapus Sr. and my mother Maria Kapus who got us all out before the Communists got in, and all those relatives and friends we had to leave behind.

For Bonnie Belle for her encouragement and patience

For my daughters, Christina and Gizella,
Hope you'll like my story.

To Karen Nelson, a good friend who went through my manuscript with a fine-toothed comb and corrected my wayward typing, many thanks

From the *MIRIAM WEBSTER* online Dictionary:
dis·place/ displaced

To remove from the usual or proper place; *specifically*: to expel or force to flee from home or homeland <*displaced* **persons**> Example: WWII *displaced* hundreds of thousands of people; me being one of them.

We lost our home and all our belongings. We lost relatives and friends. But, we never lost hope.

CONTENTS

RETROSPECT

But for the grace of God, our bones might have been swept away by the winds of time, along with the rubble that used to be our home and the rest of the waste left behind in the wake of the multitude US B-24 and Russian bombing raids of WWII. I was born in Budapest and up to that morning in the spring of 1945, I was a happy child, my parents fully expecting me to grow up a happy Hungarian, as soon as mankind regained its sanity. But, Mankind doing what Mankind does best, it kept on making war. Along with thousands of other weary and disenfranchised human beings with no voice for either side of the conflict, we marched indefatigably toward the west, to Austria and safety, where my parents and I would become, with thousands of others, *displaced persons*. With every intention of returning home as soon as the machines of war ground to a halt, we waited and waited until fate nudged us further and further west and returning home vanished from sight and hope led to hopelessness. Following several iterations of this *ism* or that, the Blue Danube turned Red and Hungary was swallowed up by the worst kind of *ism*: Communism. A friendly hand hailed us and we sailed across the Atlantic and rode the iron rails as far west as we could get; California! Here, we settled and within a short time, I became as American as Baseball and apple pie, though I could still speak my native Hungarian and some German and French that I had picked up along the way. This had certainly not been planned by us mere mortals. A divine and much higher power had set in motion a series of perplexing events that would whisk a little kid from Budapest and send him on a long, circuitous route all the way to of all places, Berkeley, California, US of A in nineteen-hundred and fifty-six. And, here I still am, several decades later, telling you my story. As perplexing and devastating as my story started out, in retrospect, my childhood, growing up and all wasn't really that bad; it was what it was. As you will see, by the time we settled down in Berkeley, I got to travel a lot, learned a couple languages along the way and made a ton of friends. To me, it was like one big adventure. What more could a growing boy want?

INTRODUCTION

As you can see on the cover, the secondary title of my book "How I Got from Budapest to Berkeley in a Roundabout Way" implies, my quest for a permanent address started out in Budapest, at a very early age I might add, and ended up in Berkeley, California, many miles away and several years later. I suppose if I had wanted to put it all in a song, I would have picked one entitled "Boy, I've Been Everywhere" and it might have gone something like this:

"Traveling, boy I've done my share
By the age of fourteen, I'd been everywhere.
I'd been to Budapest, Paris and Reno Nevada
I'd been to Toledo, Chicago, Omaha and Alameda
Berkeley, Oakland, Ogallala and Sacramento California
I'd been everywhere boy.
By the age of fourteen I'd been everywhere..."

So had I thought at fourteen when we finally made it to the United States. I could go on and make up a couple more verses, but my story will tell you where I'd been. The point is, when I counted all the cities at which I (with my parents of course) stopped at on the way to Berkeley, it came to around seventy five. These of course were the dots with a name next to them on the map. With all the smaller hops and stops in between, the count could have gone higher. By the way, everyone should know that the lyrics to the song 'I've Been Everywhere' that became a hit, originated from the magical pen of Geoff Mack, way back in 1959 and were originally made popular by Hank Snow and a slew of others. Got to give credit where credit is due.

Naturally, for years, my daughters Christina and Gizella have asked me about my childhood; where had I lived, what had I done, how come I could speak Hungarian, French and German in addition to English, and how come I ended up coming to the United States of America; and why of all places, Berkeley. And then, what did I do when I finally made it here.

Over the years, I have shown them old photographs and given them glimpses into my past as well as that of the Kapus family with little snippets from our past and the journey that got us here. They however wanted more and of course, they wanted it written down for posterity, or at least for them to read… This was the most important reason for what follows.

My only regret is that it took me so long to get to it, because the longer I have waited, the harder it was to conjure up and corral all the details. Most of the events and memories from about age five forward, are pretty much first-hand, while the very early ones, you know, the stuff that happened before I turned five, were related to me by my father and mother as well as older family friends along the way; all of whom have now sadly passed on.

Just like every story, this, the story of my early days on this planet and my formative years, will have a beginning, a middle, full of travels and travails and will conclude right around the time I turned nineteen. After that, I became your average, ordinary American high school graduate on the way to college, in my case, Junior college and trying to stay on the straight and narrow and out of trouble; or at least keeping the damage to a minimum. The other reason I ended my story a few months after my nineteenth birthday because shortly thereafter, well actually two years after, right around the time I turned twenty one, I became a United States citizen. The test and ceremony took place on October first, 1963 at the US District Court, Northern District of California in San Francisco. By the way, I had to actually take a written test on the history of the United States and, it was in English. Of course, by then, I spoke it as if I had been born right here in the San Francisco Bay Area.

On November 4 of 1956 when the Communist government of

Hungary backed by the mighty Soviet armed forces squashed the Hungarian Rebellion with the help of a few hundred Mongolian tanks; because even the occupying Russian military was unwilling to kill the people they had by then gotten to know and respect. It was then that my father knew for certain that our return home would not be forthcoming, although a very tiny little thread of hope still persisted; even though the little optimist inside him was being beaten down by the big fat pessimist...

As the Communist oppression became more and more brutal and gained more and more power, the Hungarian people lost not only property and freedom; many lost their lives. The rest slowly lost hope because they firmly believed that beyond the barbed wire of the Iron Curtain, nobody really gave a damn.

By that time, the border to Hungary might as well have been a hundred light years away. Millions suffered and thousands died, and that was not the kind of life my father wanted to foist on his family. Not when we had finally made it to the land of the free and the home of the brave, with opportunity for every individual. Of course by this time, I was firmly entrenched in the American culture and it would have been very difficult to drag me away from my new Coca Cola and blue jeans lifestyle; after all, up to this time, I had never heard of Coca Cola or blue jeans, and candy bars were for special holidays. And lest I forget, Hostess had some products that became habit forming, like Ho-Hos, Ding-Dongs and my all time favorite Snowballs; those rounded, pink and white, coconut dusted, mushy marshmallow covered chocolate cakes that belonged in a training bra; but I digress. My apologies, whenever I talk about food, I get carried away. Which is why, battling bulges became a continuing struggle.

Until that very last moment in 1958, when my father died, all three of us had somehow clung on to the hope, way in the back in the furthest recesses of our minds anyway that someday, we just might return to our native Hungary. However, with my father's passing, that hope also died.

Also, since my father passed away shortly after my sixteenth birthday and my daughters never got to meet their *nagypapa* (grandpa), I felt it most important that I should introduce them to him as best as I could along with my mother from that time before they became acquainted with her. After all, where would I be without their *nagypapa* and **nagymama** (grandma)?

Although my mother was alive when my daughters were born, and spent a great deal of time with them, there are still a few things of interest to pass along to them from her past.

Thinking back, the reason it took me so long to get started on this project in the first place was that I could not ever decide what format I would use and what exactly I was going to write about. That had been the convenient excuses I used to give, and a very good one at that, I thought: I was trying to organize my life's story into some sort of logical form. Sounded good, didn't it?

Then again, there have always been distractions, such as Bocce ball, and Bowling; someone even tried to get me into golf. Heaven forbid. Also, for years, the garage had to be cleaned out and organized: by the way, it's still waiting for that cleaning. Someone suggested a large dumpster that I could toss everything in to.

Eventually, I just started writing. The more I wrote, the more the old memories slowly bobbed to the surface. So, I gave up any hope on the idea of organizing my writing in any sort of form and just kept writing down all the events as I saw them in my mind's eye.

I developed several short stories of particular episodes of my life that could stand on their own and then I realized that they would fit rather well into some sort of chronological telling of my (early) life's story. The more I wrote, the easier it seemed to get and I eventually realized that I had covered several interesting episodes of my life, but maybe not nearly all that I would have wanted to cover if I wanted it to truly reflect what I had gone through. So I spent some more time connecting the dots between events with additional writing, to make more sense of the whole thing and to make the story flow better. Did I succeed? Who knows? I'm almost certain that someone will come up and tell me that that wasn't the way to do it. Oh well, it's the way I did it.

On occasion, I had to flash back or depending on the chronological perspective, forward to June 2008, because during that one month, after more than fifty years, I was able to sort of reconnect with my past; to come, shall we say, full-circle.

To make a long story short, my Daughter Christina wanted to get married in Europe, specifically in my native Budapest in Hungary. However, a parent's or relative's citizenship, barring that, one month's residency was required by Hungarian authorities to be allowed to accomplish this. There were no relatives of my mother or father that I was I able to locate. The fact is, my mother had kept in touch with her siblings and when they passed away, that connection was severed. Here, I must also add a caveat: back in 1963, when I became a US citizen, one of the requirements was to renounce all other foreign citizenships and therefore, I no longer had my Hungarian (citizenship) standing, which would have allowed my daughter to get married in Budapest. Another one of those things that has since changed.

At the time, the lowest residency requirement was by Italy; one week. So, I told my wife Bonnie that if I was going to be that close to Budapest, a short flight or train ride away, I was definitely going to spend a few days in my Homeland.

She countered with "If you get to go to Budapest, well I have never been to Paris, and so I would like to go there."

Upon hearing of our plans, my old high school buddy from Holland, Karel Bemelmans threw in his two-cent's worth and insisted that we come and visit with him and his wife Marie-Louise for at least a week at their home, before we returned to the United States.

The trip took on a life of its own. We spent one whirlwind month skipping and hopping through at least a dozen cities in four European countries. We travelled by trains and planes and automobiles…

And, very importantly, because of our visit with Karel and Marie-Louise, I got to revisit the little town in France, Algrange, where I went to school to age 14. Bonnie got to see Paris where the Kapus family had visited the American consulate, way back in 1954, to file all the necessary paperwork so that we could immigrate to the United States together. And best of all, I got to see the city of my birth, Budapest. It seemed that everything had come together perfectly; exactly as I had planned!?

My favorite rock group from Hungary, called Kormoran, sings a song which goes something like this: "In his dreams, he often returns home…" Of course, home for me now would be in California, however, the song is about the home one has left and longs to return to, for me that would be my place of birth, Budapest. I was surprised that I had learned more about the city where I was born, in our eight days' visit there than I had learned over the past five decades.

Now, the Displaced Person (DP) camp, which is the name they called the Refugee Camps after WWII, in Austria where we first lived after leaving our native Hungary, I hardly ever dream about. Perhaps this is due to the fact that from that early age, whatever I remember about living there seemed so natural that I have no need to revisit it even in a dream.

However, Algrange in Moselle district in France is one of the regular places that I still frequent in my dreams. That is where I grew up and where I spent my early youth, my formative years, so to speak. I went to three different schools there. I fell in love for the first time; if puppy love counts. And of course, I learned French. And I discovered later that it was a big deal to speak French; it was the only A that I got my first year at Willard Junior High in Berkeley.

After France, my story continues as we arrive in the United States, travel to San Francisco via train and eventually settle down in Berkeley, California. Now, here again, I don't dream much about my time in Berkeley. That may be due to the fact that I worked at the Lawrence Berkeley National Laboratory for thirty five years and can hop in my truck and drive there in twenty five minutes, just in case I forgot what the place looked like.

At those particular times in my life, all of those places or stops along the way were considered 'Home'. All those locations have a special place in my heart; especially this great big, wonderful country that took us in with just the clothes on our backs and the contents of three suitcases, way back in 1956.

Just so you know that I didn't leave anything interesting out, I have even included an event that I witnessed back in 1954 which may belong in the woo-woo, *Way out there category*: my encounter, along with a whole bunch of kids, of an Unidentifiable Luminous Object (ULO); well it happened in the early evening and the thing was luminous, and I didn't know what it was or where it had come from, also referred to as a UFO. And that's all I'm going to tell you here. You'll have to read the chapter entitled 'French Fried Saucer' for all the particulars.

What follows is the story of my early youth and travels through Europe, looking for a home and how we finally landed in the USA. It was a rather long and costly journey. We, like perhaps millions of others were displaced by a war that killed many relatives, destroyed our home, robbed us of our possessions and forced us on a trek halfway around the globe before finally planting us right here in the United States of America.

• • •

Just so you know, our trip to the USA wasn't free. We travelled on borrowed money that had been advanced to my father by Church World Service as a legally admitted immigrant. My father did his best to repay the amount of $756.00 ($6,810.54 – Current 2017 value) before his untimely death in 1958, leaving my mother, literally just one final installment. The reason he and many people chose this journey was to be part of something better, to be an American. As for me, I didn't mind the journey, though at times my emotions swung back and forth like a pendulum, between the joy of looking forward to something new and exciting and great sadness of having to leave all my friends and the places I had gotten so familiar with, behind. Was the journey worth it, you ask? The answer is a resounding yes. With all the travel to get here, the places I'd seen, it wasn't at all bad.

And here are some thoughts on this life-changing epic voyage: our sponsor here in the States was required to look after us for ninety days or three months and make certain that my father was gainfully employed within that timeframe. It took him less than a week to find a job. If he hadn't gotten employed in that ninety day period, by law, we would have been required to return to our country of origin, France. My father never received a penny in unemployment nor any other governmental financial assistance. We didn't even get food stamps. We spent about a week at our sponsor's home in San Francisco and then, we moved on to our own place in Berkeley. My father paid taxes from day one until he died. He didn't want anybody to think he was a freeloader. He told me, he would rather have worked three jobs than to take money from friends or the government.

My father always told me, there is dignity in any and every job you do well, even if it is cleaning toilets. As janitor, he cleaned his share and when he died, the baton went to me. So, I really did start at the bottom and worked my way up to a college degree and a rather nice job following that. However, that's a story for another book.

• • •

As I said in the beginning: by age fourteen, I thought I'd been everywhere...

One last thought: I had waited all these years to write my story: I wish I'd have done it much sooner. So, my advice to you out there: if you have a good life story in you, don't wait and put off writing it for decades. Don't find excuses. Write your story now. Get it out so you can share it with the world.

Just remember, this story is from my perspective about my experiences. I am certain that others have written of similar experiences in their own way.

This is my story!

1

A TIGHTNING NOOSE

One morning, I woke up and I found myself four borders, one ocean and ninety-eight hundred kilometers or about sixty-one hundred miles away from where I was born. This had not been my choice. I had had no say-so in the decision. My parents told me when I was old enough to understand that it was because of the War. That would be World War II. Although much later, I learned that we weren't the only ones who had to have made the same difficult decision. In fact, several million people had been affected by this war in addition to my family. We had to leave our home in Budapest and escape Hungary because of one particularly bloody battle over who would control the capital city in the waning days of WWII. Essentially, the Allies used our country as a pawn for the salivating, murderous Joseph Stalin, the dictator who led the Soviet Union. However, the butcher of Nazi Germany, Adolf Hitler had something to say about this tug-of-war (pardon the pun). I could blame all the parties involved: Hitler, Stalin, Roosevelt, and Churchill and to a very small extent, the governor of Hungary, Szalasi although there wasn't a whole hell of a lot he could have done and ironically, he was the only one out of the whole bunch who was executed.

Had they been able to capture the psychotic, delusional Hitler, I am certain the Allies would have had him executed but the coward killed himself and his bride of one day, Eva Braun; so they say.

Sadly, the Communist mass murderer Stalin hung around long enough to enslave almost half of Europe while killing as many as 65 million people, mostly his own, thanks in part to the clever agreement he managed to squeeze out of his fellow Allies, FDR and Churchill at a plush, little resort on the Black Sea by the name of Yalta.

Franklin Delano Roosevelt died in office and was promptly replaced by Harry S. Truman who unfortunately stopped General
Patton from marching his Third Army all the way to Moscow and
wiping out the Soviets and Stalin, once and for all.

The real irony in this whole thing is that although we were
made **Displaced Persons** by the Armed Forces of the United States
and her allies, it was also the United States that gave many of us a
second chance at a new life. Be that as it may, life wasn't always
that bad in Budapest, before I was born.

My father, George Kapus (Sr.) and my mother, Maria Pelikan
were married in Budapest in 1939. I came along on April 12, 1942.
When I had asked my parents, many years later, why I didn't have
any brothers or sisters, they told me that, had World War II not
broken out, they had seriously considered it even though my
mother was already 40 years old when I was born and my father
was 45. They told me that the war was already raging practically
all over the world and the European Front was exploding but a few
dozen kilometers from Budapest; my city of birth.

Up to that point, my father had been a manager in the accounting department of a Multi-national Corporation manufacturing
ball bearings of all things, by the name FHG Golyoscsapagy or
FHG Ballbearing. My mother had been running her own cafeteria-
style restaurant. These types of restaurants had been very popular
with all the business and professional people in the financial district of Budapest since the nineteen twenties as they could get a
good, nourishing and rather fast meal during their busy schedule.
This restaurant was where my mother had honed her talents as the
best cook in the world (according to my tummy) and pastry chef.
She didn't need a cookbook, she could have written one.

In mid 1943, George Sr. and Maria had made a deposit on what
was called at the time in Hungary, a Permanent Residence, *aka*
today as a condominium, at #20 Nap Utca or Sun Street; a four-
story structure with a square courtyard with balconies surrounding every floor. They told me that we lived there happily; living
the good life of Budapesti (Budapestians?) urbanites. My dad

would take me to the park in a large red toy truck called Mateosz: or Magyar Teherautó Fuvarozók Országos Központi Szövetkezete (loosely translated as Hungarian Truck Transporters National Association). We visited relatives and friends in the country, and we celebrated holidays in our little 'condo' at Nap Utca #20. My grandparents, who had lived in Erdely (Transylvania) for many years, had moved to the suburbs of Budapest to be close to their son and his family, after the Romanian government dispossessed them of their land and properties. All was going nicely in Budapest until late summer of 1944, when the war moved very close to the Capital; too close for comfort.

Suddenly, things were no longer so nice. Up to this point, somehow the inhabitants of Budapest had managed to, for all intents and purposes, ignore the war out there or better yet live with it. They had learned to deal with shortages of food and other goods, including wine and in fact carried on an almost normal life. For a few extra Pengős (Hungarian currency at the time) they managed to get luxury items such as ham, bacon and even Brandy from various underground sources. In fact, everybody knew somebody, who knew somebody, who could get you whatever you wanted, for some extra Pengős, naturally. Then again, everybody had relatives out in the country who were always willing to help since the war had not affected them as severely as the folks in the capital city where almost ten percent of the Hungarian population lived.

Sometime, in late December 1944, as a matter of fact, just a couple of days after Christmas, everything in Budapest seemed to explode. As my father told me years later, Stalin wanted desperately to capture Budapest as quickly as possible because he knew the strategic importance of the Capital, as Hitler himself had known before him. In late October of 1944, Stalin had ordered his commander of the Ukrainian Front, a man named Malinovsky (Malinowski?), to get in there and rip the Capital city of Hungary from Hitler's hold within the next twenty four hours. I guess it took Malinovsky a few extra days, because Hitler wasn't willing to give up control so easily.

Whether this did happen as I was told; a few days before Christmas of 1944, my dad had actually gone out and bought a small Christmas tree that he and my mother set up and decorated in our small front room as though the war wasn't even happening. My parents told me that for a few days before Christmas, the radio stations were broadcasting Christmas music; oblivious of the rumbling of tanks and cannons, only twenty kilometers from the Capital city.

My mother told me years later that the everyday howling of the sirens did however make me scream hysterically. She would then whisk me out of my bed or playpen and quickly wrap me up in blankets. She would lift me in her arms and while my father grabbed a bag stuffed with emergency supplies and some food, they would hurry down the stairs all the way to the cellars. Down from the fourth story, it took a couple minutes as the other tenants were also jockeying for position to get down there quickly. And of course, nobody wanted to fall down the stairs in the process of getting to safety. Pushing and shoving was discouraged by the building emergency team.

Most all of our neighbors were families, which meant a lot of screaming and crying little kids; all the way down the stairs. The screaming and crying didn't stop in the cellar with a lot of grownups joining in. She tried to calm down not only me but also some of the adults that had gone hysterical. She would then soothingly explain to me that the sirens were our friends and were warning us of coming danger. At two years of age, I didn't understand most of the words she used. The loud booms and the ferocious rattling of the building above our heads were even harder to explain though eventually I got the jest of her reassurances. At the time, the concept of death and destruction were beyond my comprehension. I had no concept whatsoever of the importance of the situation at hand.

The Soviet Army backed by their turncoat allies, the Romanians, encircled Budapest with a million man noose, to keep the Germans from being able to bring in any reinforcements and also to keep people from escaping. Hungarian and German troops that had defended the city because of its strategic importance to both

Hitler and Stalin, found that they had been cut off from any Axis military support or deliveries of badly needed equipment and supplies. The besieged troops were decimated and they were running out of ammunition and food: so was the population.

At two, I was totally oblivious of the war, except for the rare occasion when we had run downstairs and hide in the cellar because the bad airplanes were coming and dropping big, bad things that went boom. I wasn't starving. My parents made sure of that. I didn't miss a meal, while throughout the city, they explained years later, people had resorted to going after horses that had been killed in the air-raids and laid dead in the streets to butcher them for some meat. Back then, they actually had numerous draft horses throughout the capital city, pulling carriages and carts delivering produce and so on, and many got killed during the numerous air raids. It is very possible that I might have eaten some of that meat myself; of course, my mother would have cooked it, spiced it up, made it tasty for me, and pureed it. I couldn't tell the difference between horse meat and beef or chicken or pureed potatoes. All mashed up, the stuff just tasted delicious!

• • •

I didn't learn until many years later that they had actually given a name to the events taking place as all hell was breaking loose in and around the capital city; and Hungary wasn't even a major player in this whole mess. We got dragged into it under threat by Adolf Hitler, the Nazi dictator of Germany, because the Hungarian government at several points had actually attempted to exit the conflict by trying to negotiate with the Allies. Hitler of course would have none of it and put the squeeze on Governor Horty. To put it mildly, The Hungarian Government was ill-prepared for Hitler's sneaky takeover of the business of running the country.

As a result of this unholy alliance with Nazi Germany, Budapest was being destroyed bit by bit and today, more than sixty years later, she is just starting to recover from all her wounds. Even to this day, many buildings carry the scars of the Allied and Soviet bombardments and the destruction by the Soviet ground forces.

Over the years I have read that this engagement had been given a name, well actually, a couple names: **Battle of Budapest** and **Siege of Budapest** and several books had been written about the event. According to a number of observers at the time, it was one of the bloodiest battles of WWII. Whatever name they gave it, the results were the same: bloodshed, death and destruction; and we were smack, dab in the middle of it.

• • •

As we were living on Nap Utca, we were a little over a mile from the Danube River. Of course there was always some sort of artillery fire or bombs dropping, but one day, my folks told me, they heard and earth-shaking explosion. It rattled windows, almost like an earthquake. What had happened was that in early November 1944, what was deemed an accidental explosion destroyed the eastern span of the Margit Bridge. As the Nazi military, by Hitler's orders, had been practicing their demolition tactics on that bridge, there had been an accidental detonation. The Margit Bridge connected (and still connects) the Buda side of the Capital with the Pest side, while linking Margit Island to the two banks. By some accounts, several streetcars, cars, commercial vehicles, bicycle riders and several hundred people were crossing from one side to the other when the inept demolition squad, accidentally (?) lit the fuse sending the eastern span of the bridge into the roiling waters of the Danube with a giant explosion. Estimates at the time were, my father told me, about eight hundred people on the bridge and of that number about six hundred perished, including about forty German soldiers. Several streetcars and other vehicles also plunged into the murky waters.

• • •

In early January of 1945, as my folks had made up their minds that it was time to evacuate our home with a few meager belongings, we would be heading west in the direction of Austria. At the same time, the Ukrainian Front and the Soviet Army were coming in from all sides like a giant, tightening noose. The invaders were starting to detain civilians and anybody else who crossed their paths. Specifically, they rounded up all police officers, office workers, train conductors, bus drivers and anyone else they deemed enemies of the Soviet Liberators. They marched all the prisoners into POW camps they had set up right in the heart of city of Budapest. By their very nature, high schools and other school which were designed as 'closed-campuses' were perfect for this function and then they surrounded them with several layers of barbed-wire fences. The Soviets didn't care who you were, upper class gentry or working class folks. You shared the same treatment.

As it so happened, my mother's girl friend Emilia who had decided not to leave Budapest and wait out the war, ventured outside her apartment building one day, to see what some commotion was all about, got rounded up and spent several days in detention behind the barbed-wire fenced POW camp until she was finally able to sweet-talk her Soviet captors into letting her go as she promised not to give them any trouble. Maybe her good looks and pretty smile helped; or it could have been something more. Emilia never told my mother. Many were not as lucky as Emilia. Police officers and captured soldiers were brutalized and ended up in places like Siberia; from where, many never returned.

Interestingly enough, the Russkies didn't bother the long lines of refugees fleeing the environs of the Capital. They probably figured that these people were now out of their hair and they wouldn't have to feed them or shoot them and then have to bury them.

• • •

Years later, my father gave me a history lesson of these events. He explained that Admiral Miklos Horthy who had been the regent, or governor of Hungary from 1920 to 1944, tried in vain, to stay out of the conflict Altogether.

However, Hitler dragged Horty into the war through a clever ploy. A bombing of the city of Kassa took place on 26 June 1941, when still unidentified aircraft conducted an airstrike on the city, then again temporarily part of Hungary, as it had been reclaimed by the Hungarian Army, after it had been given to Slovakia under the conditions of the treaty of Trianon in 1920. As the story goes, observers identified the three bombers as Soviet Tupolev TB-3's. However, to this day, it has not been made clear whether the observations were correct; as other observers claimed that it was actually 3 Heinkel HE-111's, disguised as Soviet bombers that had dropped the bombs. Some twenty nine bombs were dropped injuring or killing nineteen civilians and damaging several buildings.

However, one bomb missed the target and didn't explode. It was later found outside the city of Kassa and was identified as a Russian bomb. Had that been a bombing run by the Soviets, hitting the wrong target or was it in fact Hitler's Luftwaffe pulling off a fast one? No one will ever know; although, it would make sense that Hitler would have been the one who had orchestrated the clever deception.

Whichever story you believe, Hitler was able to convince Horty that it had indeed been done by the dastardly Soviets and therefore Hungary had no choice but to respond with force, by declaring war on Russia.

As the conflict dragged on and more and more Hungarians were dying, especially in the capital city, Horty again tried unsuccessfully to contact the Russians and negotiate an end to the conflict. In early 1944, he yet again attempted a parley with the Soviets, mainly because by then he had lost nearly 200,000 Hungarian lives, mostly soldiers. Unfortunately, before he had a chance to get to the negotiating table with the Soviets, Hitler's army entered Budapest and Hitler's people grabbed Horty and forced him into an untenable situation. He even went so far as to have Horthy's son kidnapped to use as leverage for his demands and to keep Horthy from getting any more bright ideas about contacting the Russians. The brutal dictator eventually had the poor son shot and Horty had no choice but to go along with the Nazi plan lest he be killed.

My father explained that although Horty was not what you would call a great leader; he had managed to keep Hungary out of the conflict on a number of occasions. Dad also told me that Horty had done an admirable balancing act; which I didn't get at the time. With Hitler and his Nazis taking control of the Hungarian government, they eventually forced Horthy to abdicate. In his place, Hitler helped install as governor, a Hungarian counterpart, the leader of the (Nyilas) Arrow-Cross Party, Ferenc Szalasi, who was more amenable to Hitler's plans, to a point.

Following his abdication, Hitler had Horty arrested and tried for treason, in his own capital city. As he was being transferred by train to Berlin for imprisonment or more than likely execution, the train was held up by an armed band of Horthy's followers, somewhere in Austria. After a brief but ferocious battle with the Nazi guards, Horthy was freed and secreted away through Austria and Switzerland all the way to Spain where he lived until his death of natural causes on February 9, 1957.

Once Hitler had Horthy out of the way, he took charge of all military action in Hungary without much input from the newly appointed governor, Szalasi who also wasn't as cooperative as perhaps Hitler had originally envisioned he would be.

Here, we could insert that Hitler was not always telling the truth (Surprise!); which is what Szalasi soon realized. As a result, he only lasted 163 days as governor, before he too was forced from office. On his way to Vienna for prosecution by the Nazis, he was dragged off the train by the US Military and put on trial in Budapest by the new Hungarian (Socialist) regime and promptly hanged in 1946 from a lamp post on a Budapest street.

I wish I could say that this ended the Siege of Budapest but I cannot. When it was all over, Hungary became part of the glorious Soviet Empire even if not in name, most definitely in philosophy. For all intents and purpose, for the next forty five plus years, Budapest still had a noose around her neck.

From that point forward, the Communists kept a choke-hold on Hungary but more specifically on my city of birth, Budapest, until 1989. Of course, the Poles, the Czechs and the East Germans

didn't fare any better. In the Eastern Block in general, transportation was terrible. Trains and busses were antiquated and in bad
need of repair. Trains ran alright, except they were never on time;
being late by as much as 3, 4, 5 hours. Food was scarce because
everything the Hungarian farmer produced, be that meat, poultry,
grain, fruits or vegetables, went directly to the Soviet Union, leaving but scraps for the Hungarian population. The postal service
couldn't be trusted because any letter, especially from a foreign
country such as the United States would be opened by the postal
Inspektor Elvtárs (Comrade). If some nice relative who had managed to escape the carnage, sent someone a few Dollar bills, hidden
between the pages of a letter, they were promptly removed and
pocketed by the good Elvtárs. If the opinion of the letter writer did
not coincide with the ideology of the wonderful socialist regime,
the recipient of the letter was dragged down to the AVO (Secret
Police) office for questioning and further brainwashing and at
times physical punishment.

My mother's friend Putyu (Emilia), having her letter from my
mother opened by the postal Elvtárs, was dragged down and
threatened with severe punishment if she didn't write to tell her
friend to stop besmirching the character of the great new regime;
so she wrote my mother to stop writing. As a result, my mother
lost touch with her childhood friend for several years until she was
able to reconnect almost a dozen years later, when we had gotten
to the United States.

• • •

We were now at the point where our family got affected by the
events of the time. On the 13th of February 1945, The Hungarian
and German units defending Budapest, unconditionally surren-
dered, which opened the way for the Allies to speed up their advance towards Berlin. As the city was close to sixty percent
destroyed, it was the right time for my parents to make a very hard
decision. If the cease-fire held, everything would eventually be alright. On the other hand, with Hitler, you never knew.

They quickly packed some of our belongings in a suitcase and a rucksack, taking clothing, valuable papers and whatever other incidentals might have been needed, as well as cookies and crackers and some canned goods. They bundled me up in a thick bunda (furry winter coat like Eskimos would wear). On their person they hid some jewelry and every bit of cash in the house; since my dad had recently collected his severance pay, as he had resigned his position just weeks earlier. His severance pay in 1944 had been 50,000 *Pengő* (About ¼ of the value of the American Dollar at the time, or about $12,500); mostly in brand new bills. Had they not left, this bundle would have paid for our little condo. But as my dad used to say "the wind blew that one away". At the time, until it became impossible to safely navigate the streets of Budapest, people actually kept going to work, shopping; basically going about their business and trying to ignore the war. Then, reality set in.

On our day of departure, my folks switched off all the lights, secured all the windows, pulled down all the shades and locked all the doors as if we were going on an extended stay with some relatives in the country. The expectation all along was that within a matter of a few days, perhaps a month or two at most, we would be returning home. They had every intention of waiting out the conclusion of the war in a safer place across the border and then return. I remember my father recounting years later that he had said "In a couple months, at most six, the war will be over. Like everybody else, we'll be going home to Budapest" all this in the secure belief that our little flat would be awaiting us.

Our whole building was leveled by a bombing raid just a few days after we had left. We however didn't find this out from Putyu, for a couple years.

As we left our building, my parents knew that there would be no transportation of any kind available. To make matters worse, as our feet touched the cobblestones of the main street, ready to get out of Dodge (Budapest), Hitler, in one of his final, cowardly acts, had all the remaining bridges on the Danube blown up by his Wehrmacht Sapper troops. That was in January 1945 during his retreat to the Buda side of the Danube River, away from the advancing Soviet and Ukrainian troops.

Rail lines had been knocked out and roads were severely damaged. Busses in fact hadn't been running for quite a while and several hundred were actually lined up, abandoned, in the bus yard.

We fell in line with scores of others from all walks of life who were just as anxious to escape the fracas and destruction. A long line of many hundreds, perhaps thousands of refugees were anxiously escaping the environs of the capital city. We, well actually my parents, carried our possessions while others pushed wheelbarrows loaded with their belongings, while others yet pulled small garden carts filled with whatever they were able to load on them and occasionally with small children sitting atop the contents.

As we worked our way through the streets of the capital city, even though I was not yet three years old, I would notice a lot of human forms lying helter-skelter on the street, on top of piles of debris and some even looking like they were just sitting still in doorways.

"Mommy, mommy, why are those people sleeping," I would ask my mother.

"They are not sleeping, Gyurika (Georgie)" she would reply. "They've gone to heaven."

At this point, my concept of heaven was very limited. I knew that at Christmas, Baby Jesus came from heaven to bring me a Christmas tree and presents; so it had to be a good place.

Years later, as the topic was brought up again, by me of course, I asked her "If all those people lying on the streets had gone to heaven, does that mean we were in hell?"

"Yes my son, we were." She replied.

By then, my folks had taken me to church a few times and I had heard the priest and the minister mention the opposite of heaven, of course in context, relating to the evil doers who had managed to destroy our country.

In my little brain I was trying to figure out how those people could all have gone to heaven, but they were actually still lying around on the street. I had obviously not delved into the mysteries of the separation of soul from the body. A few years later, I was beginning to understand.

The refugee column had to trudge along day and sometimes night toward the border. The faster you got there, the sooner you would get to safety and be out of the war zone.

The Austrian border was roughly 200 kilometers away. So if you were driving that route today, it would take a good couple hours, three if you were a slow driver. Back in the spring of 1945, having no transportation at our disposal, all the bridges on the Danube having been destroyed, daily air strikes on towns and railroad lines along the way, with very little food in their bellies, it took this ragged column, many carrying small children, over a week to finally reach the Austrian border. The roads were wet and slushy from the melting snow and occasional rainfall mixed with the slush. We slept out under the skeletal remains of the trees along the river.

Some people were more anxious then others to make it to the border and would keep on trudging ahead to eventually succumb to the exhaustion. Some would fall asleep in midstride next to their meager belonging, never to wake up. The column also had to make every effort to avoid situations where it might be caught in some sort of military action; most of the time from the air. This meant a lot of detours through muddy fields and flooded country roads, under miserable conditions.

The way to safety was littered with the debris of the vanquished. Hungarian and German hardware of all sorts, trucks, tracked armored vehicles and tanks with their turrets blown to bits had turned the countryside into a giant wasteland; like an immense junkyard. Along with the rusting tools of war, hundreds, maybe thousands of bodies of dead soldiers of the defeated armies formed a macabre display not unlike mutilated statues, frozen in time. It was everyone's hope and prayer in our refugee column that these poor souls would be properly put to rest soon so that their souls wouldn't wander around restlessly forever. We could no longer help them and time was of the essence in our quest to escape the carnage.

Unfortunately, aerial attacks by Russian bombers very often did not distinguish between armed, uniformed soldiers and unarmed civilians; just more people to be sent to heaven.

Of course at this point, there was no turning back

Churchill, FDR and Stalin joking at Yalta meeting (P/D Photo)

The lion guarding Lanchid (Chain Bridge) is down – 1944 (GK Drawing)

Mussolini and Hitler goose-stepping at a parade, before their downfall (P/D Photo)

Ferenc Szalasi with bodyguard and driver, a few weeks before his hanging (Author's archives)

2

WAS SOMEONE
WATCHING OVER ME?

As I mentioned earlier, I came along on April 12, 1942 after some two days of labor according to my mother who often reminded me of this fact. At times, she stretched her labor time to thirty-six hours. The event took place in Budapest, Hungary at the Children's' Hospital just a few blocks from where my parents lived at #20 Nap Utca (Sun Street).

• • •

By the way, in 2008 when I finally got to return for a visit, I was very disappointed to find that number 20 had pretty much been an empty lot since the latter days of WWII, when the condominium complex was taken out by a wave of B-26s or more than lightly Russian bombers. A very ugly concrete bunker style two-story structure was erected on part of the property by the then glorious communist administration sometime in the 1960s. The rest of the property was but a pile of rubble covered by weeds, like a giant abandoned grave.

• • •

We lived at the Nap Utca address until the spring of 1945. We had to eventually escape the city as Budapest was being bombed on almost daily basis by B-24 Liberators of the 451st Bomb Group which had also wiped out Csepel. After the allies took out all the bridges to cut off transportation and supply routes, they tried to take out everything else. They went after railways and highways and eventually all other important buildings which also suffered near destruction.

We then wandered our way with thousands of others across the border to US occupied Austria. By then the B-24s had destroyed about 50% of the city and several of the bridges spanning the Danube River, and the Führer took care of the last five, in order to cut off the enemy's supply routes.

Before we did escape the devastation, there were a couple years when we lived a rather pleasant and comfortable life in our permanent apartment (which is what they called condominiums in Hungary, way back then anyway). My mother told me that we were happy. Until the last few months, it almost felt like there was no war going on at all; the clatter of conflict was so distant, we couldn't hear it. It almost felt normal to mom and dad.

• • •

For some strange reason, I have this one very clear and recurring dream of an outing with my father. In the dream, it is so clear as though it just happened a couple days ago. It must have been on a Sunday afternoon since he worked during the week. I remember him sitting me into my big red MATEOSZ truck of which I wrote earlier. This big red truck was something akin to the big red Radio Flyer wagon kids got pulled around in over here in the States. Anyway, he would pull me to the park and get me an ice cream cone. Most of it I am told ended up all over my face and the nice clothes my mother always dressed me in, though some of it made it into my stomach; by the chubby looks of yours truly in some very early photos.

On this particular occasion which I still have a clear mental image of as I close my eyes, I am sitting in the back of that red truck. We were in the courtyard of the apartment/condo complex we lived in. My father was holding the pull-rope of the truck when my mother yelled down something from the third story balcony. I am looking up at my mother, holding a paper sack over the railing. My father let go the rope to look up and my mother dropped the paper sack that he caught in both hands. In my dreams I still see the paper sack dropping almost as if in slow-motion out of my mother's hands.

"Well Gyugyu (a diminutive nickname akin to Georgie or Jojo, given to me by my father), Anyuka has made us some sandwiches for the park," he said. "We'll go and have a picnic".

This is one of those inexplicably fond memories from when I was barely a year and a half old. But for some reason, it has stuck with me all these years and has been a recurring dream for the longest time; my mother's smiling face as she was waving us good-bye. Go figure.

• • •

Now, there are numerous other events, I don't remember at all and they were related to me both by my mom and dad later on, when I could actually comprehend what the heck they were talking about.

This next little episode happens to be one of those that I have absolutely no recollection of. Again, sometime at around a year and a half of age, I got really sick. The doctor informed my parents that what was ailing me was something called Diphtheria. You more than likely have never heard of this nasty disease, unless you are in my age group or read about it in a medical publication.

You probably also don't know of anybody else who has ever had it, that is until now, unless you lived in an underdeveloped country. This is an acute, infectious disease caused by the bacteria *Corynebacterium diphtheriae*. The infection started in my nose and spread to my throat making my parents think I had caught some nasty cold or flu. Very quickly, it worked its way down to my lungs. Toxins formed which were destroying all the healthy tissue and was causing an ugly green-grey membrane to form over every orifice and surface of my air passages, producing even more toxins.

As this nasty stuff grew all over my throat and windpipe, I was experiencing great difficulty breathing. In addition, my parents were told that I couldn't be laid down in my crib because once I was lying flat; I would be more susceptible to choking to death.

Hence, until the antitoxins and antibiotics that had been pre-scribed, would take effect and quell the nasty infection, my mother and father had to hold me upright in their arms and walk me back and forth throughout our apartment for something like forty eight hours straight, in order to keep me from falling asleep and choking.

The doctor, who had been their friend, told them to take me to the Children's Hospital just a few blocks from our home so that the nurses could do the walking back and forth but they didn't want to entrust my well-being to anybody else. After the forty eight hour period, the infection started to slowly break up and they told me that I started breathing easier. But even after I started looking and feeling better, my mother was still nervous about laying me down for fear that the infection would return. Fortunately for me and for the folks, I recovered as is obvious by my writing this story. They said that after the ordeal, I slept for what seemed like a week, with my mother frequently checking in on me to make certain I was still breathing. So in retrospect, I owe both mom and dad a big one, just for those forty eight hours.

Fortunately today, they have a vaccine for Diphtheria. As a re-sult it has all but been eradicated from most developed parts of the world. Back in 1944, it wasn't an easy task dealing with the disease and a great many children did in fact die from it...

•••

As if my bout with Diphtheria hadn't been enough, I had an-other incident which actually landed me in the hospital this time. On his way back from the Russian Front, my father had acquired a beautiful icon, which is a religious painting done in gold and framed in a gilded, inlaid wooden frame with glass in front for a couple Rubles. My parents had decided to move it from its former location to hang it above my crib so that the saint pictured therein and the golden angels would guard over me.

They should have known better by this time that I was a curious little bugger, and perhaps the icon should have been hung a bit higher on the wall or on a totally different wall altogether. I was at that curious stage when I had discovered that my reach had gotten longer. I could grab things off of the ornate little table next to the crib and bounce them off the floor; and so mommy had to move the little table. With that challenge out of my reach, I started admiring other nearby things and eventually, the icon. I stretched to reach for it, but it was just too high, I thought.

One day though, I figured out that I could actually raise my leg all the way up and over the top rail of the crib. Very ingenious, I thought. Now, I speculated if this might give me a boost and assist me in reaching my goal which was of course a closer examination of the icon; know what I mean? It was so pretty and shiny and I wanted to look at all the angels and the saint, up real close. No harm in that, right?

As the folks were sitting on the divan (couch), relaxing and listening to the radio, I made my move without much fanfare, sort of nonchalantly. After a few disappointing slips, my leg was firmly hooked across the rail. The next thing, my hand was reaching for the icon. With a little grunt and an extra push of my diaper-wrapped popo, I was finally able to touch it. With a grunt and a final push, I dislodged it completely.

The next thing, the icon came crashing down along with yours truly and we ended up in a heap of broken glass and the icon separating from the frame and me being eyeball to eyeball with the saint and the golden angels pictured therein. I let out a blood curdling scream (I was told) which got mother and father's attention. As they rushed over, they realized that not only had the icon broken apart and there were glass shards everywhere, but the obvious fact that I had a piece of glass stuck in the top of my little skull. I was bleeding profusely (I was told) and screaming at the top of my lungs. This time, a trip to the hospital was definitely warranted.

When they told me the story years later, my parents said that I had been lucky that the glass hadn't pierced my thin skull and all I had needed was but a few tiny stitches to seal the cut on top of my head. Which brings me to my puzzlement as I was growing up, when on occasion I had been called 'thick skulled' or hard headed. Now which one was it, thin skull or thick skull? But I digress. To this day, if I softly run my finger along the ridge of my skull, I can still feel the inch and a half or so scar from 1943. I suppose, it could have stretched with my head expanding. Of course, it could all just be my imagination...

By the way, my parents actually had the icon restored to its former appearance after the incident and hung it back up on a totally different wall, far, far away from my crib. It was one of the items my father regretted leaving behind. It would have taken up too much space in either suitcase they packed with essentials. Besides, they had believed that in a few weeks' time, they'd be back...

By the way, when he brought the icon back from Russia in the 1930's, the icon cost him a couple Rubles and a few Kopeks. By the 1950's, we could have bought quite a bit of food for it, In France. But, as the French say: "S'est la vie Mon ami!"

Out and about with Anyuka (Mom) in the winter of 1943 – (Author's archives)

The good life in Budapest with Apuka (Dad), in the spring 1943 – (Author's archives)

3

BY THE GRACE OF GOD

While negotiations for Hitler's surrender were taking place, aerial bombardments, mostly by the Soviets had resumed. They had never been known to play by the rules; or else, hadn't gotten the message. Anyway, somewhere along the way to the border, our refugee column was unable to avoid such action near a small settlement along the Danube River.

As the Russian planes started raining hellfire over the town and strafing the countryside, the column was forced to head for cover under the trees along the sloping banks of the Danube River where quite a bit of snow still covered the ground. My mother had been carrying me at that time because I had gotten tired of walking. My father was carrying the suitcase and rucksack and had lagged a bit behind. Often times when the going was slow, I and all the other smaller kids were allowed to toddle alongside our parents to give them a bit of a respite; until us wee-people started whining.

On this particular occasion, my mother had picked me up to stop the complaining. Nobody really knew what the planes were bombing. They had pretty much destroyed all bridges, supply lines and factories. There wasn't much left of the little towns we passed but great big mounds of busted brick, splintered wood and chunks of cement. Then again, maybe the Russian pilots didn't want to run out of fuel so they just dumped their load of bombs; as they were often accused of doing. Who knew?

The planes got very low to the road we had been following. It would have been impossible for the Russian pilots to mistake us for Wehrmacht troops, since none of us wore any sort of uniforms. Besides, unless they were blind, they could see little children hanging on to men and women and sitting on top of carts filled with people's belongings. It didn't seem to matter to them. Following a couple of low flybys, they began their bombing run.

The column of hundreds broke up; everyone scattering for cover in all directions. Russian pilots were well known for strafing anything that moved on the ground, be it soldiers or grandmothers with little children. They would later claim that they couldn't tell civilians and military apart from way up there. Can you believe it? Through the smoke, the dust and the stench of cordite from all the bombs, people were desperately looking for safe places to hide.

As my mother was running for cover under the trees along the bank which sloped down toward the river, the bombs kept going off everywhere, rocking the ground underneath her feet and adding to the thick haze and the stench. She was holding me as tightly as she could, me in my big fur-lined coat when she slipped in the slush and the concussion ripped me right out of her arms as she fell.

I was sent flying and bouncing down the steep bank toward the swollen, swiftly flowing muddy, bloody river. She of course let out a scream, terrified that I would keep on hurtling right into the water to drown.

My father, who had dropped the suitcase and rucksack he had been carrying as he himself hit the ground, scrambled to his feet and took off after my mother. They were both slipping and sliding in the muck while ripping their clothing and getting all scratched up on the bramble and brush. They later told me that all they could do was watch me sliding and bouncing downhill. They were certain that I would end up plunging into the turgid, mucky waters.

As I kept sliding and bouncing along the snowy, slushy river bank toward oblivion, my descent was suddenly halted. A rather large boulder, very close to the edge of the surging river, stopped my progress. Someone 'Up there' must have been watching over me. Others weren't as lucky as I had been. Some ended up in the river and had to be pulled out by the others; while some went under and succumbed to the treacherous swirling waters.

When the folks finally got to me, my mother said that I was laughing like this had been some sort of a whacky winter carnival ride. I was completely unhurt. The worst thing that had happened was, my face was smeared with muck. Here I must interject a small factoid: my mother was a clean-freak. She had always kept me spotlessly clean. "Wash your hands before you eat", she would say. "Wash them afterwards. Don't pick up dirty things from the ground. Don't pick your nose", and so on .You know what I mean?

Anyway, the first thing she did was to pull out her handkerchief, wet it from her mouth and start furiously cleaning my face. The other thing I want to remind you of is, this happened around March timeframe and as I said, it was still rather cold. There was still snow and slush all over the place, so my folks had me bundled up; bundled up might be an understatement. I was wearing this thick large fur winter coat which was called a Bunda in Hungarian. As it was a couple sizes too big, it went down to the top of my shoes and was topped off with a fur hat made of the same hide, tied under my chin. This getup made me look like I belonged to some lost Eskimos tribe, way up there at the North Pole; Nanook Kapus at your service.

With all that padding, no wonder I hadn't felt a thing.

My mother thought for sure that it had been divine intervention that saved my life that day. I on the other hand firmly believe that it was in fact that big boulder; however I never challenged what she wanted to believe. Anyway, how did that boulder just happen to be there, in that spot? She might have been right. But, whatever it was, I am here writing the story about it. Amen!

• • •

As related to me many years later by older friends, refugee columns of several hundred just like ours, had followed the very same route along the river and some town had been hit by some Russian Petlyakov Pe-8s, Migs, or maybe a Tupolov or US B-24 squadrons that had flown up from Italy. They were laden with cluster bombs (or chain bombs as the refugees called them) which they dropped regularly on industrial, communications and military targets. The people would run for the trees by the river. Unfortunately, the number of drops and their succession caused such a fracas that literally hundreds were thrown into the river. Those who could, swam to safety. Those who couldn't swim had to be rescued. However, hundreds perished due to the concussive impact.

• • •

My parents had no intention of moving abroad. My mother was awaiting the end of the war to return to Budapest and reopen her restaurant. My father was going to try a new career at just forty eight years of age. The trek to Austria was a temporary solution to the problem at hand. Obviously, neither had been psychic. You will see just how wrong they both had been. At some point, I even thought we would be going back to our home in Budapest and wouldn't have to live in the forest or barracks or church basements. So yes, even I had been very wrong.

Escaping Budapest, my mother holding an unknown child's hand – 1945
(I accidentally discovered this photo on the web)

4

MY DAD

Oh My Papa or 'O Mein Papa' as it was written in German by Swiss composer Paul Burkhard in 1939 was one of my father's favorite songs. It brought tears to his eyes as he remembered his own dad who had died before I was born. When I heard it sung by Eddy Fischer and countless others after we had gotten to the States, I could understand why. The song was about a little girl's admiration for her father, who happened to be a clown. Yet more than that, it showed the humanity and love for a father, any good father; one of those things missing today.

So, it is time to get to know my father a little bit better, mainly because he was the most important man in my life; not only for being responsible for my being born, but also because in the short sixteen years I spent with him he was able to help me lay a reasonably sturdy foundation to build my life on. I often felt cheated because he had left me so early in my life. I have always felt that there was still a lot left for me to learn from him and he wouldn't be able to help guide me through some of the rough patches and whack me on the backside when I strayed from the straight and narrow. And yes, getting whacked on the backside was OK back then. It was the exclamation point to a lesson I occasionally needed. And guess what? I wasn't scarred for life.

I missed him a lot because at sixteen, I had finally gotten to a point where some of what he was saying, was actually starting to sink in. But mostly I missed him and fifty-five years later I still do because we never got to that point in life when we could do all those 'guy things' other kids got to do with their dads. He worked very hard the two years here in the States prior to his death; he didn't have much time for fun. Whoever claims that dads are a footnote or of no importance, should come and talk to me.

Up to the last days of his life, my father tried to instill in me the importance of hard work and the power of knowledge. In other words, he would say," Whatever job comes your way; do it to the best of your ability. Don't ever be ashamed of doing a job well; whether it's cleaning a toilet or running a bank".

He got me to read all the classics and I was very close to attempting Dante's Divine Comedy; which I have perused and let me tell you, it ain't just simple fiction. He also tried to pound in me all the information he possibly could that might end up helping me at some point later on in my life. Maybe premonition on his part was a driving force.

Unfortunately, at age sixteen, some of that teaching was still going over my head. It's not that I was a dumb kid; it's just that I listened with only one ear, to my detriment.

He would also tell me tales about his early life back in Transylvania. That is where at age sixteen he enlisted in the Hungarian Army fighting the Bolsheviks somewhere on the Russian Front. After only a few months of service, he was promoted to Sergeant. He was a leader and a real go-getter and he was rather proud of that. He was eventually captured by the aforementioned Bolshevik troops and as a result spent two years as their guest in a Siberian prison camp. There through the long winter months and totally unhealthy living conditions, he lost partial use of his left arm due to the hideous and freezing temperatures. Through the use of ointments and heat treatment he eventually regained most of the arm's function. However, even years later, the pain would come back throughout the varying seasons even until his final days. Following his stay in the Bolshevik Paradise, he returned home to Transylvania.

However, being the youngest son, with no chance of inheriting the family fortune and title, which in those days would go to the eldest son, he moved up to the capital city, Budapest. He had always had a knack for the fanciful use of the mother tongue. So, he went to work for one of the big Budapest newspapers as a cub reporter. He spent several years pounding the pavement. When he grew tired of chasing news stories, he enlisted in the River Police on the Danube and chased after bad guys. The River Police back in the 1930's would have been considered akin to the U.S. Coast Guard in functionality. There he would spend several years tracking down shady characters such as smugglers and other assorted scumbags. These they would turn over to local or state authorities. After several years of this, he switched careers again. This time, he started out as a clerk in the accounting section of a large ball-bearing manufacturer where he excelled and soon began moving up the ladder all the way to the rank of manager, in charge of the whole accounting section. He was very successful and made unusually good money until the day he finally called it quits allowing him to escape Budapest.

• • •

Sometime in the time period of 1935 to 1939, my father met Maria. The only thing I remember either of them telling me with certainty is that sometime in 1939 they got married and three years later I made my big entrance.

• • •

There is an interesting side note on my father's early childhood. I had recently rediscovered a picture of him taken on the eve of the new century (1900) dressed in a girl's pinafore dress and with hair down around his shoulders. I was a little kid when he had first shown it to me. What could I say, I thought it was hilarious; a little boy in a girl's dress. With a very serious frown on his face he explained that (for some strange reason, to me anyway) mothers dressed their little boys to look like little girls, back in those olden days. Now don't get me wrong, I think he positively looked cuter than a button in girls' clothing, but I told him then "No way, no how would I have stood for such humiliation".

Anyway, what could he do? He was only three. Then again, he had a smile on his face in the old photograph like he was enjoying it.

Maybe girls' clothes were a lot more comfortable? Of course, there are a lot of famous people who wore girl's clothing in the olden days, like J. Edgar; but apparently the famous Mr. Hoover managed to keep it a secret for most of his life… Again, I digress. I apologize.

• • •

My father was also a very good writer; excellent in fact at poetry, patriotic speeches, newspaper articles and of course stories. All along, his intention had been of someday, writing our family history. Unfortunately, his illness and untimely death left it up to me to write something. Of course, I can only write about what I know from firsthand experiences as well as what I absorbed from the stories told me by my parents and friends. Alas, my father's writing might have been superior to what I can come up with but here I am, writing.

Now, ever since he had been a youngster, my father had been very interested as to origins of the family name Kapus as well as where exactly did the Kapus clan originate. This was in fact one of the most interesting stories he had ever told me and fortunately I still remember much of it.

He had done all this research about our family's origin in Transylvania when he first arrived in Budapest. He had in fact been successful in tracing the family name and numerous references back about 700 or 800 years as best as I can recall. He was even able to discover the family coat of arms which had elements that also appeared in some Transylvanian coat of arms. When he told me about his research, we already lived in Algrange. He sketched out for me what the coat of arms had looked like. He said he had an actual copy which unfortunately was safely stored away in one of his bureau drawers, back in Budapest. When we would return home, he promised he would show it to me.

I will try to go back as far as I can, regarding the Kapus Family's history which my father recounted to me. The name itself originated in about 1150 A.D. but since I wasn't around back then, whatever I write comes from second hand information, so more on that later. Let me instead start a little bit before I came along so that I can talk about my father who is actually the one who had researched the origins of our family.

My father, Kapus György (George), was born on October 10, 1897 to father Samuel Kapus and mother Hedvig (maiden name-Kabos) in Zillah, Erdély (Transylvania) Hungary.

Off course today, Transylvania is part of Romania and has been part of that nation as a result of the treaty of Trianon of June 4, 1920, for what it's worth. This was one of those incredible injustices that ate at my father all his life. Because of our Triple Alliance with the German Empire and Italy, as the Austro-Hungarian Empire, when World War I was lost, the losers were punished by the victorious Triple Entente of France, Britain and Russia. As a result, The Austro-Hungarian Empire was dismantled. Hungary took the brunt of the Allied punishment.

Hungary lost nearly a third of her former territory. Austria, which was our partner in the empire, actually benefited from the breakup by actually gaining territory instead of losing some. Anyway, this is all ancient history but to my father, back some sixty plus years ago, it stung because of Hungary's loss of his beloved Transylvania to Romania. Alright, now back for the rest of the for history lesson...

• • •

As I stated earlier, our family name originated at around 1150-1200 A.D., this would put our family's beginnings even further back in history...

In the court of either Andras (Andrew III) or Bela (Bela) IV or even perhaps Karoly (Charles) I, possibly, there was captain of the guard in charge of the access to the king's castle. If I had my father's notes, I could tell you the exact king and wouldn't have to guess which out the list, A, B or C the king would be. Now again, I don't remember what my father told me what the captain's name had been, so let's just call him György (George) for argument's sake. Alright, so for many years of bravery and unfailing service, guarding the gate to the king's castle, often from incursions by Ottoman Muslim hordes, the king rewarded Captain George the Gatekeeper (the kapus), with a rather nice estate in Transylvania and the title of Baron. So, from that day forward, the captain was no longer plain George the captain of the guard, he was now Baron George (the) Kapus (or gatekeeper), thus formalizing the family name as well.

Of course, along came the game of futbol (soccer) in the late 1800's and the position of goalie in Hungarian is also called the kapus or goalkeeper, more popular but certainly not as noble, unless of course you're really into soccer.

The Kapus barony in Transylvania was passed down the bloodline until my father's eldest brother would inherit it. However, somewhere in the 1920s, the Kapus family lost most of their fortune to the world-wide stock market crash and with that went the barony and pretty much the rest of the estate. Of course, none of this would have mattered because the Socialist government of Romania confiscated all privately-owned land and property from all native Hungarians following the Treaty of Trianon which effectively removed most of Transylvania from Hungary and attached it to Czechoslovakia and eventually to Romania.

One of the many talents that I inherited from my father was that of artist. He himself was rather good at drawing in pencil and pen and ink, and I still have a couple portraits he did of my mother and me. He also designed a number of posters for events in the camp in Austria as well in Algrange. He was also an excellent public speaker. He made patriotic speeches at Schmitzberg as well as Algrange. As a matter of fact, he actually spoke at one of our Mach 15th (Hungarian National Holiday) celebration in San Francisco, to a rather large crowd and was well received and even got a standing ovation. Unfortunately, a few months later, he died. He was a man of many talents.

He passed away in 1958 at the relatively young age of 61, never having met his granddaughters; and he would have loved both of them. He died of psoriasis of the liver brought on by the continuous breathing in of fumes from the Carbide lamps used while working in Austrian and French coal and iron ore mines for some seven or eight years. That had been the diagnosis.

•••

Through those early years, I learned to appreciate my father's writing talent especially in Austria. By then, I had grown old enough so that I could understand what he was talking about, most of the time. He wrote speeches, articles, poems and even songs. He also wrote five or six plays which he produced himself, with talent from the Schmitzberg population for the Schmitzberg audience. Did I mention that he actually composed the music for most of his songs?

That creative side of him makes you wonder what he could have accomplished had WWII never happened or, had he lived beyond 1958. We'll never know.

•••

When I became a US citizen, back in 1963, on the application for citizenship, one was required to renounce any foreign titles or citizenships; which I did. Apparently today, you can keep your titles and have multiple citizenships. The times, they have changed.

My father used to tell me that someday, if we ever got home, to Hungary that is and Transylvania was liberated from the Romanians, I would become Baron Kapus, because his other brothers had been killed. So, being a kid, I would ask, "Would my friends have to call me Baron or could they still call me just George?"

"They could call you George just fine," he would say. "By then, Baron won't mean much."

It's another issue I won't have to worry about.

•••

Here, I must bring up a brief story of what kind of a man my

father was. As Hungary was slowly swallowed up in National Socialism, everybody working in a good job had to be alert to the fact
that any criticism of the government and of course of the Führer
who had taken up residence in Budapest, was unadvisable, lest
your status would become untenable and perhaps eliminated with
the possibility of your being sent to prison or perhaps, worse. So,
it came to be that an edict came down from the government that a
census be taken of the religious affiliations of the workers; a not so
cleverly disguised counting of Jews in particular. Everyone was assured that this was only to be a census; nothing more. And we all
know that the Führer always kept his word. Because by this point
in time, he was really in charge!

My father, being a good company man, was all for cooperating
and getting the census done. That is until, one of the 'party' repre-
sentatives let lose over a drink at the pub down the street that the
Führer was ready to round up all the Jews and send them to some
camp. My father wasn't a dumb man and had for the most part figured this out by himself, however 'Lose Lips' had just confirmed
what he had suspected all along.

As this supposed census would take several days if not weeks
(they didn't have computers back in 1944) he went in to work the
next day and discreetly told the seven Jewish guys he worked with
that they should go out after work for a beer to a pub of their
choice. I know that there were certain restrictions about what Jews
can drink, where and with whom; however, these were challenging
times.

After work the next day, they met at a pub, most of the guys
frequented, sat in one of the quiet corners and ordered their beers.
After their order had been delivered, my dad quietly explained the
situation. So far, Jews had been pretty much left alone but since
the takeover of the Hungarian government (for all intents and purposes) by Hitler, stirred up some ill winds. Still, these guys didn't
feel in any danger.

"You all know that the new government has ordered all employers to do a census of their workers," my father said. They all
indicated that they'd heard something to the effect. They didn't

think much of it at the time.

"They want to know how many of you are working throughout the city and put you all on a train to one of the camps, as soon as the census is concluded" my father continued. "This could happen any day. If I were you, I would leave Budapest and go visit some relatives in the country or maybe even across the border".

"Are you sure this is what's going to happen?" they asked

"One of the party acolytes blabbed at the pub the other evening that the purpose of this so-called census was to get an accurate count of how many Jews there are in the city," replied my father.

"We need our jobs," they replied. "We have families to support."

"If you stay, it may not be tomorrow or the day after, but very soon, they will have an excuse to round you all up and put you on that train. Especially, since Hitler has taken everything over".

"That Hitler, he's a real bastard! (they actually used harsher epithets than that) I wouldn't be surprised," said one.

"The sooner, the better," my father said, "before the census concludes.

"Thank you Gyuri (George)," said one. "It might not be a bad idea to just disappear.

As they all left the pub, my father knew that he probably would never see them again but at least, they wouldn't be caught up in the eventual, inevitable roundup.

The seven didn't show up for work the next day and my father showed due outrage at their absence, as would be expected. He of course couldn't tell anyone what he had done and for many years he never talked about it. He finally opened up to me about it when we had finally made it here, to the States. That was the first time that I heard this story. Although, at a Hungarian gathering back in 1957, he ran into an old friend from Hungary he hadn't seen since 1945. He knew my dad's story. They are both dead now, but I had to tell this episode of courage that very few knew about.

My father's seven co-workers had family and friends who had family and friends; and so on. My father never knew or even imagined how many innocents he might have saved because he didn't have a giant ego and what he had done; he had not done for fame or glory. He had done it because it was the right thing to do.

• • •

Here is a final note about my dad's family. I have included a photograph taken in 1907 of the Kapus children and their cousins. My dad's sister is standing next to him, his other brother is standing next to his sister and his older brother with his rakish hat is at the other end of the group. His seven younger cousins are standing or sitting in front of them. Unfortunately, his sister Esztike (Esther) got ill when she was in her twenties and committed suicide. His two brothers and seven cousins, my father was never again able to make contact with after we left Budapest. My mother's friend Putyu wrote her telling her that several of the cousins had gotten killed during the bombings and the others, she was never able to track down.

What a sad ending to a big family!

Of course, my mother's family had been luckier, that is staying alive and she was therefore able to reconnect with her brother and sister. Now, their fate and how the new Socialist government dispossessed them and made them destitute, that's a different story which I will tell you in a later chapter.

The Kapus cousins at a 1907 family gathering. My dad is the little bald kid on the far right of the group. His sister is next to him an older brother to her left and his oldest brother is on the left, with the hat on. (Author's archives)

Dad at age 22, returning from the Russian Front in 1919 – (Author's archives)

The 'kapus' or gatekeeper, defending the king's castle against barbarian invaders – (my illustration for the book by Irene Tosaky 'The Heroes Will Return Again' – 1996 Ed.)

5

THE U.S. ZONE

Except for the bomb blast that almost sent me to oblivion, the rest of our wandering toward our goal, seemed tame by comparison, like a big, exciting weekend outing. You would have thought the same thing at age three. The official date that we entered the US Zone was April 15, 1945; three days after my third birthday. The train took us to Linz in Oberösterreich or Upper Austria. From Linz, where we transferred to yet another train already practically full with other refugees from Hungary, we were taken to Attnang-Puchheim, where we were herded into out-of-service railroad cars and straw laden cattle cars sitting in a rather large railroad yard. We were to live here for about three or four months. Whatever we needed came out of the two suitcases we had left Budapest with as well as some canned goods, courtesy of the US Military. Besides some changes of clothing, the suitcases contained all the documents we might ever need to identify ourselves since the hope was that after a few months, the war would wind down and eventually be over and we would be allowed to return home to our securely locked apartment with all of our nice stuff inside, intact.

• • •

I have to segue here briefly, to explain what happened after we left Budapest. It wasn't until a year or two later, when my mother was finally able to write her best friend Emilia, and she wrote back telling my mother that pretty much if we ever returned, our flat would be empty. The few good neighbors that had stayed behind broke in and slowly removed all the good stuff and then eventually the hooligans roaming the streets cleaned out what was left. Soon thereafter, the whole complex was leveled by Soviet bombers in advance of Soviet tanks as they moved in to secure Budapest, thus making us, for the time being anyway, totally displaced.

Interestingly enough, I saw this for myself, for the first time when my wife Bonnie and I flew to Budapest on a visit in 2008. In the 1960s the then Communist administration had put up an ugly two-story gray, concrete bunker style apartment complex with small windows on part of the property. The rest of the space that the four-story complex had formerly occupied was now just a giant pile of rubble left over from World War II. It had been overgrown by tall weeds like a giant, unkempt graveyard.

A planned rehabilitation of the area had been slated for 2009/2010 by the current democratically elected government.

• • •

Now, back to the US Military Zone; living in the railroad yard wasn't actually that bad. It was dry and safe and we didn't have to walk mile after mile every day in the snow and slush; and nobody wanted to blow us to smithereens. Besides, as I looked out the passenger car windows, I day dreamed that we were travelling; even though the scenery was stationary. In my little mind's eye, it was moving. I even made choo-choo sounds to add to my imaginary travel.

Some unpleasantness hit us in the first few days as some unscrupulous GI's managed to relieve many in our caravan of some of their valuables claiming it was illegal for refugees to possess them; and you didn't mess with guys holding M-1's and Tommy-guns. Some people who actually believed this managed to part with some irreplaceable heirlooms and other valuables such as rings, necklaces, gold and silver coins, brooches and other pocketables.

We were pretty much at the mercy of these connivers, until a unit of MP's took over the security duties and sent the wayward GIs on their way, back to their units. I must admit that as a result, some of the valuables actually found their way back to their owners.

Of course, by then the women had learned to hide valuables by sowing them into the lining or hem of their coats and even bras and could tell the scofflaws that they had "nichts" (nothing in German). So, when the men were finally allowed to go into the town of Attnang Puchheim, they had something to barter with for bread, butter and milk, so their families wouldn't go hungry.

After a few days however, the U.S. Military finally got organized and began to hand out regular rations for the remainder of our stay. As I said, after almost six months we were moved to more suitable and permanent housing. I was three, so, as far as I was concerned we had just moved up...

The U.S. Army eventually decided to move us en-masse from the railroad yard to a now unoccupied and recently cleaned and painted P.O.W. camp near Ampflwang which was a small municipality in the district of Vöklabruck in the Austrian state of Upper Austria, at the time, under the U.S. Military's control. The name of the camp was Schmitzberg Lager and we were relocated there at around October 14, 1945. There were around a thousand to about fifteen hundred souls who eventually moved in along with us. At the camp, everyone was issued an official identification card. And I mean everyone, including all of us tiny tots.

• • •

The card issued to me had the number 288833 printed on it. I had actually completely forgotten about it until I recently came upon it while rummaging through the garage, trying to organize it; a never-ending process. I found it in a box with a ton of other old mementos, photos and documents my mother had saved after my father had passed away; some going all the way back to my grandparents' wedding papers. I didn't even know these things existed anymore. But I digress.

The point of bringing up the I.D. card was that I got a chuckle upon seeing it again after all these years. I literally had not laid eyes upon this little piece of folded cardboard for almost sixty years. For the first year or so in camp, everyone had to actually have their identification card with the big number in the upper left corner on their person at all times to prove that they had been in fact properly processed to live in this particular camp. Mine was pinned to the front of my jacket, until they told us to remove it.

Besides the number, it gave a description of the holder not unlike your driver's license of today would have. But the funniest part was the official name of this card: **EX-ENEMY DP IDENTIFICATION CARD**. At age 3 ½ and all of about 28 and a half inches tall, I had been designated an ex-enemy. I must have presented a pretty terrifying image.

• • •

Life at Schmitzberg Lager (Camp) was not all that bad. My introduction to camp life however, had been somewhat traumatic, though. Before we were allowed to occupy one of the newly cleared out clapboard units which had formerly held WWII POWs, we had been lined up in single file in the main plaza and moved through a decontamination station which was not unlike a chute that cattle are forced through from their holding pens on the way to railroad cars. We all went through the chute single file while we were told to hold our noses and cover our eyes. Then from both sides we got sprayed with DDT from above. We all came out looking like a troop of Himalayan Snow Zombies all covered in white powder, with our eyes blinking through so we could see where we were going. After this humiliating and stressful experience, we were finally given the keys to our new accommodations and allowed to enter with our belongings. Well, it was actually after we stomped all the way to the door to shake off the excess white powder. I might have exaggerated a bit, the amount of white powder we were covered in. Although the experience had been humiliating, nobody had died.

We were assigned an end unit in one of the large barracks somewhere near the center of the camp. There were around thirty to forty barracks of various sizes, each housing twenty to thirty people. Larger families got more space and single men and women shared units. Our unit had a small room with a stove, table and four chairs, which served as kitchen and dining room and another smaller room with two cots. As I said, I hadn't gotten used to too much stuff thus far in my short existence, so having two whole rooms instead of straw covered cattle car floor to sleep on, looked pretty darn good. In addition, since I was only three and a half when we had arrived there, going to the bathroom was easy. There was a pot behind a curtain that I could use anytime. As far as taking a bath; that for me was done in the middle of the kitchen in a washtub. There wasn't much privacy but it was always warm. Grown-ups went to communal showers in another building. While we lived in the camp, I only visited the showers once. A hot washtub in the middle of the kitchen was just fine with me.

From the day I was old enough to hold a toothbrush, (for a while, I think we had just one) I had to brush my teeth daily; even though there weren't too many of them (teeth). Until my father finally got a hold of tooth paste from the US Military, we all used baking soda. If there wasn't any, my parents told me to run the toothbrush across the bar of hand soap and brush with that. It wasn't a great taste and was only too happy to go back to baking soda; happier yet when toothpaste came along, and even happier when I got my own toothbrush.

By the way, privacy curtains as well as curtains for the windows were made up from surplus parachutes, sheets and sometimes even empty potato sacks. Eventually, someone enterprising had somehow gotten their hands on an old foot-operated Singer sewing machine which was then lent from one family to another and when my mother got a hold of it, the window coverings became real curtains.

Very soon, I also outgrew all my little clothes and not having much money, well actually, almost none, my mother went about altering hand-me-downs using the old borrowed Singer sewing machine. She eventually turned into quite the little seamstress and altered clothing made for larger kids to fit my petite size. She did this with pants, with shirts and even jackets. She even picked up knitting so she could knit me socks and sweaters. This went on for quite a few years until I started growing a little bigger after my first grade in France. So, finally, at age eight, I got a pair of store-bought pants and even a nice shirt; which by the way were both a size or two larger so I could wear them for a couple years. Until I got those new items of clothing, I thought most people only bought underwear in stores, everything else, their mother made. And also by the way, my outgrown wardrobe was handed down to some other family with smaller kids. No piece of clothing ever went to waste in Schmitzberg!

• • •

Soon, I also outgrew the pot behind the curtain in our little domicile and I had to adapt to using the grown-up facilities, which were outside.

There were spots where there was a single outhouse. Then, there were little shed-like structures in various locations with four to six stalls which were shared by three or four surrounding build-ings. Rain or shine or snow, day or night, that's where I had to stand in line with the rest of the folks big and small. Fortunately, two large lamp poles offered plenty of light and safety, though at times I would ask my father to stand in line with me, especially late at night. The one drawback of these facilities was the size of the deposit hole. My father always told me to hang on to the edge with both hands until I got done and then jump off. I followed his instructions to the letter.

This one little kid didn't.

One morning as we were sitting around the table having break-fast, we heard all this shouting and commotion. We looked out the window to see what the hub-bub was all about and saw all these people running around waving their hands in the air. We all went out to find out what was going on. "Little Pista (Stevie) fell into the outhouse," the woman was yelling. "Did he slip and hurt himself?" my father asked. "No," the woman replied, "he fell through the drop hole. We got to get him out." This outhouse was fortunately not very deep and was only about half full. Couple large guys finally reached in and pulled the little bugger out. He was crying, mostly from embarrassment as he dripped you-know-what and desperately tried to rid himself of all the clinging crumbled papers of all kind used for wiping. Very rarely did we get to use toilet paper as it was considered a luxury. So, old newspapers, catalogs and heaven knows what else, were the 'papier du jour'.

I must inform you here, little Pista missed a week's worth of first grade at the camp's Hungarian school, due for the most part, to his embarrassment. The other kids thought they were funny when they asked him if he had swallowed anything... Little kids could be mean at times?

• • •

My father would at times parlay some of the family's limited valuables for occasional luxuries such as a chunk of fresh meat, some bread and butter, eggs and occasionally a bottle of cheap Austrian wine. I remember him coming home this one time and triumphantly showing us that he had traded away to a farmer, his best pair of dress shoes for eggs, a good size chunk of bacon, butter and some nice cheese. He said he didn't mind the trade.

"I have no use for fancy Sunday shoes to work in the mines, or even at Sunday church," he said. "God doesn't look at what is on your feet anyway. He looks to see what is in your heart."

• • •

By the way, the reason my father had to trade away for food, some of our possessions is that the 50.000 Pengős he had received in severance from his employer; that same 50.000 that would have been worth 12,500 Dollars just a few months earlier, that very same money that could have paid off our condo back in Budapest, had turned into scheiss (that's kaka or excrement in German) the minute we had crossed the Austrian border, as the Pengő had been devalued. Back in Budapest, if you could find a loaf of bread, it would have cost you ten million Pengős.

• • •

A nearby coal mine having lost a goodly number of their workers came to the camp to recruit many of the men who were willing
and able and all too happy to start making a little income. Since
we all had been dispossessed by the war, the US Military obviously
didn't charge us rent, but everything else folks needed, cost Geld,
that's German for Money, even in Austria. Things went well
enough. We had a roof over our heads, I thought and food in our
bellies. What else could anyone want?

Mostly all of the thousand to fifteen hundred souls wanted to
desperately return home, to Hungary. The war appeared to be
winding down. Treaties were being signed. The World Court was
to assemble in The Hague and mete out punishment on the hierarchy of the Nazi Regime. It was only a matter of time before news
of going home would reach Schmitzberg.

Now, all this didn't happen overnight. We actually spent four
and a half years as guests at Schmitzberg Lager Resort and Spa
(which was our inside joke!). After the initial introduction and
early anxieties of having to deal with your former enemy, in a few
weeks' time tensions eased and everyone went about the business
of living. Soon, the administration of the camp was turned over to
the Austrian authorities. Most every one of the men had jobs. They
raised their families. They kept the Hungarian school going. We
all went to church. There was a Catholic mass and a Protestant
service on Sunday and Jewish services on appropriate days; although, being a small community, most people crossed over and
attended one another's religious services. Of course, some didn't
attend any services. But there weren't many. Everyone wanted to
talk to God when things weren't going well. There were weddings,
baptisms, and even a small number of funerals. We celebrated all
the holidays.

The men in camp, old and young, organized a soccer league
wherein several teams would compete and occasionally would
venture outside the camp and play one of the local teams. It was

all in good fun and gave a chance for the D.P.s to interact with the local town folks. The team my father played on called themselves 'The Galoshes Brigade' as they all worked in the mines and had to wear the aforementioned footwear.

There were also activities for the kids; among them scouting. The folks formed a decent size troop of Boy Scouts, Girls Scouts, Cubs and Pee-Wees; I started out as a Pee-Wee. I'm not really sure that was the name they gave us, but that's what we were. The scouts even held occasional Camporee (Little brother to a Jamboree) to get together with all the other DP scout troops from around the area.

There were also periodic dances held in the big hall as well as theater nights. My father was the writer, the composer, the director and the producer of many of the plays.

• • •

While at Schmitzberg, my father wrote newspaper articles for the mimeographed weekly, as well as patriotic poems and speeches and five or six plays. As best as I can recall all his plays included music and especially songs and were melodramatic or of patriotic nature except for this one which was more of a 'fantasy travel adventure' musical.

This particular play, called *"Harry's Adventures in Transkukutchin"* for instance was a musical comedy period piece, which took this traveler (akin to Marco Polo) sometime in the eighteenth century on an adventure to a place called Transkukutchin, a made-up name for some imaginary region of the Ottoman Empire. The hero got involved with harem girls and fell in love with the sultan's favorite redhead. He then had to do battle with the evil sultan and his guards before he could escape and take his sweetie back to his homeland barony. Even as the hero fought the sultan's guards; naturally done tongue in cheek, he did it with appropriately sung humorous lyrics. Errol Flynn would have been proud! And, no human or animal was ever hurt or killed.

I can still remember some of the lyrics of the song sung by the sultan as he introduces himself (in Hungarian of course) to our adventurer, Harry.

"Ali Ben-Bimbula
Török Basa vagyok én,
Transkukutyin hősi trónyán
Vigan ülok én..."

Sorry but I couldn't make it all rhyme in English:

"I am Ali-Ben-Bimboola the Turkish Pasha. Happily sitting atop the glorious throne of Transkukutchin..." Etc. I wish I could remember more.

In addition to good looks and some acting ability, the hero character also had to know how to sing. My father was lucky in casting the guys as we had several in camp who had done some stage work before the war. The trouble was casting for the female roles. All the young ladies in camp wanted to be on stage and be the star. Some were very pretty. Some could even sing, and some could act. Unfortunately, a lot of them only wished they could sing and act. Some couldn't remember any of the lines. Some couldn't carry a tune to save their lives. Many could wiggle and shimmy but couldn't dance. Needless to say, they all thought they were beautiful and that it should have been enough. My father actually found some of the more mature women who had beautiful singing voices. For the rest of them, he got them into the harem where they danced in the background and still competed for the spotlight: all in good fun.

Dad was very diplomatic. He convinced all cast members that all their parts were extremely important to the production and managed to keep the peace, mostly between the younger and more immature gals and guys. He always managed to give everyone who came to tryout, a part if at all possible or a promise of a part in the next production. He even got parts for my mom who actually had a great singing voice and had taken part in some amateur stage work back home in Budapest. There were also enough people in the camp with musical instruments, so there was always an orchestra of sorts to back all the productions.

These events usually took place on Saturday evenings, which

meant that we rug rats got to stay up late, mostly because all the babysitters above the age of twelve wanted to be on stage. Like I said, it was all great fun and after all the plays, there was dinner and dancing. Us kids, we ate and after running around all the dancers like crazed chipmunks, we would fall asleep in a corner of the hall atop the pile of coats, until our parents carried us home.

Of course, the grownups kept partying until early morning sometimes. My dad liked to indulge in a little vino and at times got a bit tipsy like most of the attendees. But then, how could you hold it against any of them to occasionally get a little happy, after what they had gone through during the war years, with daily air raids and their country being reduced to rubble all around them. Everybody needed to loosen up and party a little to forget!

That's me at three and a half, sitting on the US Jeep with my Ex-Enemy ID card – 1945 (Author's archives)

Ex-Enemy DP Identification card issued to me on April 15, 1945 - (Author's archives)

Family portrait in front of our Schmitzberg Lager barrack – 1946 - (Author's archives)

Panoramic view of Schmitzberg Lager DP Camp – 1945 - (Author's archives)

*Schmitzberg Lager scout troop – I'm the little kid sitting
at the far left of the group -1946 (Author's archives)*

6

KRAMPUSZ

The little Austrian kids were singing "Bald kommt Nicklaus Abend da…" (Lyrics from a German St. Nicklaus song: Soon it will be St. Nicklaus eve…) These were happy times for the tiny tots; including yours truly.

Since I could remember our family celebrated what was known as Mikulás (or Szent Miklós) on December the 6th. It's St. Nicholas's birthday and is celebrated in many European countries including Hungary and of course, Austria.

It's was just another holiday that gave us little kiddies and opportunity to score some goodies to rev up our little engines.

"Put your shoes on the window sill," my father would instruct me, "so that Mikulás can fill them with treats for you."

So, before I climbed into bed, I put my shoes on the window sill. My father also advised me that the shoes should be clean and polished because Mikulás preferred them that way. I understood the reasoning behind that. Who'd want to put candy and stuff in dirty shoes?

The next morning, to my surprise, the shoes would be filled with goodies such as chocolate bars and marzipan and gingerbread cookies shaped like Mikulás, if I had been good throughout the year, if not; I would have gotten chunks of coal or rocks or even potatoes. I believe this is why some ingenious Hungarian candy maker had created something called Potato-candy. Oddly enough, I liked the stuff. It looked like little potatoes and had a taste that was truly different, but what the heck, it was sweet…

Now in Schmitzberg Lager, we also celebrated Mikulás eve in the community center and kids got some candy there as well. However, at the communal celebration, we discovered where the coal and rocks in our shoes came from.

You see Mikulás had a sidekick named Krampusz (Crum-puss). Whereas Mikulás went around handing out goodies and patting the little kids on the head, Krampusz accompanied him and handed down punishment to the bad kids.

This one particular Mikulás Eve I still remember clearly, because it was the first time that I actually became aware of this nasty creature known as Krampusz. Up to this point, I had only been told about him by my father, to keep me in line, I think. The image he painted was enough to scare the bejesus out of any five-year-old. So, right around that time of year, I really behaved myself. I had no desire to meet up with this nasty Krampusz who up to this point, I only had an imaginary image of. And well, I had very good imagination for a five-year old.

I remember my father telling me about him just as I was about to go to sleep on the night of the 6th. So, whenever I would hear anyone slogging through the snow late at night, probably some poor soul having to use the outdoor toilet, I would imagine that it was Krampusz going around the camp, meting out punishment on the bad kids. I half expected to hear in the middle of the night, the screaming of the boys I considered to be especially bad. I prayed extra hard that he wouldn't stop at our door. Those footsteps in the snow might actually have been the pounding of my little heart pumping blood past my little eardrums.

As I was saying, this one year, probably 1947, we celebrated Mikulás; I finally got to go to the communal celebration where I would meet, for the first time, this scary character. Unbeknownst to all the kids, this whole thing was a setup to scare the 'you-know-what' out of them, and it worked, on me especially. Here was Mikulás who was traditionally dressed in a bishop's habit with a pointed bishop's hat, carrying a long, curved bishop's staff and a big bag of goodies, walking through the crowd.

Suddenly, there rose uproar. Through the semi-darkness of the hall as the crowd parted to let Mikulás through, from my vantage point, I could barely see a dark shadowy figure following him. Suddenly, he jumped out from behind Mikulás, and I saw the ugliest, scariest creature I had ever seen. Let me tell you, to a five, six-year-old kid, he was very scary and really ugly; a creature of nightmares. He kind of looked like a cross between the abominable snowman and the devil from Dante's Inferno. Two horns stuck out of his forehead and he had long, nasty looking teeth and evil eyes. The whole thing could have been a mask, but to me that didn't register. It was all part of the creature. He wore a raggedy black-striped pajama-like outfit over his furry body. He had a chain wrapped around his mid-section, dangling down his side and in his right hand he carried a switch made of thorny branches a couple feet long to deliver punishment; oh and a sack on his back filled with chunks of coal or maybe potatoes. By the time I saw him, I frankly didn't care what was in the sack. I wanted to hide behind my dad, or get the heck out of there.

Unbeknownst to us little tots, a couple of the bigger boys had volunteered to be the recipients of the staged punishment. So here came this nice old guy with the white beard and the pointed hat, handing out candy and saying nice things to the little kiddies and patting us on the head; followed by this god-awful creature.

All of a sudden, to our surprise, the Krampusz guy would grab the first of the designated bad-boys, Jancsi (Johnny) by the collar and start what appeared to be, a very serious and painful whipping. I almost wet my shorts and desperately clung to my father's leg; couple little kids actually did leave little puddles under their feet. I, like the other little tykes, had believed this whole scene was for real. Up to this point in my life, this had been the scariest event I had ever encountered, especially on a supposedly happy holiday. I knew I would never want to anger this guy.

I gave this event some very serious thought. So, if I stayed at home and just put my shoes in the window and got coal if I was bad, why would I want to go to a Mikulás gathering and take a chance on getting whipped? Getting coal in my shoes, wouldn't be that bad, but getting whipped, that would be very painful. I'd have to think about that for next year…

A few days later in an unguarded moment, my dad was talking to one of his friends, Feri (Frank) at the dinner table while having a glass of red wine. I was over in a corner coloring some Christmas pictures and I overheard some of their very interesting conversation. I managed to stay as invisible as possible in my corner so that grownups hardly even noticed my being there. This sometimes paid off with some very revealing information; you know the kind you weren't supposed to hear.

Their conversation centered on this guy, Zoli. I knew who Zoli was. However, the next thing that came out was like a dark secret to me.

"That crazy Zoli," my father was saying, "he sure took his Krampusz role a little too seriously."

Revelation number one: Zoli was Krampusz, I deduced.

"Yes," replied Feri. "That kid looked really scared when Zoli went into his act.

So, Krampusz wasn't real; one point for the grownups.

My dad and his pal were chuckling about the whole thing.

"I think when he said he needed a shot to work up his courage," my father said, "he must have taken maybe three or four shots."

"He did have sort of a wild-eyed look about him," said Feri. "He actually looked a bit tipsy." Feri chuckled.

Revelation two: Zoli was tipsy. At five, I had no clue what that meant. I would have to do some research on that word.

"I think he was more than tipsy," my father replied. "He looked like he was schwacked."

That didn't help. At five, schwacked could have been Martian.

"Jancsi didn't get hurt or anything," Feri said, "although, the committee should take under serious consideration, asking someone else to play the role of Krampusz, for next year, somebody who doesn't drink, until he takes the disguise off."

Revelation three: so, Krampusz wasn't real. Some grown up would dress up and play the part. Then, was Mikulás not real as well? I wasn't ready to do any research on that one just yet. That might possibly cause the end to the flow of treats. I wasn't willing to take that chance.

"That might be a good idea," my dad replied. "I'll bring it up at the next meeting." With that, they toasted with their half glass or red vino.

In my little brain, I still couldn't believe what I had heard and I had stopped coloring with my eyes trained on them and my mouth hanging open. They stopped talking and looked in my direction. I acted like I had been thinking about my task at hand and rolled my eyes up to my forehead, and then started again coloring in earnest while muttering to myself, to make it look legit. The whole concept of Krampusz getting schwacked, I still didn't quite comprehend, until I finally asked my dad one day. He wanted to know where I had heard such a word. I had said one of the older boys had used the euphemism... I didn't actually use the word euphemism.

I never did find out who had been selected to play the role of Krampusz the following year because that year I was in bed with the cold. And the following year, 1949, we had left the camp in the spring; thank goodness.

Even though I almost believed one hundred percent that the whole thing had been staged and it was nothing but a schwacked Zoli in a costume, I still never wanted to meet up with the ugly Krampusz ever again.

Krampusz, the ugliest creature I ever saw, when I was five (GK Drawing)

7

SCHMITZBERG CHRISTMAS

Christmas was the biggest and the best holiday when I was growing up in Schmitzberg Lager. The whole camp gathered in the big community hall. There would be a giant Christmas tree and the folks always managed to collect enough Schillings and Groschen from everyone to be able to buy every kid in the camp some sort of small present. No kid ever got left out. Even the not-so-good kids got a gift. We sang Christmas songs and ate Christmas baked goods like walnut and raisin logs, poppy seed logs and all sorts of Christmas cookies with sprinkles or dusted with powdered sugar. Somehow, the folks always managed to get their hand on some baking ingredients from the locals, by bartering or doing extra jobs.

Following the merriment, everyone walked home to their barracks, ate a little supper and after that everyone got ready to go back to the community hall for midnight mass; yes, even the Protestants and many of the Jews as well, showed up for midnight mass. It wasn't considered a celebration for Catholics only; it was for the whole Hungarian community.

When my family and I were returning from the hall following the Christmas celebration, a surprise was waiting for me. My father would disappear from the celebration under some pretext and hurry home to set the whole surprise up. As we would walk through the door of our little housing unit, magically a lit Christmas tree would be waiting for my mother and me.

"It volt a Jézuska!" I would cry out (Baby Jesus was here).

"Of course, he was here, Gyurika (Georgie)," my mother would say. "That's because you were a good boy"; For at least two weeks prior to Christmas.

According to Hungarian tradition the presents had been delivered by the Baby Jesus along with the Christmas tree.

I never questioned the logic that it would have been an insurmountable task for a baby to deliver a lit Christmas tree and presents to every one of the three hundred or so kids living in the camp and for that matter, the rest of the world, without anyone ever catching a glimpse of him. Then again, as long as I believed that it was so, I kept getting presents. So even as a little kid, I figured, why mess with a good thing…

• • •

A few weeks before Christmas 1948, my father let me in on the mystery of how Baby Jesus selected a particular tree for Christmas Eve delivery to your house. One morning in early December, right after breakfast he said "Gyere (come) Gyurika, let's go pick out our Christmas tree." I was definitely interested.

As best as I can remember, the whole camp was laid out on a leveled piece of land about the size of about four football fields, maybe a bit more. To the north, there were two roads exiting the camp, both merging into the street that wound its way to the town of Ampflwang if you turned right. If you turned to the left, the street ended in a gravel road which eventually turned into a dirt road. This road climbed directly to the woods. So, we followed this road and went on a long, slow hike. The snow on the road was not very deep as we left the environs of the camp. But as soon as we got nearer the tree-line, the deeper the snow got. It went from about six or eight inches to a foot and even foot and a half in places; some places up to my nose. Around and under the trees it got so deep that my father had to carry me, although I insisted that I was big enough to walk on my own. And, I tried. I really tried. It was hard work. I was all bundled up in that fur coat that had saved me from the raging Danube River. Of course, my mother had to enlarge it a bit as I had gotten a little taller. Still, when I fell over, no matter how hard I tried I couldn't upright myself. But, I never got hurt.

We hiked what to me at the time seemed like many kilometers, but in fact was only about three quarters to one kilometer. And there, right alongside a frozen creek, stood the most perfect little pine tree I had ever seen.

"How do you like that one Georgie?" my father had asked.

By about the age 6, I had learned a number of big words that I could use in a sentence, and one of them was "gyönyörű" which means beautiful in Hungarian; though I'm not certain how well my pronunciation had come out.

"We'll have to mark it so that the Baby Jesus will know to bring it to our home Christmas Eve" my father said.

He had brought out a length of red ribbon from his pocket. On it he had already printed in large, precise letters 'KAPUS'. He handed it to me. Then, he lifted me up and said "tie it on that high branch." When he finished rechecking my knot, he said "let's go home and have some (kakaó) cocoa", aka hot chocolate.

Well, guess what? On Christmas Eve, when we got back from the community celebration and we opened the door to our little home, like a miracle, there was that very same little pine tree, sitting on our little kitchen table. It was beautifully decorated with a multitude of shining Salon Cukor (Parlor Candy, a Hungarian Christmas tradition); some cutout ornaments and garlands as well as lights on every branch tip. The reason for the lights being at the tip of the branches was that they were in fact small, lit candles, like birthday candles, in holders that clipped to the ends of branches. There were no electric Christmas lights in the whole camp. If I remember correctly, years later my parents told me of a couple of Christmas tree fires. I'm glad I hadn't been made aware of them at the time...

Normally, children were taken for a walk if weather permitted, or if you had a big house, they were told to play somewhere, away from where the tree and presents would magically appear. And most importantly, before we took off for Midnight Mass, all the candles on the tree were blown out.

Now back in 1948, I was certain that that tree sitting on our kitchen table was in fact the very same one we had picked out and clearly marked on our hike in the woods. Some of the older kids tried to convince me that it came from a tree lot in town and laughed at my gullibility. But I knew better because my father had made certain that a piece of red ribbon would be tied to a branch at the back of the beautifully decorated tree sitting on the table; just like the one I had tied on that little tree by the creek.

Bottom line Christmas was my favorite holiday of the year, even better than my birthday. Every year, no matter how poor we were, how little money my parents had, they somehow always managed to put away enough so that Baby Jesus had some spending-cash. There were always presents for me under the tree; even if they didn't have enough to get each other anything. That is probably why I never realized that we were poor. I just thought that, that was the way things were for everybody. All the other kids got presents too. If their folks couldn't afford it, good people like my father, would chip in so that no child would be without presents at Christmas time, even when things were tough.

At Christmas, every Christmas, something magical happened and to this day, it is still my favorite holiday of the year.

• • •

In Hungary, back then (in the old days), Christmas Eve was celebrated with your immediate family; siblings and grand-parents. Christmas day, you went about visiting all the relatives and taking them gifts. On the second day after Christmas, you visited all the good family friends that had made your list...

I also discovered many years later that all the Salon Cukor on the Christmas tree had been fabricated, not by Baby Jesus or even elves for that matter; my mother had made them up and hidden them out of site until they magically appeared on the tree, wrapped in tissue paper with a strip of foil wrapped around it and a piece of thread attached to one end. My mother could do magic in the kitchen. When I got to be old enough, she let me help her make them and I became the taste-tester on all the ones she didn't consider perfect for the tree...

I miss those Salon Cukor; those real Salon Cukor.

8

CAMP GERMS AND WORMS

In addition to the DDT spraying upon our arrival to camp, the US Army made certain that all the kids got immunized so that there would be no outbreaks of any kind of diseases. The camp nurse, Piri Néni (Miss Piri) gave us csuka-máj-olaj (cod liver oil) regularly which tasted yuckier than the bottom of your shoes, so she gave all of us kiddies a cube of sugar afterward. Occasionally, I was able to make the absolutely ugliest face after taking the spoonful of oil, that I actually scored an extra cube of sugar. Some of the kids upon observing my strategy copied it and soon it became a contest as to who came up with the ugliest face to score the extra cubes of sugar. In general, kids were in reasonably good health under the circumstances and didn't get sick except for the occasional cold or stomach ache. Me, I was the exception. As I wrote earlier about my bout with Diphtheria, the doctor had forewarned my parents that depending upon how well my lungs recovered from this nasty disease, I might have lingering effects as I grew older.

• • •

So, it was that right around my fourth birthday, I contracted what was then diagnosed as Bronchitis. With the usual treatment and bed rest, I should have recovered in a matter of a week or two. However, when the ailment persisted beyond the third week, the camp nurse took me to see Dr. Kleinsasser (I have no idea how I remembered his name!) in Ampflwang who prescribed an extended stay at a sanatorium high up in the Austrian mountains near Lake Attersee. A little clarification here: this place was not for insane people; it was a sort of wellness center, for people with respiratory problems. The good doctor told Piri Néni that the clean mountain air would be good for my lungs.

I had never been away from my mother and father for more than a few hours. Needless to say, this pushed me into total panic mode. I thought that I would never see my parents ever again, a very scary prospect at age four. The closer we got to the date of departure, the more panicky I got; hiding under the sink, worked for only so long. The arrangements took only a couple days and I would be on my way for all intents and purposes, to the end of the world.

The trip to the sanatorium took the better part of a day. Thanks to my mother's girlfriend Terry who was sweet on the US Army captain in charge of the camp, I got to ride to the train station in Ampflwang, in a U.S. Army Jeep along with Piri Néni and my father. Apparently, they couldn't afford a train ticket for my mother, so she had stayed behind. Just as well, because even I can remember the tears running down her cheeks as I waved from the backseat of the jeep. From there the train took us to *Vöklabruck* by the lake Attersee. From there the final leg of the journey up the mountain to the Saubere Luft Sanitorium (I was four. I can't remember the real name of the sanatorium) was by bus.

I got checked in and had a bed assigned to me in the children's wing, in a room with four or five beds on each side of the wall with an aisle down the middle. Six or eight of us kids were assigned to this rather large room, all about my age. I discovered that there were even a couple little girls in the mix.

My father had told me since I'd been old enough to comprehend that brave soldiers didn't cry. Well, let me tell you, I must have been a lousy soldier because I cried so much that I didn't even have to get up at night to pee…

Years later, I was told that I was ready to pack it in about every other day but eventually stayed the duration of prescribed treatment; which was three months. There must have been something about the clear, clean mountain air because when I got back, I felt truly better. Also, after a while, I had made friends with some of the other kids. I had learned a bit of German by then so I could communicate with the local Austrian kids and even the doctors. As it turned out, there was a little Hungarian girl I made friends with. She unfortunately hadn't come from our camp. As she was leaving, she said "Bye-bye". I didn't know it then, but I would never see her again.

There was a time about half of the way through my stay that my mother and father came for a visit. They spent a few hours with me, and of course I was certain I would be leaving with them and was ready to pack up my stuff. It took great effort on the part of the staff to keep me there. I just really wanted to go home. At this point, home to me meant Schmitzberg Lager.

• • •

Going home had been the dream of every person in Schmitzberg Lager. For them, going home meant the place of their birth. After all, Hungary was but a bus or train ride away. The war was winding down. It would have been but a few hours ride to be back in your own home again. But for many of the refugees, repatriation was not to be…

Most everyone in camp had ways of communicating with relatives and friends back home. Through the camp grapevine, we soon found out that much of the enticing news coming out of Hungary was for the most part fake news; some of it put out by the Communist government and their lackey media.

Yes, the war was indeed over, but the country was not free.

About half of Hungary had supported the alliance with Hitler's Nazi Germany while the other half opposed it; but both sides ended up paying equally to the new benefactors. All those in the Hungarian National Socialist hierarchy were tried and hung. Many of the grunts and the poor run of the mill foot soldiers in the military suffered at times fates worse than death. Many were imprisoned, and some were sent to Siberia by the glorious Soviet liberators, never to be seen again. Unfortunately, from the conquering alliance, instead of oversight by the United States, Hungary fell under the jurisdiction of the Russians, which meant a Soviet Socialist Style Hell for the next fifty years and from which, Hungary is still reeling.

Besides the two main political factions, there were those who were already fomenting trouble from within, in eager anticipation of the Soviet takeover. Of course, they immediately aligned themselves with the liberators. They then helped them track down anyone and everyone they deemed opponents to the new regime. They shot and hung civilians on lampposts in the town squares, if they voiced opposition to the new regime. These were the useful idiots of the Soviet occupiers.

• • •

As I was told by my father, these turncoats were laying the groundwork for the Communist takeover of Hungary, way before any Russians marched down the main street of Budapest. My godfather Ferenc (Frank) from whom I got my middle name was a comedian and political satirist and regularly appeared on stage in Budapest nightclubs. It was sometime after my baptism, that he was performing in one of the nightclubs my parents frequented. He tended to poke fun at the National Socialists, the opposition and the Soviet sympathizers. As he was in the midst of his performance, a group of these 'anarchists' tossed a grenade on stage which killed him instantly as well as injuring many in the audience. The culprits were of course never caught due to all the chaos that was stirred up by the winds of war. This was just another example of the tolerance exhibited by the cowardly followers of 'isms' such as Socialism, Fascism, Communism and Totalitarianism…

They just didn't have a sense of humor or courage.

• • •

Meanwhile, back in Schmitzberg Lager, people didn't find out right away what was going on back home. As a little kid, I glimpsed into the hell that Hungary had descended into from the photos in the expatriate publications, of people being hung from lamp poles on street corners; photos, which had been smuggled out by the many who were still escaping to freedom.

From what my father explained to me some years later, a couple of hundred well-meaning refugees from Schmitzberg had been convinced (connived, actually) by agents of the new regime who had insinuated themselves into camp life, into believing that everything was hunky-dory back home in Hungary. They packed up and left for what they thought would be a joyous welcome after giving away their meager possessions.

Only when they crossed the border, did they realize that whoever was waiting for them, weren't friends. Instead, what they discovered was that they had returned to a hellish situation. Those who were lucky enough and managed to escape made their way back to camp within a few weeks after being concealed by relatives or hidden in barns and stables. They made certain to warn everybody of the dangers facing those who were naïve enough to believe that returning home at this time was the thing to do.

Once the cat was out of the bag so to speak, these instigators quietly and swiftly made their escape, in the middle of the night, but for a couple diehards who had decided to stay behind. These worms wanted to see if they could still work quietly on some of the more homesick and gullible in camp and convince them that the others had just run into some unfortunate situation. It would never happen again, they persisted.

However, by this time, everyone had learned their lesson. Those two conniving infiltrators were set upon by a group of very angry DPs and were beaten to within inches of their lives and then advised to get the hell out of there and to never return to the camp again. They licked their wounds and dragged their sorry carcasses back to their Soviet masters, thankful that they still had their lives.

Of course, upon hearing of this episode, the local authorities were in no hurry to investigate. They figured that DP justice had been rendered and the Soviet agents had failed to make incident reports. As neither the Austrian nor the American military had ab-

solutely any sympathy for them or the government they represented, there was no action of any sort taken. Also, local law en-
forcement had very little if any occasion to visit Schmitzberg, for
any reason.

The authorities knew that the DPs were a hardworking and
honest lot that never gave them any reason for concern.

9

YOU CAN NEVER GO HOME

News from back home in Hungary slowed to a trickle, due to new regulations and for a while actually stopped completely. Overnight in 1945, a barrier of ideas as well as hard steel and concrete went up between the Soviet occupied countries and the rest of Europe, the Iron Curtain. Eventually, walls and barbed wire fences with occasional lookout towers with machine guns and patrolled by submachinegun armed soldiers reinforced the not so ethereal curtain.

Initially, the joke from the captive citizenry was that all the protection in place was there to keep people from trying to sneak in; ha, ha.

The fact was, many of those who had stayed behind suffered worse than the enemy. Those who took over from the National Socialists considered all people traitors if they dared to raise any concerns or speak up against the new Socialist Regime. Many small-town people of course had never tried to escape or immigrate to foreign lands because they didn't want to leave their farms and land unattended and in fact the war had not greatly affected their lives unless they were in the direct path of the advancing enemy.

Many had acquired status before the war and were living in reasonable prosperity, so they felt that leaving would mean losing everything and having to start all over again somewhere else, so they weren't willing to risk leaving. You know, like some people who sit through major disasters like tornadoes and hurricanes, protecting their homes and property, and at the end come out mostly unscathed. Well, many of these people didn't. In fact, since all the air raids were directed at the major cities along the Danube and major transportation routes, smaller communities hardly suffered much ill effect of the war that is until the Russians ground forces marched in and took control and by then, it was too late.

A young cousin of my mother's whose name was Esztike (Little Esther) and who happened to be pregnant at the time, found herself in the path of advancing Russian troops and was run through her midsection by a bayonet wielding Soviet liberator and died instantly; along with her baby. My mother found this out quite some while later, after we had already escaped and were living in Schmitzberg Lager.

And if you thought the Russians were bad, the Romanians were even worse. As they took back the towns and villages of Transylvania that had been part of Hungary for hundreds of years, they killed and raped, looted and pillaged with no one to stop them.

In one particular incident, as the returning Bolshevik soldiers, who had been pretty brutal themselves, observed the savagery and brutality of the Romanians, were so shocked, perhaps as they recalled how they themselves had behaved. Out of pity or perhaps embarrassment, the Russian Captain ordered his soldiers to shoot every last one of the murderous Romanians.

Other relatives wrote to my parents of similar atrocities while they fared somewhat better, but not a lot, mainly because they had managed to stay alive and so were able to tell us about it.

Take for instance my aunt Rozsi (Rosie) who was my mother's older sister and her husband Janos (John). They had a little boy and two little girls. The Egyed family lived in Mezőtúr where Rozsi as well as my mother were born.

Rozsi and Janos operated a beauty salon out of their big two-story house. This property had been in their family for seventy-five years or more and they owned it free and clear because of the labor of their parents, grandparents and great grandparents. They lived rather comfortably before the war and the ravages of combat had barely touched this town which happens to be about ninety miles south-east of Budapest; which by the way was forty percent destroyed by Allied aerial bombardment, while Mezőtúr managed to stay mostly unscathed. For them, the war had always been somewhere, way over there…

The family felt safe being away from the battlefront, so they had no reason or desire to leave. As a matter of fact, in retrospect, my folks had been told that they could hold out at their home until the end of the war. Of course, at the time of the bombardments, my parents felt like they simply had to get out from all the destruction. As the end of the war came and went, business started to pick up and Rozsi and Janos were making a decent living again. Then as the 'Socialist Operatives' came out of the shadows and adopted their new moniker 'Communists' they and their local minions, took over every aspect of civic and municipal life. Things began changing in a hurry, and mostly for the worse. All the formerly elected officials were kicked out of office if they were lucky or simply locked up if they resisted the changes; even some of the Soviet sympathizers. Some were actually executed for putting up too much of a fuss. The newly appointed mayor and council members were now members of what was simply known as the Párt (the Party) and greeted each other as Elvtárs (Comrade). These corrupt sellouts held an economic stranglehold and the power of life and death over the citizenry.

In other words, former crooks, liars, backstabbers and Communist sympathizers became Komiszárs (commissars).

The biggest bullies in town became cops. Hot dam, it almost sounded like the Old West, where the crooked sheriff ran the whole town; except in this case, these crooks were all deputies of Uncle Joska, *aka* Joseph Stalin. You had to keep your mouth shut and play along; or your life would be made unbearable or perhaps terminated.

It is thus that Rozsi and Janos kept prices for their services reasonable and tried to minimize their earnings so as not to attract too much attention to the fact that even under these bad circumstances they were still able to feed the family and pay off obligations with something left over.

Unfortunately for them, they couldn't remain totally invisible to the many curious little spies working for the Komiszárs of the new benevolent city council. Eventually, it came to the attention of the comrades at the city hall of Mezőtúr that there was at least one family in a particular part of town that was living rather beyond their means and in a really big house; way too big for a family of only five.

A committee of comrades came for a visit and determined that in fact Rozsi and Janos and the three children didn't need such a large house, even though they also ran a business on the premises. This committee of envious bureaucrats decreed that the family would have to share with fellow citizens and be moved to the back of the yard where there was a very small two-room bungalow which in the past housed the caretaker of the estate and his wife. In other words, their house was confiscated for the general welfare of the town.

Just imagine, the big house was fully furnished and contained many family heirlooms throughout, some over a hundred years old, which the Egyed family was unable to move to the two-room cottage and had to thus leave in the big house. After all, they had to leave the big house habitable and welcoming for those less fortunate, whether they liked it or not. The 'share-equally' city council then, moved three large 'welfare' families into the big house.

The adults of these families were for the most part unemployed and unemployable and therefore lived under the auspices of the Socialist state with their numerous offspring. I believe my mother told me that there were eleven or twelve kids between the three families. Eventually, most of valuable heirlooms were slowly disposed of by these enterprising freeloaders who could live rather large while the Egyed family had to scrape to get by. They were now practically dispossessed and were struggling. This is how the glorious Communist government rewarded hard work and self-reliance. The unwritten motto of the new administration was something to the effect of "the People Sharing the Wealth Equally". The part they didn't advertise was "If you didn't like it, we had a cell for you to think it over "or, you could vacation in Siberia.

You would think that a story such as this one, would perhaps have a happy ending, but it didn't. Rozsi and Janos Egyed lived in the little bungalow in the back of the family estate well after the children had left. When Janos died, Rozsi moved away to another town where she was still at the mercy of the Socialist welfare system.

The government never reinstated the property to Rozsi, even though it had been owned outright by the family for generations. In 1979, my mother was sending both Rozsi and her sister-in-law Erzsi (Elisabeth) living in another small town nearby, postal money orders in the amount of $20 each, to help them out as they were now both widows and without much support from the government. My mother had on previous occasions slipped a $20 bill in between the pages of her letters to them. However, we eventually discovered that none of those Jacksons made it into their hands as the letters had been steamed open and read by officials and then re-sealed, minus the money. You see, the communist government was so paranoid that they had to know what the correspondence was about. They also did not punish local officials for removing whatever was included in the letters. They told the recipients, and there were many, that the money had been lost. "File a complaint" they advised and they would look into it; when pigs flew!

One of my father's sayings regarding the reassignment of property and wealth by the new Socialist overlords was: "This new regime works until they have squeezed every Filler (WWII era Hungarian coin equal to less than a penny) out of you to give to the Party loafers and bums and then everybody gets to share the big nothing that is left."

● ● ●

As I wrote at the beginning of this chapter, news from Hungary were not encouraging. I must also say in retrospect that at one point, both my mother and father almost fell for the tale of how great things were going, back in Hungary and for a very brief time considered leaving the camp and returning home. Thank God, they didn't make that mistake. I might have ended up in some nasty state run school, being raised by that socialist state, wearing a blue shirt with a red scarf and marching with the little commie kids in the May Day parade singing joyfully about living in the wonderful Red Paradise.

With all the distressing news coming out of the homeland, people slowly gave up on the idea of ever returning and started planning on moving further away from Hungary and Schmitzberg Lager, to better job and housing opportunities and a more normal life. They were packing it in for other parts of Austria, Germany and eventually France; whenever, wherever jobs were becoming available to refugees. Some were going to wait as there were rumors floating around that the United States congress was working on legislation that would allow displaced persons from former enemy nations that had been thoroughly vetted, to immigrate to the USA. Of course, you can imagine how slowly the wheels of government turned, even under well-meaning administrations.

The whole time we lived in the camp, my folks had always strongly resisted the idea of moving further and further away from Hungary. They felt that where they were, was just a few hours away from home.

Some of the people, who had connections Down Under, were invited to go all the way to Australia, where manpower was in great need since the end of the war. Many left. But that was one place my mother and father would not even consider. They said that was on the other side of the globe and would be a place of no-return. They didn't realize then that, we would end up in a place of no-return.

More and more of the buildings in Schmitzberg Lager were slowly being boarded up as families left.

Then, one day in early 1949 when there was talk of the French needing workers in the mines and were not only accepting but actually requesting former enemy refugees to fill those jobs due to the decimated workforce, my parents made the decision to move out. They accepted the invitation to immigrate to the Southern part of France where these jobs had become available in a coal mine. Even though it was farther away from home, it certainly wasn't as far as Australia, or the USA, which was now also moving on the legislation to accept applications for work from former enemy refugees as long as they were able to secure sponsorship for themselves from relatives or acquaintances already in the United States. However, the wait at that point was still a year or two away due to the long lines trying to get in as well as the processing time and annual quotas.

We packed up our meager possessions into three suitcases this time, giving the rest away to friends who were to remain at Schmitzberg Lager for the foreseeable future. Meanwhile, we were getting ready to immigrate to the southern part of France with a group of about a fifty or sixty of our camp neighbors. These were mostly families but a small contingent of single men and women had also joined the group. We took a two-and-a-half-day train ride to Cavillargues in the South of France. It might actually have taken somewhat longer as we often had to detour around areas where the tracks had been bombed and repairs were still under way.

I was barely seven and here we were moving again, for the fourth time and further away from our home yet.

Welcome to the Iron Curtain. Just don't try to leave! – (GK Drawing)

10

CAVILLARGUES

Change was in the air. I was now seven and it all seemed fun, like a big adventure. I was starting to enjoy myself and war was no longer a threat. The train took us to the South of France, a few kilometers above Avignon. The town of Cavillargues in 1949 was not a bad place to live. The people were nice and the area had not suffered much from the effects of war; they did however need workers.

We didn't actually get to live in the town of Cavillargues but somewhere in the hills a kilometer or so out of town at a place designated the Pougnadoresse mine's workers' housing complex. Housing complex might have been an overstatement. The place was a two-story concrete structure that looked like an old motel from that era, stretching out to accommodate about a hundred people in single room living quarters.

It was sufficiently large for our group. However, bathroom and shower facilities had been built without much forethought and were therefore shared by everybody. The right end of the long structure formed an arch which straddled a sizable creek and had a giant mill wheel built into the end of the structure. Behind the building, a concrete dam held back the water and from there, the water could be pumped to the mine. That's to the best of my recollection

The rooms were of acceptable size for a small family such as ours, until we all realized that lizards would be sharing the space with us as they were able to come and go under the doors and through the rather loose-fitting windows.

At times, we believed that the lizards were actually able to walk right through those walls. After a while, we just got used to the idea that at any time you could encounter them. I would sometimes wake up in the middle of the night and there would be one of them scaly little creepers sitting on your chest. "Daddy, there is a lizard sitting on my chest" I would mumble, "and he's staring right into my eyes."

"Don't worry son," my dad would say in his very serious tone, "He'll go away when he gets tired of looking at you." And, he would turn over and go back to sleep.

I would watch the lizard for a while longer and I actually believed he had hypnotized me, because I would quickly fall asleep.

It was the weirdest experience, but they never bit me. After a while, I just got used to them. They just seemed to like human company; or maybe, we just kept them warm.

The rooms themselves were square and rather plain, with metal bed frames topped by rather thin mattresses. Looking back, they did look like cheap old motel rooms that you see in real old movies or maybe county jail cells, except that today's jail cells have a heck of a lot more amenities. Calling these rooms Spartan, would have been a compliment. I actually started missing our accommodations from Schmitzberg Lager. My father encouraged me to think of the whole episode as an adventure because he would say, "I have a feeling we are just passing through and probably won't be staying here very long."

He had an uncanny talent for foreseeing our future.

As I had mentioned earlier, one of the many problems was that there weren't sufficient bathrooms for all the people; say if more than four had to use them, you stood in line for a while, day or night. That is why, when the lines grew too long and the folks got impatient, they would wander off and on up into the hills behind the building to take care of business, in the bushes, behind some trees along with the wildlife; that is until one day one of the women came running, with her skirt still hanging down and screaming about being chased by snakes. Everyone laughed. "They're just little sikló (shick-low) or Couleuvre (coo-l'oevre) in French (garter snake)" they laughed.

"They won't bite you, they're harmless," everyone said.

They were wrong. Upon closer investigation by a couple of hardy young guys, it was determined that they were in fact a rather small snake from the viper family, actually called Vipera (or Viper). These little snakes are only about ten to twelve inches long at most and are in fact the distant cousins to such nasty creatures as the copperhead, the cottonmouth and the bushmaster. Being smaller only meant that they didn't leave big bite marks; but they in fact did leave some (bite marks). They were also poisonous but not nearly as dangerous as their larger relatives.

One problem with these little green slithering critters was that they didn't bother to warn you with a rattle like their larger American cousins. Another problem with them was that they were relentless and persistent; once they spotted you, they wanted to be your best friend. The more you wanted to shoo them away, the more they persisted in coming after you; that is, when you could actually see them. The very last problem was: due to their coloration, they blended right in rather well with nature. So, you didn't know they were around until you squatted down and suddenly realized that the little brownish green stick that had been sitting by your feet just opened its eyes and was about to sink its pointy little fangs into whatever tender part of your anatomy happened to be exposed close to ground level.

Squatting right down so close to Mother Nature, I don't need to explain which parts of your anatomy were exposed to danger. After two or three sightings and actually only one bite, everyone decided to return to standing in lines for the only four available bathrooms, except when you had to do number one. Don't even let me get started on showers. Compared to these facilities, the accommodations at Schmitzberg Lager would have been considered luxurious...

• • •

While in camp in Austria, I started attending a basic or first grade Hungarian class, which was unfortunately interrupted due to our departure. The Austrian authorities also required the young to attend a half day's school in town to learn German which was and still is, of course the country's official language. So, by the time I arrived in Cavillargues, I could communicate rather well in two tongues, Hungarian and German. However, the French had no interest in learning the languages that I and all the other refugee kids spoke. Almost immediately upon my seventh birthday, I was introduced to my third language, French. I was slowly becoming multi-lingual. Of course, I had no clue as to what that meant at the time. It was just something that we all had to do.

One of the easiest ways to learn new languages is to sing songs in that language. We started out with *Frere Jacques*, then *Sur Le Pond D 'Avignon* which of course was a-pro-pos since Avignon was just a skip and a hop away. Then, we learned *Alouette, Gentille Alouette* before moving on to the national anthem: *La Marseillaise*. It was rather funny at first, because you got to understand that French is as different from German and Hungarian as Russian is from Swahili or Martian.

The teacher would tell us very slowly in French: "chantez (sing)." At this point, we didn't even understand what chantez meant.

Then he sang "Sur le pond d' Avignon, on y dance, on y dance…"

And we went "La, la, la, la, la, la, blah, blah, and blah, dancy, dancy… "

He would say "Non! Non!" and repeated the lyrics. We would raise our shoulders like we didn't understand and cocked our heads to emphasize the point. We would even say it in German, "Ich verstehe nicht, or "I don't understand." And boy oh boy did the teacher get annoyed with us speaking in German.

We all had this suspicion that he actually did understand full well what we were saying, but that French national pride being what it was, kept him from admitting it. He was determined to teach us little *étrangers* (foreigners) French even if it killed him and us.

Of course, we weren't a bunch of dummies. We were learning

quicker than he thought. We were just pretending not to get it, for a little while anyway while having a good laugh; like a bunch of little wise guys. And of course, all the local kids were laughing at us and clapping and pointing fingers. We were having great fun not understanding each other, but after a few days' time we were all singing "Alouette, Gentille Alouette," skipping along on the way home, like we'd been born there.

This didn't mean that all of a sudden, we had mastered the French language. It just meant we could sing that particular song and we could now move on to: *Sur Le Pond d 'Avignon*. Of course, in about three months' time, we did learn to speak it sufficiently well to do our assignments in French and converse rather well with the local kids. At that point, they stopped laughing at us because we could answer them back in their own language. Suddenly, fate and *la lingua Franca* had made us equals.

It didn't take very long for the teacher to start warming up to us as well, as he discovered that we were really making an effort to learn. There was even a sense of appreciation that a bunch of displaced, foreign kids could overcome a difficult language barrier and in a short time pretty much excel in it. When the time came for us to leave the environs of Cavillargues, all the teachers were really sorry to see us go. We had finally been accepted into their society and the school community; unfortunately, it was again time to move on. I remember the teachers giving us some very nice French books with their farewell handshakes.

The reason for us all having to leave yet again was because the Pougnadoresse mine had been forced to close as it had run out of coal. So, six months almost to the day after our arrival, the group of fifty some odd family members and singles, was breaking up into smaller groups and slowly dispersing to the four corners of France as news of job openings started to come in through the aus- pices of the refugee organization that had gotten us moved from Schmitzberg Lager to this location.

As I was forming friendships with the other refugee kids and starting to warm up to the locals and the area, we were moving yet again.

I was probably never, ever going to see my little Hungarian buddies that I had known since the early days in the camp. I was also saying goodbye to my new French buddies who were sad to see us go. I was sad again for having to leave but glad that those little kids had liked me enough to accompany us to the train station for a last goodbye. Come to think of it, the teachers actually brought out the whole class we had been in, to wave us *Bon Voyage*.

The only thing I wasn't going to miss even a little bit was the accommodations of the Pougnadoresse Housing Authority and the long lines at the bathroom; and let's not forget the vipers. I do have to admit that all of us boys left our marks on the backside of the old concrete building. When you had to pee, you had to pee. "C'est la vie!"

Next stop for us would be in North-Eastern France, in a town called Algrange in the province of Alsace & Lorraine and the Department (county) of Moselle, famous for its grapes and wine production, a fact of which I had not been aware of at the time, since I was not allowed to drink vino, just yet.

Getting ready to board the train that would takes us to Cavillargues in the south of France — My little buddy Jancsi is almost in the middle of the picture and I'm at the far end in front of dad -1949 (Author's archives)

11

YOU DON'T PICK
YOUR NEIGHBORS

Our little group arrived in Algrange in early fall of 1949. Well, we actually arrived at the train station in Hayange, about four miles north as there was no passenger train service to Algrange. Our small group was now made up of my mother, father and yours truly, a couple by the name of Bodogni and their three kids, the Magenheims and their little boy Jancsi (Johnny) and four single guys. There was Fredi (Freddy) who was a friend of the Magenheims, Springer Karcsi (Charlie Springer) who wanted to be called Karoly (Charles) and his buddy, this big, slow, lumbering guy who had been a meat cutter back in Hungary, by the name of Bajor Feri (Frank Bayor). The one thing I always remembered about this guy Frank is that he had hands the size of shovels. Once, he actually threatened to beat up my father. But, I'm getting ahead of myself again.

The fourth single guy to tag along with us was Bartha Berci (Bert Bartha) who had been a mechanic in the Hungarian Air Force and was also damn good at fixing German cars.

As it turned out, when we got to Algrange, the work promised to the Magenheims and their friend Fredi had been filled. It appeared to have been some kind of paperwork mix-up. As a result, they were sent along to Colmar, in the Haute Rein (Alsace region), where there were apparently many more jobs available than applicants. So, right off the top, I lost my best little buddy Jancsi.

• • •

I was now stuck with the Bodogni kids and man, were they ever a strange lot. Hey, I was seven but even I could see that something wasn't totally right with this bunch. There was Karcsika (Charlie named after his father Charles). He was the oldest and according to his daddy, could do no wrong. Charlie had a younger brother they called Öcsike, which literally means Little Brother and a little sister named Katika, meaning Katie. Charlie was a nice enough little kid, well actually, he was about my age but a smidgen taller and he was afraid of his own shadow and stuttered uncontrollably. Besides the stuttering, he also mumbled all the time; which meant that I had a hard time understanding what he was talking about, half the time and I had to make him repeat everything he said.

"Say that slowly and loudly, so that I can understand you," I would have to tell him.

Sometimes, even after he repeated himself, I still didn't know what the heck he was saying. Come to think of it, Papa Charles stuttered a lot himself. The only time he didn't was when he sang, and he did have a rather pleasant mellifluous singing voice; and as a matter of fact, he also played the violin rather nicely.

Back to Little Charlie though; he couldn't sing a lick. For some reason, the poor kid even stuttered when he sang, if you can believe it. The other thing about Little Charlie that was quite annoying was that he had leaky-teaky issues. This meant he had to constantly run and pee. Since I was only seven and not a doctor, I couldn't figure out what his problem was. I thought perhaps, it was some kind of childhood bladder issue. If he didn't like the game you wanted to play, he would jump up, grab his crotch, lift one knee and then the other and run off to pee.

This brings up yet another issue; he would take forever to come back. The reason for that, I soon discovered was that he couldn't pee like the rest of us, up against the back side of the house or the fence or the old bush. He had to go inside, sit on his little pot; yes, I said pot and even at seven and eight years of age. He always had to pee in private. If he lost the game that he had actually wanted to play, he would run off to pee. He would just grab the front of his shorts, let out a wail and run off. See where am I going with this?

Poor Charlie, he had a lot of issues. One more irritating thing about Charlie was that whatever toys were lying around, he always declared them his possessions, even when they were not. I had to use some clever diplomacy to reclaim some of my very own property. Let's just say that the kid wasn't very good at sharing. Thank goodness, they didn't hand out grades for Sharing back in those days, nor for feeling good about yourself. I don't believe he felt good about himself.

Öcsike, the poor little kid, had communication issues himself, from birth. He just rocked back and forth against the wall of the building, mostly outside in the front yard and usually in a sunny spot, where we all played, while mumbling incoherently and rolling his eyes to the top of his head and back down. It was somewhat enthralling to watch him while he performed this ritual, but also rather disconcerting. For years, people thought the poor kid was simply retarded. I know it's not politically correct to say that today, but that's what they said back then; not me. Some went as far as calling him an idióta (idiot), but definitely not a savant, because he couldn't speak a coherent word.

Anyway, poor Öcsike wasn't ever able to attend school because the minute you tried to drag him away from the wall he was glued to, he would let out the most blood-curdling wail while falling to the ground, flailing and kicking. For some reason, every day, he had this uncanny ability to locate the very same spot on the wall where he had rested his hands the day before; like he had some kind of homing ability. Sometimes, he even went out there in the rain, in his little raincoat and hat. The day we moved away, I could still see his hand's imprint on the surface of the wall. Nah, he was actually rocking in that same spot. As I walked by, he actually winked at me. It could have been the sun getting in his eye. Then again, you never know…

It wasn't until many years later, long after we had moved to the States, that we heard from our friends the Magenheims that they discovered that there was nothing wrong with the kid mentally. What they found out was that he had hearing issues; something about his ear canals being severely obstructed. So, he had simply been repeating whatever strange, distorted sounds would make their way through the blockage. Once the problem had been medically rectified, he was able to learn to speak and his life finally began to normalize. Good for you Öcsike! The eye rolling however, I don't know if that was ever corrected...

Now little Katie was a pretty little girl, the youngest of the three. She all but mimicked her older brother Charlie's eccentric behavior; including frequent runs to the pee pot. I could never figure that one out either. She was sweet as can be if you could stop her long enough to say so. The problem was when you started to say "Hi!" or "How are you?" to her, she would take off running like a scared rabbit. Again, it was many years later that we found out that both Charlie and Katie had gotten married and were actually raising their own families and that Öcsike had become a drummer or was it a plumber? No, I'm pretty sure they said drummer. It must have been because he had gotten that beat down, from all that rhythmic rocking back and forth glued to that wall. Either way, it was quite a surprise.

• • •

I can't leave the Bodogni clan just yet, without telling this little story about when I was left in their care. My mom and dad hardly ever took any trips very far, mostly because it wasn't in their budget but also, if they both went, I came along as well. However, this one time, I remember them going to visit the Magenheims in Colmar by train and staying overnight. For some reason, I hadn't been invited, or maybe there wasn't enough money for three tickets. I never questioned their decisions. Anyway, they asked Mrs. Bodogni to watch me for that day and a half of their absence.

Erika was her name. She was a rather big, bosomy redhead, who lisped, so her name came out as 'Eh-hee-kah when asked. She wasn't very good with the letter 'R' either. It was hilarious, for a little kid anyway. You had to have been there. On top of that, the more she got annoyed with something or someone, the more Erika lisped and the funnier the words with an **r** in them came out.

So, my parents' trip meant that I would be forced to spend way more time with the Bodogni kids then I would ever have wished. In addition, I had to eat what Erika cooked; another punishment. Let's just say that cooking wasn't one of her fortes. When she cooked, you could smell it in our apartment and up and down the hall, because almost everything was well-done and beyond and soaking in Margarine. Besides, in my mind, my mother was the best cook in the whole world, ever. To put it mildly, I was not fond of Erika's cooking and therefore, I was not a very good guest. However, her family seemed happy with her culinary creations.

I ate very little of Mrs. Bodogni's concoction if I could help it. But I ate a bit, out of necessity and courtesy. "I'm just not very hungry," I would say. They all just stared at me like I was green all over and horns had just grown out of my head. Did I mention that every one of them had great big, bulging eyes; and they just rolled them at me?

The second morning's breakfast was however the last straw for her, and me. She had made scrambled eggs. Such a simple dish; who could possibly mess up scrambled eggs, you ask? It didn't look bad at first glance; however, the strange odor emanating from the fluffy yellow pile on my plate, initially clogged my nostrils, stuck in my throat, made me visibly gag and my eyes water. I might be exaggerating a bit here; but on second thought, I don't think so. To understand my reaction, you have to realize how my mother made her scrambled eggs, by comparison; a light vegetable oil or a little bacon dripping to coat the pan and whipped up eggs with a tiny pinch of salt and paprika for flavor. That was her favorite way of cooking eggs; no additives like milk or buttermilk, or water and certainly not fried in Margarine. You have to remember that back then, Margarine had the consistency and taste of axle grease; it might actually have been used in auto repair; yuck!

Hey, I had been spoiled by my mom's cooking. Even during the toughest of times, she could make the humblest dish taste like a meal made for a king. My mother could make ordinary food taste extraordinary; need I say more?

Well, I had decided to give it a try. Taking that first bite of Erika's scramble actually constricted my throat and I gagged. In retrospect, I could have had a Margarine allergy; anything is possible. No effort on my part could make it go down. I was about to chuck it up and was barely able to finally force it down with some water followed by a slice of toasted bread. That first bite turned out to be my last bite. The Bodogni clan just stared at me with bewildered looks again with bulging eyeballs like I had just morphed into some evil troll.

I said "I'm sorry but I don't think I'm feeling too good this morning" as I got up from the table and walked out into the hall for a deep gulp of air.

Erika's feelings got hurt, naturally. She could tell I hadn't taken too well to her scrambled eggs. When I returned from the hallway, I was sent to stand in a corner without the rest of my breakfast; thank God.

When my folks returned from their trip that afternoon, they got a less than favorable report on my behavior from Erika, in her lisping voice which got more and more hysterical as she recounted all of my trespasses over the past thirty some odd hours. Thank God, I was still in the corner because the more hysterical she got, the more she lisped and the more I wanted to bust out laughing. I had to bite my knuckles to keep from irrupting and embarrassing my parents. Bottom line, Erika would never, ever again watch me; or feed me for that matter. Praise the Lord!

The folks promised the Bodognis that I would be severely reprimanded. Unfortunately, it almost turned into a laugh fest. Both mom and dad had had a difficult time containing themselves as poor Erika tried to recount the events of my visit. They of course were well aware of her histrionics and my less than acceptable behavior at times; most of this due to the fact that I was a rather opinionated child. Back in our apartment, my dad did a lot of yelling, mostly for the benefit of our neighbors; to show that I was really getting my well-deserved comeuppance. The three of us had to cover our mouths to keep control of our laughter. My mother who actually liked Erika, couldn't help letting out a couple of chuckles herself.

"Now tomorrow," my father said so loudly that the neighbors

could actually hear, "you go over there and apologize for you behavior to Erika Neni", which I did. As a family, we always presented a united front.

And after all, the Bodognis were our neighbors and fellow countrymen; and in a strange sort of way, our friends.

Mikulás in Algrange – the Bodogni kids are between Mikulás and me – 1950 (Author's archives)

12

LA CANTINE

Housing had been arranged for us in Algrange at one of the mine's housing complexes called *La Cantine* meaning the Cantina, through the auspices of the French Refugee Relocation Administration. Why this complex was called La Cantine, no one knew. Maybe in the old days they actually served food or drinks there. The local iron ore mine was called Mine d'Angevilliers and its entrance was located only about a half a mile from where we lived. As it was, you had to walk out to the street and cross over a railroad bridge to get to the entrance of the mine. Let's just say that it was but a skip and a hop to get home after work.

Now, the definition housing complex was somewhat of a misnomer. About a hundred feet above the tracks that moved rail traffic from the mine to the foundries, this piece of real estate had been leveled. On it, two elongated bunker-like concrete structure had been built. They contained eight large rooms roughly sixteen feet squared, on either side of a four-foot-wide hallway. At the end of the hallway, there were a half a dozen toilet stalls and a couple showers with no doors for any privacy on half of the long back wall. The other half contained one long deep trough divided into four, for washing oneself and doing one's laundry. It had obviously been originally intended for male mine workers. Now there were men, women and children, but no one had thought of modifying the accommodations.

Now let me further explain to you all who are used to nice comfortable sit-down, flush toilets, in lockable bathrooms; these facilities were not. Privacy had not been considered in the design of the Cantina. The toilets basically consisted of two pads, shaped like oversized footprints, poured in the concrete floor for your two feet to fit on, with a two-to three-inch-deep circular depression behind about a foot diameter with a six inch hole right in the center of that; the bomb bay. There was actually a flusher activated by a chain, and that was a nice thing. The tricky part of the whole operation was avoiding the deposits made by previous occupant(s) if he/she had not been an accurate bombardier, or sleepy, or what have you. You were in grave danger of stepping into some doo-da, especially after dark. Are you following me?

I meant to tell you that the rest of the rooms in La Cantine, were occupied by single men who worked in the mines. They had come from France's North-African colonies such as Algeria, Morocco and Tunisia mostly; although some had come up from Italy and Sicily. Let me generalize here. Hungarians stuck together as did all the other ethnic groups, and some of them didn't care for each other very much. For example, the Italians and Sicilians got into it, fairly regularly. That's actually how I picked up some Italian phraseology; mostly not usable in mixed company…

• • •

As you can imagine, La Cantine was truly a melting pot of the various cultures, none stranger to me than the workers who had come from North Africa. Up to this point in my life, I had never run across anyone who wore a turban, except in the movies, in other words someone who had come from that part of the world. As it happened, all of us Hungarians happened to have been assigned to Building 1 along with some of the men from Algeria, Morocco and Tunisia.

In Building 2, there were Italians, Sicilians, a couple Germans and more North Africans. The occupants in that building were all men. I hardly ever saw any women of any nationality besides those from our little Hungarian group in either building. Although at some point I did observe that some ladies would come to stay there for short visits, mostly at night. Some returned on more than one occasion. They might have been relatives or overnight bed buddies.

They didn't tell me and I didn't ask. They always smiled at me and I smiled back.

All the various ethnic groups kept pretty much to themselves, so I never really got to know any of them except some of the guys from North Africa. Since there were a number of them living in our building, I not only had occasion to observe some of their communal activities but also had the opportunity to interact with them more frequently. I addition, they all seemed to hang around in one of the rooms in our building.

They were mostly younger men in their twenties with some closer to thirty and even a couple who looked quite a bit older. They had all come to Algrange for the work in the mines and the foundries. Although many spoke French at some level as I had occasion to speak with them, in their gatherings, they all spoke Arabic with each other. Some of them were reasonably polite and friendly with us and greeted us in passing while others didn't say anything and just stared openly, appearing to hold us in some sort of contempt or at least looked at us with suspicion. We must have been just as strange to them as they were to us.

Remember, this was 1949 when I first encountered them.

I had always been taught to be polite but cautious with strangers. I would say "bonjour" to them as we passed each other in the hallway. Eventually, I got to talking with some of the younger guys; I was curious. They would ask about where we had come from, what I learned in school and in turn I would ask them about where they had come from and what they were doing and so on. It went on like this for a long while. I was a precautious child, but, I was also a curious child and that got me into some interesting situations.

• • •

As I said, I had gotten pretty good at learning a couple of new languages; I was now sailing along in French. Of course, sailing is only good until something or someone rips a hole in your sails.

At *La Cantine*, as I said, I had frequent contact with the younger

North Africans and we were on civil if not totally friendly terms with one another. So, one day, this young guy being funny he thought, invited me inside one of their rooms where they just happened to be gathering.

They were lounging about, toking on their shisha, sipping tea from little glasses and having an animated discussion. There were bowls of different snacks sitting on a low table in front of a divan. I could see an assortment of nuts and chickpeas, olives, merguez (spicy, North African mutton or beef sausages) and Brik (a Tunisian dish consisting of thin pastry with filling and deep-fried, sort of like a stuffed wonton). They were all laughing and seemed to be having a good time and I just stood there, staring like a dummy, with my mouth open. They all turned and started laughing at me, I thought and commenting at my sudden inexplicable appearance in their midst. I couldn't understand a word of what they were saying, as it was all in Arabic. They must have thought I looked funny. I just wanted to run and hide but my feet wouldn't move.

The younger guy, Farris who had invited me in decided to try and teach me some words while telling me their meanings. There were about ten or twelve men in the room. Some got into the banter while others appeared disinterested and even bored by the whole thing. One of the men who happened to be sitting on a bed in the corner appeared to be totally annoyed by my visit and probably felt it was an intrusion into their special space, even though it had not been my idea. He just kept jabbering in an angry guttural. Farris, who had claimed to be my friend tried vainly to calm him down. The older man, Hamza just yelled back at him "Why you bring this stupid little étranger to our gathering?"

Of course, I understood étranger. The rest, I was told later. It was in Arabic.

So, Farris came over to me and told me to say something to Hamza in Arabic. "Go tell him haloof," he said. I should have asked for an immediate translation. I only found out much later that the word Farris had told me to say meant pig, pork, warthog or some such thing which was not at all complimentary in their culture as in anyone else's. What possessed this knucklehead to think that telling the old grumpy man that he was related to a pig or even a warthog, would be funny?

So, innocently, hands behind my back, I walked over to the older man and told him what Farris had told me to say.

Hamza literally growled as he jumped off the bed and lunged at me. All the others let out a gasp. I barely got out of the way. Farris got between us with his hands up, saying "He was just saying what I told him. It was a joke."

With a lot of expletives, I couldn't understand and a spray of spittle, the older man said in broken French, as he pointed at me "Next time you say that, little étranger boy, I will cut your throat from ear to ear". I could imagine a gleaming scimitar clenched in old Hamza's right hand as I stood there in shock, like a deer in the headlights of a 1939 Peugeot.

Farris had to shove me out the door saying he was sorry. I could see that his eyes had that glassy look, like I remembered seeing on a drunk or two. But these guys weren't supposed to drink anything alcoholic. Perhaps, Farris had been smoking something stronger than tobacco in his shisha? Or maybe North African tobacco was a lot stronger that I guessed. Anyway, I ran like the devil was on my tail, down the hall, to our room and promptly hid in the corner, behind the bed.

When my father finally got home from work, my mother made me tell him what had happened as best as I could, between gulps of air. He firmly told me to stay away from that end of the hallway unless I had to go to the toilet. "Better yet," apuka said, "If you have to pee, just go outside and pee behind the wall."

Later on, Farris told me that the older man was just trying to scare me. I believe I wet my shorts. Others from the room told me the same thing. I smiled. I didn't believe a word they said.

After that incident, every time I saw old Hamza, I made an effort to go as far in the opposite direction as I could. I can still remember the crazed look in his eyes. That guy had been really pissed. And no one could tell me different.

• • •

In my quest for learning other foreign languages, besides Arabic, I fell into another trap set by an older, wiser (ass) construction worker. This time, the guy was from Italy and rode a great looking motorcycle.

It was the first time that I had ever seen a motorcycle called **Indian Scout**. This bike was **Made in America**. It was in the summer of 1952 or 1953. I was on the way to the butcher shop about a kilometer down the road from our house, with one of my buddies, Michel (Me-shell), when we came upon the bike, parked alongside a construction site. It was like nothing we had ever seen.

Glinting in the late afternoon sun, there sat a 1941 Indian Sport Scout in powder blue with yellow wavy lines through the blue and lots of chrome. There was even what looked like a chrome, curved bar around the back fender, sort of like a small bumper. The handle bar bent way back in a big chromed swoop and the seat was made of tan saddle leather. Attached to the luggage rack was something I had never seen before until I got to the States. It was a double, leather saddle bag with long leather fringes. Needless to say, the Paisan was very proud of his American made motorcycle. It must have cost him a few million Francs (Francs weren't worth much back then). As we stood there admiring it, I said to Michel, "wouldn't it be nice to live in a country where they make motorcycles like this?"

"Oui, oui," replied Michel. The Italian worker was watching us and told us not to touch it but seeing our interest, he started to tell us about it and even offered to take us on a ride, "someday, after work."

"Mama Mia," we both replied. The man laughed and said, "You boys want, I should teach you some more words in Italian?"

I should have known there would be a catch; but we both agreed. He started teaching us some Italian words. Michel and I were eleven. We did not know Italian. Actually, our friend Mouchi (housefly) whose parents were Italian, but had been born in France, had taught us the few words he knew, but not enough to actually communicate with anybody and mostly unsuitable in a civil dialog. We both repeated the words as best as we could. We should have seen a trap closing. Because by the time we realized what we had been taught, it was too late.

As we had been standing there, getting our lesson in Italian, we had noticed a very nice looking dark, curly haired woman across the street that our new mentor Casanova, appeared to have been admiring and was apparently already acquainted with. So, he told us "go across the street and you say to that nice lady, "Signorina vacca bella. She will really like it"

Dutifully, we crossed the street and standing in front of the nice woman, with our hands behind our backs, just like in school, we delivered our newly learned compliment "Signorina vacca bella" with the sweetest smile we could muster, like a couple of little, brainless parrots. She let out a screech and started yelling at us in Italian; things neither Michel nor I understood but could tell were not of a complimentary nature.

She then reached into her shopping bag and pulled out a three-foot-long sourdough baguette, which she began swinging at us like Excalibur, still screaming. Our friend Casanova was all doubled up, holding his stomach, he was laughing so hard, over across the street. We took off running. The woman ran after us and we could hear the clicking of her high heels on the concrete sidewalk. We ran faster. You'd have thought her big bag of groceries would have slowed her down; no siree! She ran faster. The baguette finally broke in half. She flung the other half in our direction. It missed me but hit Michel in the back of the head almost knocking him over.

The signorina's footsteps finally slowed and she stopped. I could see her taking deep gulps of air and coughing. Back in those days, smoking was considered sexy; however, it did affect you in a hundred-meter dash. Even with our shorter legs, we had outrun her. As we got near Michel's house, we slowed down and turned around to see that the woman had changed directions and was now charging after our buddy Casanova, with a foot-long salami swinging in her right fist with a colorful verbal assault emanating from her red lips. Michel and I figured that it must have been some sort of domestic misunderstanding that we had gotten ourselves unwittingly stuck in the middle of.

The next day when we got to school, we asked our pal Mouchi what exactly we had said that got that nice lady in such a tizzy. Mouchi burst out laughing.

"That was no compliment you idiots," he said. "You called her *miss beautiful cow.*"

After that, I was very careful before I repeated anything that I had learned from Italian construction workers. And boy oh boy, did I learn a few doozies, mama mia!

"Scuzami per la mia colpa e mille grazie"

• • •

Back at the Cantine, as a family, we got assigned one of the square rooms for the three of us, while the Bodognis got two adjoining rooms because of the three kids. The three single guys ended up sharing one room, like many of the other single guys in the complex.

Our room had one big bed; somewhat narrower than your average everyday American queen-size. There was of course no room for another, even smaller bed. So, of course that meant that we all had to sleep together like a bunch of Gypsies, with me in the middle, most of the time. And don't ask. I played outside whenever possible and went to the movies whenever I had saved up enough centimes to afford it, or my dad would give me his pocket change. I went to the circus a couple times and one time I was sent to scout camp for a whole month.

We had a coal-burning stove for cooking, baking and heating in one corner. However, if my mother wanted to bake more than one thing, we had to walk it to the baker about a kilometer and a half away and he would put the pans in his big oven in the evenings when his baking was all done, for a few centimes. Around Christmas time, there would be a line of women with more than one pan to bake. Not many had double ovens like we have here.

We had a little table with four chairs around it for dining and homework, between the stove area and the bed, a built in wooden closet for all our clothes about four feet wide and a utility case sort of contraption with no drawers that my father had slapped together out of scavenged shipping crates and palates in which we stored cookware, utensils, canned food and all the clothing that didn't fit in the closet.

My mother sewed little curtains for each shelf to keep the dust out and the contents out of sight. The bed occupied the space opposite the dining area with a little corner left for me to keep toys and other necessities in a wooden crate, as well as for staring at during punishment. Eventually, we acquired a couple of simple, small armchairs to complete the furnishings. I still think back in amazement that with the little space we actually had, my parents managed to throw dinner parties for ten to twelve people. They would sit everywhere including the bed and my toy crate, and they ate my mother's tasty cooking and drank cheap French wine.

I can still recall the aroma of her Chicken Paprikás (Paprikash), stuffed cabbage, Wiener schnitzel and Hungarian Gulyás (Goulash) wafting all the way outside where I'd be playing. And let's not forget her desserts: Dobosh torte, hazelnut torte, apple and peach tart, Pogácsas (bacon biscuits which go well with beer and wine, also milk), various strudels and a few other sweets; too many to list. Now, you have to remember that when we got to Algrange in 1949, we ate beans a lot. It took a year or more before we got comfortable enough to have a dessert after Saturday and Sunday dinner.

• • •

I really enjoyed those Saturday parties. After a few glasses of vino, everybody got very mellow. As they ran out of beverages, one or another would send me to the local grocery store to get more.

That was possible, because back in those olden days in France, there was no age limit for purchasing alcoholic beverages. And of course, I didn't mind. As a matter of fact, I actually volunteered most of the time, to go as often as necessary for beverage runs. With a few glasses of Mouton Cadet in them all the guests got very generous and donated tips for my quick return from these errands. When they were all about to leave, which most of the time was late at night, if I had fallen asleep, I would try to wake up to say good-bye with a smile. This never failed to score me a few more cen-times, on occasion even a one hundred Frank note; which by the way back in the 1950s was worth about thirty-five cents, American. What did I know from dollars and cents? To me, it was real money and that meant going to the movies with my buddies or getting pastries at **Monsieur Schmuk's** pastry shop at the school lunch break; more on that, later.

• • •

Throughout our seven years in Algrange, our most expensive possession was a beautiful, multi-band radio which sat atop our storage chest with one my mother's lacy embroideries underneath it. The unit which was encased in a beautiful wooden cabinet was made by Blaupunkt and we got many hours of entertainment and news out of it as well as Sunday Futbol (soccer) games. I believe that my father put in a lot of overtime at the mine to be able to buy the Blaupunkt which wasn't cheap. I remember he was always pretty tired.

The Blaupunkt was also our source for Hungarian news and music courtesy of Radio Free Europe. When the folks didn't have enough money to go to the movies, we would all sit around the radio on Saturday evenings and listen to some mystery theater presentation or a comedy-variety show. My mother and father sat around the little table relaxing with a cup of tea or if there was any left, a glass of wine while smoking a cigarette or two. I would lounge on the bed with my toy soldiers all spread out and one ear tuned to the broadcast. Those were happy, peaceful times.

At other times, we read; all of us. The folks read some serious Hungarian novels or non-fiction they had gotten a hold of in trade or on loan; although my dad would sometimes read German books or magazines like Stern (Star), Spiegel (Mirror) and Schweitzer Illustrierte (Swiss Illustrated).

Me, I would read anything interesting in French. Early on, I really got into all the Jules Verne novels such as ***Twenty Thousand Leagues under the Sea* and *Mathias Sandorf,*** and from Alexandre Dumas, ***The Musketeers Trilogy*** and of course Edmond Rostand's ***Cyrano de Bergerac*** and some lesser known titles like ***Les Cubes OZZ***, an early French science fiction effort. Let us also not forget some very nice comic books, such as ***Spirou*** about a boy with a talking squirrel and ***Tintin et Milou*** about the Belgian cub-reporter's adventures all over the globe (Why, Steven Spielberg even made an animated movie about one of his adventures in 2016).

Thank goodness, I had learned to read in French so quickly. Interestingly enough, when my father asked me, what I wanted to pack to take with me to the US, my erector set and other toys or my books. I was about to turn fourteen at the time, so the books won out. The toys went to my buddies' younger siblings. To this day, I still have my collection of about twenty ***Library Hachette***

Everyone's in a jolly mood as Dad aims at the photographer, Bert Bartha — Jean is left of him and the Bodogni kids are to the right, with me at the end -1950 (Author's archives)

Friendly gathering at the Cantine, with the Mine D'Angevilliers in the background – Charlie Bodogni is standing in front of my mom and I'm the taller one one with my arms crossed -1951 (Author's archives)

An early movie hero I started watching in France – Jean Wayne (GK Drawing)

13

CULTURE CLASH

Now, let us revisit our neighbors from North Africa and their culture. Over the years, I got accustomed to them and their ways. But it was their weekly celebrations which even after all these years, I still remember with vivid fascination.

As best as I can recall, on Friday they gathered for prayers and on Saturday afternoons, they would celebrate with a big bonfire in the middle of the grassy field alongside La Cantine. You couldn't call it lawn because no one watered or mowed it. The men threw a makeshift roasting rack atop the fire; something one the men had welded together out of steel bars, with a spit and a crank for turning. They would then skin and gut a fat mutton and stick it on the spit of the roaster and let it roast for several hours, while dancing wildly around the fire. Now, during the rest of the week, all these guys wore regular westernized clothing, but on weekends, everything changed. They switched to more traditional garb, like caftans, long robes and even turbans.

I sat in amazement on the stoop at the side entrance to our building overlooking the field and observed the activities from thirty to forty feet away, making certain to stay as invisible as possible. At times, Charlie would come out and stand behind me to see what I was watching. I could hear his breathing behind me. He was as curious as I. I would turn around and say "Hello Charlie, I didn't know you were there."

"I just wanted to s-s-s-see what you were w-w-w-watching," he stuttered.

"Sit down here, next to me and we can watch together" I would say.

"I can't sit down," he would reply. "I have to go p-p-p-pee..." and holding his crotch, he would run off.

Some of the men out on the field, sat around well back of the fire on blankets and stacks of pillows they had brought out and puffed on their Hookahs while others got into the singing and dancing part of the celebration. Drums, cymbals, bells and a couple flutes accompanied the singing. There were also guys taking turns on making certain that the carcass on the rack was kept turned in a timely fashion while basting it with some pungent, spice laden liquid mixture; not bar-b-queue sauce and nothing with alcohol in it. There were also some big cooking pots at the edge of the fire in which they cooked a couple of side dishes for the dinner. I later found out it was Couscous and Haricot; that would-be Couscous and beans. Sometimes they made fried bread and even fried egg-plants at the edge of the fire pit. Of course, everything was eaten using the five-fingered-fork method.

They were not keen on allowing outsiders (in other words, everybody else) to attend these affaires and weren't very happy even when observed from afar. So, I tried to cautiously watch the event from a reasonable distance and stay as invisible as possible; that is until old Hamza walked by and growled at me something to the effect of "nosy children will have their nose cut off". The rest of the words he added in his own tongue and those I couldn't un-derstand. He still scared the bejesus out of me. Another of the younger guys, Haddid that I regularly encountered and talked with tried to calm him down and drag him back to the party, say-ing "The boy is just curious. He isn't doing any harm." To which Hamza replied something in Arabic that I still couldn't understand but got the message loud and clear. So, I went inside the door and peered out from the corner, mostly out of sight.

Over the years however, as they got more acclimated to the local culture, they also eased up on trying to keep outsiders away, though nobody from the outside joined their weekly celebrations; they no longer scared strangers away.

As I said, these wild parties were fascinating, especially from my perspective as a kid who had never, and I mean never, ever been exposed to anything like it before except possibly from the pages of Jules Verne writings. Heck, when I saw this for the first time, I was seven. I just stood there with my mouth wide open, probably eyes popping out of my head, completely transfixed, mesmerized.

All those loose caftan and pale flowing robe clad, dancing shadowy figures with turbans atop their heads, whirling and jumping up and down around the flames emanating from under the roasting sheep, formed a hypnotic image forever burned into my memory banks. Their songs, of which I couldn't understand a word, would rise in the starlit night sky chasing the exploding ambers from the fire like a million crazed fireflies.

Those who didn't have knives in their hands, to cut the roasted meat with, carried long walking sticks. As the rhythmic chanting transitioned into high pitched whooping, they would thrust their sticks and knives, sometimes the tip of their hookahs up towards the sky in emphasis, as they would finish one of their songs in a prolonged drum beat and ululating refrain.

Now, my understanding was that they weren't supposed to drink alcoholic beverages, but something got them going because as the night wore on, they got louder and their celebration got more boisterous and the ululations more intense.

As I watched transfixed, I found myself transported to the Sahara Desert where a band of Tuareg tribesmen were celebrating by an oasis, some victory over an opposing tribe, instead of just watching my North-African neighbors letting off some steam after a long week's work, on a Saturday night.

After they had worn themselves out with all that exuberance and shouting, they finally sat themselves down to devour the sheep which had been roasting on the spit and was quite ready to fall apart. Haddid, the one that had befriended me, once offered me a piece of the meat for which I thanked him profusely and as he was turning to leave, I actually tasted it. I am sorry but at that age, I wasn't yet versed in the intricacies of flavors of ethnic foods; in other words, I had not yet developed a sophisticated pallet. When I put that piece of mutton in my mouth, I almost gagged and had to spit it out lest I choked. Watching them skin and gut and then cook the poor animal and being exposed to the pungently greasy aroma of the roasting carcass for the past few hours, it literally made me dizzy. My folks had told me to tell him it was very good and to not hang around the next time, lest I be offered some more.

Bottom line, to this day I can't eat sheep, mutton, or anything that bleats. Ok, so I know that on the menus it's called Lamb. Sorry but to me, it will always be mutton.

• • •

This one time, several years later, as I was desperately trying to lose weight so that I could drop a few pounds to qualify for the lighter weight classification on my wrestling team, our doctor suggested that I eat lamb chops instead of beef or pork as it was less fatty. So, I told my mom to cook me up some Lamb chops. She grilled them to perfection with some garlic, just the way she made me pork chops, with a light dusting of Paprika. I used to love those grilled pork chops of hers. She even made some potatoes and sweet and sour red cabbage with it. It smelled good when she got it done and put the plate in front of me. I took one bite and it was like déjà-phew (vue taste-wise). Without even trying, my brain dredged up the old memory. I made a b-line to the bathroom. That was the last time I ever tried grilled bleat. That was in 1962 or maybe 1963. I really was a fussy eater.

• • •

For the most part, life for little kids in this part of France was very safe. We ran the streets and played in the hills without fear of being abducted or molested by some degenerates, but at about the time we were ready to emigrate to the States, the big story in the local papers had to do with the kidnap and murder of an eleven-year-old little girl, in a town about ten kilometers down the road from Algrange. The police were having a hard time solving the case, mostly because this type of crime was all but unknown in this rural part of the country. As a result, parents started to watch their kids with a little more attention. A few years earlier, a friend of my parents wanted to give them a day off; like I was such a big problem. Anyway, this friend, Takacs Pali (Paul Takacs) lived in Thionville which was about fifteen kilometers away. He would come over on Saturdays and have dinner at our house and then the folks would get together with all the Hungarians for a little party.

So, one Saturday, he came over and picked me up. We rode the bus from Algrange to Hayange (the town next door) and then the tramway from Hayange to Thionville. He took me to a movie in Thionville and then bought me lunch. He then took me to a fair and after a few rides got me cotton candy and other goodies. On the way back to his place, we walked through the apartment complex where he lived. He was holding my hand and we were talking about stuff when this Algerian fellow approached us. "Very pretty boy," the man said.

"Yes, he is," replied Pali, "merci!"

"He is your son, non?" the man asked in broken French.

"Non, he is the son of my friend," Pali replied.

"How much for him?" the man asked.

"What are you talking about?" Pali asked, somewhat taken aback.

"I just want to buy him for a few hours," the man said.

"Go away!" Pali yelled.

The man did leave muttering unintelligibly. Pali was bigger and I didn't think the man would have challenged him, but even he was taken aback. "He was joking of course," Pali tried to reassure me. I was only about ten but even I could see that the man had been serious and by no means was he joking, even though he had a wide grin on his face.

I was somewhat shaken by the whole thing and of course wanted to go home.

Pali told me we would tell my folks about the incident but we would both claim that indeed it had been a joke. So, after we told my folks about the fun we had had, upon our return, we breached the subject of the incident. My parents listened. They weren't getting the joke of the whole thing as neither was smiling. Then, I was sent outside to play. Although I stayed close to the door and heard most of what was being said.

The jest of it was that my outings with Pali, especially to Thionville, had been rescinded for the duration. Pali would be welcome anytime but until he moved to some better location, I wouldn't be making any more visits. I felt bad for him. He was a genuinely nice man who had been forced to leave his family behind in Hungary because of his military service; besides, he always had funny stories and jokes to tell me. I might have mentioned this before: my parents were very protective of me. I had time limits for playing, going to the movies and even to the circus. If I broke the curfew, I paid dearly, staring at the corner wall, sometimes on my knees; other times just banned from going to the movies for a few weeks.

It was almost as if my parents had perhaps glimpsed the future or else they really understood what that strange North African might have had in his mind; something I still couldn't comprehend at the time. Instead my dad reminded me of the incident when that little girl got kidnapped. "But that was a girl," I had said "I'm a boy. They don't kidnap boys." He then went and told me about the Lindbergh boy's kidnapping in America. That got the wheels turning. For a while then, I was extremely careful of strangers. Of course, after the revelation of the Lindbergh boy's kidnapping, whenever the topic of moving to America came up, I would just shake my head no, no. I wasn't at all sure if I'd ever wanted to move here.

For a while, the incident remained on my mind but eventually I forgot. However, my mind had it all carefully catalogued away

• • •

Because of all the job opportunities, there were almost as many refugees in town as were French and Germans: who were both the native inhabitants of Algrange. You see, this region of France, known as Alsace-Lorraine, had changed hands between France and Germany on at least a couple occasions. This region was annexed by imperial Germany from France in the 1870s. It was part of Germany through World War I, and was again returned to France at the end of 1918. This particular corner of Lorraine where we ended up had several iron-ore mines and as a result was of strategic importance to both countries. During WWII, as they invaded France, the Germans again wasted no time in grabbing control of the mines and industries in and around Algrange. There was therefore great celebration when the US Army formally liberated the mines in 1944, after the retreating German army had blown most of the bridges in and around Algrange to slow down the Allied advance; just a bit of historical reference here.

Without further bogging-down into history and for the sake of argument, let's just say that the population of Algrange was split almost evenly between those of French ancestry and those of German ancestry. As a result, those with long memories, hated each other in private, however they all waived the French tri-color and sang the Marseillaise on July 14th, whereas some thirty years prior they might have been singing **Deutschland, Deutschland uber Alles** or **Rally Round the Kaiser**.

With the end of World War II just a few years earlier and the workforce decimated by the war, the influx of refugees had added to the ethnic mix of the region. Algrange having one of the mines in the region and a rather large foundry had attracted a large number of workers from Italy and the French colonies of North Africa, such as Algerians, Moroccans and Tunisians. Added to all those, were a mix of refugees from Hungary, Poland, Russia, Czechoslovakia, Ukraine; basically, all the ethnic groups whose homeland had been forced under the control of the Russian Bear which didn't waste much time in reorganizing these free nations into the glorious Union of Soviet Socialist Republics.

Bottom line, at that particular time, the population of Algrange which had grown to around eight thousand, had changed to two-thirds native and almost one-third foreigners.

From about the time we arrived there in 1949 until about 1951, my father and the other men in our group all worked at the Angevilliers mine, right across the railroad bridge from our housing complex. Sometime during 1951, the mine production dropped and many workers were laid off, my father being one of them. For a year or so, he worked at another mine, some six kilometers down the road from Algrange. He was assigned to what would be swing shift over here in the States. He could ride the local bus to work from a bus stop about a mile's walking from the house. However, busses didn't run after 9 o'clock at night. So, when he got off work at midnight, he would have to walk all the way home, bone weary. Some friend told him of jobs in a foundry in Hayange, which was the next town over and only three or four kilometers away.

He not only got hired right away, but was assigned to dayshift and got a bigger paycheck. He could also ride the bus to and from work. The name of the foundry was S.M.K. and he soon discovered that they treated their workers a heck of a lot better than either of his two previous employers. He remained there until we moved to the States. The manager of his department wrote a very nice letter of recommendation in case he would need one in the USA and gave him a copy of the history of SMK Foundry.

In the meantime, my mother kept our little home running. She cooked, cleaned and did our laundry. Upon discovering her abilities in the kitchen, the single guys next door asked if she would cook a meal for them occasionally, which she did, and they assured her that they would remunerate her, which they did, very generously.

For a while there, when we first got to Algrange, our budget was pretty tight: at times, non-existent. I remember going to the butcher shop with my mother, where she would negotiate with butcher for a soup bone. That's a bone that has no meat left on and it's only good to use as base for soup. Now, this butcher was of German descent and he looked kindly on us, so once he got to know us better, he started to leave a little more meat on the bone. Our soup started to actually have bits of meat it to the delight of my father who really needed to keep his energy up for the work in the mine. The old butcher also took kindly to me. When we would go to his butcher shop, he could see me practically drooling at the cold-cut display as he helped lady shoppers who bought sliced ham and pork chops and beef stew meat, while we waited in line for soup bones.

While waiting on the richer customers, he would go behind the counter and slice off a half inch slice of Salami. "Since you have to wait so long, here's something for you to taste," he would say. We never did forget his kindness. When my father started working at the steel processing company in Hayange, his salary went up a few Francs so we could afford the occasional pork chops and beef stew. We still went back to the old butcher, even though we could have saved a few centimes a half kilometer down the road. He knew it and my hunk of salami kept coming until the last time we shopped there, before moving away. Maybe that's why even today, a couple slices of salami are one of my favorite snacks.

As I said, my mother's cooking brought in a couple of hundred Francs into the household budget, which also helped us buy the multi-channel Blaupunkt radio, and allowed us to go the movies on Wednesdays. Let me explain this briefly. In those days, in our little town, new movies came in on Wednesdays. Also, in those days, in this corner of France anyway, there was no school on Wednesdays; however, we did have to go on Saturdays; ah those French and their ideas.

So, after my mother got her chores done and I had completed all my homework, we would hit the first showing at a reduced price. She and I both liked Tarzan and Jungle Jim with Johnny Weissmuller. My father didn't care if we went, as long as my grades were good and dinner was ready when he got home. Dad also was not particularly fond of a long-haired guy yodeling while swinging from tree to tree through the jungle and living with chimpanzees. He also knew that he didn't have to hurry home and would stop off at the Miner's Fork Bistro for a couple of cold brewskies with his work buddies.

There were Sunday matinees at all three movie houses: The Sax, the Eden and the Odeon where I got to go with my friends. We were to see Walt Disney's Snow White, with French subtitles. I also got introduced to Jean Wayne (it's French for: you guessed it.) westerns and Gene Kelly in the Three Musketeers and of course *Les Deux Nigauds* meaning the Two Nitwits, referring of course to Abbott and Costello. I believe they called the Three Stooges '*Les Trois Corniauds*' or '*Les Trois Cornichons*'; can't remember for sure. We got to see all the horror classics of the thirties and forties as well, such as Dracula, Frankenstein and the Werewolf. If some serious drama was playing, dad would also come along and we had dinner afterwards at one of the local eateries.

Life wasn't at all bad. However, it hadn't always been that way.

Weekly cultural event at La Cantine – North African mouton roast (GK Drawing)

14

YOU'RE GOING TO
POKE YOUR EYE OUT!

Now, as soon as we had arrived in Algrange, and I mean literally the next day, I was marched up to the local elementary school and enrolled. My father had been instructed to enroll me at *Ecole Chemin des Dames*; just in time to finish first grade with the rest of the class. I never even got lucky enough to get a few days off before they had me out of the house and learning the three R's in French no less.

I suppose my folks didn't want the shock of moving affect me in a negative way, so they didn't give me time to ruminate over the matter; out of one culture and tossed into the next without skipping a beat. Boy, my parents were smart. Of course, Chemin Des Dames is where I would meet a whole slew of new friends and some that weren't to be. And here again is one of those health-related issues that seemed to haunt me throughout my early childhood. For a while there, as a little kid, I was sort of a bug magnet. Whatever malicious little bugs were going around, they would find me…

• • •

Well, I never did poke my eyes out running around with scissors; but trouble did have a way of finding me. One of the first little friends I had made at Chemin des Dames was a little Polish kid named Jacek (Yah-tzeck). One day he came to school with what looked like a nasty, crusty rash on his right knuckle. As a matter of fact, it was the winter of 1949, my first year at that school. Being of curious nature, I asked what he had. He said it was warts. At seven, I had no clue what warts were or where they came from. I would soon find out. I asked Jacek if it hurt and if I could touch his hand. As I said, it was winter and apparently the crust on his knuckle had broken open and started to bleed. I was so fascinated by this giant sore that I began to feel the bumps. They felt crusty like tree bark.

Within a couple days, I had tiny little crusty warts popping up all over my right knuckle. Within a couple weeks, they had pretty much covered the whole knuckle. At that point, they weren't very big. Still, I was scared and embarrassed and I tried very hard to keep that hand away from my mother who was a super clean freak. When she finally saw my hand, she almost shrieked. She knew what those nasty things were. The next thing, my father got involved. They had gotten some topical ointment at the local pharmacy, which my folks applied to my knuckle; however, it did very little. The more they applied that stuff, the more warts grew, to the point where after about three weeks my whole right knuckle looked and felt like crusty tree bark.

One thing led to another and I was sitting in the waiting room at the local hospital l' Hôpital d'Algrange. Today they call it **Hôpital Alpha Santé**. It was only about a kilometer from the house. I was to have surgery done on my right hand because they said (at the time) it was the only way to remove this many warts. My stay was to be an overnighter.

Unbeknownst to me at that very same time, my mother who had had an examination earlier on in the week while I had been in school, had been diagnosed with having breast cancer. So, as it turned out, I was going to share a room with my mother for one night anyway, which of course made my whole ordeal somewhat more palatable.

Little did I know or understand the life changing procedure my mother was going to have to go through.

Let's just say that back in the nineteen fifties, the detection and diagnosis of any form of cancer was not as advanced as today. My dad had been told that the local doctor doing the examination was one of the best at dealing with the disease. As I stated above, I was not aware of what was happening to her; even had I, I would not have understood the implications…

The doctor had informed my father that the only way of saving my mother's life was to remove the affected breast. All along I believed that his stress and concern was over my eminent procedure, which in fact scared the poop out me; the fear of the unknown, you know. It wasn't until many weeks later that I had a revelation into what my mom had to have gone through. In a moment of weakness and with the assistance of a bottle of Mouton Cadet shared with Bert, one of the guys next door I used to call Uncle Bert, my dad had broken down about my mom.

He went on to tell Bert how the doctor had recommended the removal of my mom's left breast. This was another one of those times that I was under the watchful eyes of Erika Bodogni. She however avoided every opportunity to give me any grief. This should have been a sign. Except, that again, I thought she was nice to me because I had recently gone through my big hand surgery.

Dad told Bert that when the doctor had completed the amputation, he had brought the severed breast out on a surgical plate, covered up in gauze. My dad looked down and tears started rolling from his eyes. The doctor said that a biopsy would be performed and he would inform my dad of the results. Back then, biopsies took forever and they had to be sent out to some regional medical facility in Metz. The best that I can recall was that about a month and a half or so later, the doctor wrote a letter for my dad to come in and discuss the findings of the biopsy. I don't have to tell you, we didn't have a telephone. Actually, about seventy-five percent of the people didn't have one. Most communication was done via the mail or by telegram.

When dad went in to see the doctor, he told him that the tumor had not been malignant and he was sorry that my mother's breast had to have been removed. Unfortunately, in those days, that's how things got done. This had upset my dad even more than the fact that my mom had gone through the procedure in the first place. The cumulative effect of the whole ordeal had led to the bottle (maybe even two) of shared Mouton Cadet.

As my dad said afterwards, my mom had been a brave soldier.

She never cried or complained in front of me. I am certain that when no one was watching, she had to let it all out. Again, from snippets of conversations between her and my dad, I gathered some of my impressions of those days long gone. My mother was a rather handsome woman as a lot of people had observed, especially young men. In her younger days, she resembled a young Betty Davis. Anyway, after this surgery, she felt scarred for life. But, she didn't give up. She always dressed with the greatest of taste and hid the effects of the surgery well with her homemade prosthetic, so to speak, and never complained about it. Until the day she died in 1981, only a handful of people knew what she had gone through.

Now back to me. After all, this whole thing started out with my booboo.

My mother was still recuperating when my procedure was scheduled. In those days, after a major surgery like my mother had gone through, she stayed in the hospital for almost two weeks.

They had put me under for my procedure; you know anesthetize me. When Morpheus finally allowed me to return to a conscious state, I was in a bed in the same room as my mother. She said, "Everything will be alright and you'll be just fine in a few days". Of course, the next day, I got to go home. My mother said she would be home soon herself.

A few days after my procedure, I had to report back to the hospital to have my hand re-bandaged and my wound checked. When the doctor first removed my bandages, I couldn't believe what I was seeing.

All the bones of my knuckle, tendons and joints on the back of my right hand were clearly visible. There was some infection and lots of fluid to clean up. Then, the doctor took an electric pencil-like device, not unlike a soldering iron and applied it in and around every joint and bone on my knuckle. He explained that the warts in many cases had such long roots; he had to make sure that they were all destroyed. Let's just say that at seven years of age, I didn't have the faintest clue as to what he was talking about. I knew that celery had roots and carrots and kohlrabi; warts, I had to believe him. I had to go back altogether about five or six more times; however, after third time there was no more electrical torture. Did I mention that I felt every poke of that soldering iron as I was not given anything for pain? But like my mom, I was a brave soldier.

The doctor also did advise me that I stay away from kids with warts (duh) and to wash my hands after touching anything that was unclean. To this day, I wash my hands at least twenty times a day…

• • •

Since we're talking about my medical disasters, I had one more incident that required the intervention of a doctor; this time in 1950. There was that big grassy field outside the Cantina; the very same one where our North African neighbors did their sheep roasting and wild celebrating. That's where we also kicked the soccer ball around and played pirates with wooden swords and whatever else we could come up with.

It was also great fun to slide down the side of the hill almost all the way down to the railroad tracks, with the Bodogni kids of course. Interestingly enough, on occasion we even got Öcsike to slide down with us; usually on cardboard torn from big boxes. Öcsike would actually let out wild whoops after sliding and rock back and forth until Charlie walked him back to the top and let him slide down again.

This one time, I was sliding down and suddenly flew off the cardboard and slid face first almost all the way. I say almost because about halfway down, I flipped over and felt something cutting into my left knee. "Ouch, a nail" I yelled out.

I was wrong!

"You're b-b-b-bleeding," Charlie almost fainted.

"It's nothing Charlie," I bravely proclaimed as I looked down at my knee. "Just a little cut!"

Somebody had smashed a liter wine bottle into pieces on the side of the hill and I had just slid over the debris field. A big chunk of green glass, broken from the bottom of the bottle, was now sticking out of my aforementioned left knee; me and broken glass, aye,

aye, aye!

My knee was gushing blood. Blood was running down my shin, into my sock and shoe. On impulse, I pulled the glass out which made the blood flow even faster. I grabbed my handkerchief and held it to the cut, then limped home, still dripping blood all the way. My mother screeched and my dad jumped out of his chair and into action.

He sat me down. He got out a bottle of Hungarian *Pálinka* (eighty proof cherry Brandy) and poured some on my knee. This was the moment when both of my parents decided that I might become an opera singer, because everybody up and down the hall could hear my mellifluous screams. Dad got out some sterile gauze and patted the wound dry and wrapped it up. We headed for the aforementioned Hôpital d'Algrange. Dad had to carry me part of the way because we didn't have a car and at this time, busses weren't running to our part of town yet. Ironically, the bus route stopped at the bottom of the hill; you got it, right across the street from the hospital. I kept reassuring him that I could make it the rest of the way while hobbling for effect.

He explained to the doctor what had happened. The first thing the doctor asked if the broken bottle had been dirty. "Oui, oui" I had said. "Then," he replied "We will then have to give you a Tetanus shot".

I had had my share of shots with vaccinations and all but I wasn't crazy about them. And let me tell you, Tetanus shots especially back in those days, were the worst. I tried to be a good little soldier again, so I kept the yodeling to a minimum as I got stuck. By the time I came to my sense, the doctor had re-bandaged my knee. "See, it wasn't as bad as you thought," my dad said. Who was the old man kidding? I was in shock...

The doctor then complimented my dad on his quick reaction and rather heady first aid procedure. "Using Brandy on the wound," he said, was "très innovative."

"I took a good, stiff shot first" my dad said "before I poured some on his cut. I had to steady myself some."

Maybe I should have taken a shot...

15

GRADE SCHOOL IN ALGRANGE

As I wrote earlier, the day after we unpacked our belongings at 6 Rue de Londres, aka La Cantine in Algrange, my father marched me off to school. I was admitted there and then into first grade at Ecole Chemin des Dames. My very first teacher was a Monsieur Redt. Don't ask how I remember his name. It came to me in flash. He was a very serious educator, the size of a heavy weight wrestler, but fairly reasonable and not mean to the kids. When you'd look at the class picture for 1950, he towers over the little first graders. I pretty much sailed through first grade rather easily thanks to what I had picked up in Cavillargues. I was a quick learner and was able to complete all the required 'Lire, Ecrire and Calcul': reading, writing and arithmetic required of all French first graders. Except for the momentary glitch with the warts, I was ready to move on.

At the end of summer vacation of 1950, I returned for the second grade at the same school under the tutelage of Monsieur Montàné and managed to complete the course equally well.

However, I and my classmates all advanced to the third grade. This meant that we would all be required to attend école Saint Jean Baptiste which soon after our arrival was renamed école Wilson (Yes, in honor of our US President), way on the other side of town. That meant that I would have to walk almost three kilometers one way to get there. It was also where, let's just say, fate kicked me in the derriere and school life got enormously tougher.

Due to the population of France, at that time anyway, being around 70% Catholic, all public schools were run usually under the auspices of the Catholic Church. That in of itself would not have been a bad thing. Everybody needed religion in those dark days after the war.

In fact, it may be time to mention that my mother was Catholic and my father was Protestant or more specifically Calvinist. Before I had been born, they had decided that if it turned out that I was born a little girl; I would have been baptized Catholic and named Mariska (you know, like Mariska Hargitay) after my mother, sort of. On the other hand, as it turned out, I was a boy, and therefore would be baptized Calvinist like my father. Fate had decided and that meant I wouldn't be called Mariska, thank God. This also meant that on any given Sunday, we either went to mass or to the Protestant service or sometimes both. This was usually determined by how far we all wanted to walk and what the weather was like since we didn't own a car; as a matter of fact, there were only about a couple hundred cars in the whole town. But, to church we did go, every Sunday.

By the time I was eight, I could recite almost the whole mass in Latin and could sing along with the best of the priests; "Dominus Vobiscum. Et cum spiritutuo…"

In fact, just about the time I was to switch schools (to Ecole Mixte) I had been told that I was being considered to become an altar boy; like I needed more complications in my life. Then again, I would have learned Latin; I'd have been quadrilingual much earlier…

As I was saying, at this point I was going to attend école Saint Jean Baptiste, for third grade. In addition to having to get up earlier, I had to walk three times as far. And from the first day on, I discovered that my patriotic teacher hated foreigners with a passion. He especially hated the **Boshes**, you know, the Germans even worse. And every chance he had, he would remind those of us who were not born French of his passionate dislike for our kind. His name was Monsieur Vureclaire; interestingly enough, his name was the French transliteration of a German name (Vurklahr). And even though he really hated foreigners, the local French kids received no better treatment. Basically, I don't think he liked kids specifically and everybody else in general. So, all the kids hated him back except for the couple kiss-butts every class always had.

The worst part; in such a small-town school, teachers did double duty. Monsieur Vureclaire was the Assistant Au Director (assistant principal) in charge of torture, us kids firmly believed.

Here's a thought in retrospect: Monsieur Vureclaire hadn't gotten a regular dose of coffee and it was the lack of caffeine that turned him into Monsieur Hyde. Right around that time, good coffee was hard to get and expensive at that; so, they drank a lot of Chicory instead. Chicory smelled like dried rabbit droppings and I wouldn't have been surprised if it tasted just like it. There's also no caffeine in Chicory. So, the lack of Caffeine could have been the cause of Monsieur Vureclaire's devilishly demonic demeanor; Nah!!!

The very first time we left class for our break in the school yard, the older kids forewarned us of Monsieur Vureclaire's omnipotent power over all activities in and out of class. When we asked what specifically set him off, they said we'd find out soon enough. We did. If we didn't answer a question from him correctly, you got paddled on your derriere. He actually used a heavy wooden ruler to mete out punishment, making sure the ruler caught you on the exposed part of your leg, right below the edge of your short pants. (A note here: kids wore short pants all year around. In winter, they were made of thicker fabric and we wore extra-long knitted wool stockings to cover the rest of our leg). If you were caught chatting and not paying attention, you got the ruler or even got slapped in the face. If you didn't turn in homework, you got the ruler or slapped in the face. You see where I am going with this? Where the hell was the French ACLU???

I don't think I was a dumb kid. I did my homework as best as I could. I even tried to keep my exuberance toned down and tried to keep as invisible as possible in class. But hey, I was a nine-year-old kid. I occasionally slipped. On one such occasion, after I had over a period of time been collecting a nice set of welts on the back of my legs, old Monsieur Vureclaire, who by the way should never have been a teacher, slapped me across the face. It's the first time that I realized how many stars there were in the firmament. In addition to stars, I also got a taste of my own blood. For you see, he had hit me so hard that he gave me a bloody nose. And the reason for this very extreme punishment was actually not totally valid in my opinion.

We had been playing this game which is similar to musical chairs except we played it in the schoolyard and was called **Napoleon Monte a Cheval**; Napoleon mounts his horse. We all started by singing the words to the song Napoleon Monte a Cheval and began running all over the yard looking for one of the kids designated as horses. When the singing stopped, we jumped piggy-back style on the nearest horse. The one without a mount was out of the game and became the game caller. We were all running around, screaming the song at the top of our lungs, which Monsieur Vureclaire didn't care for to start with. That's it, he had a Napoleon Complex; brilliant! Naturally by this time, every kid playing had learned to really dislike him so we kept on. The next thing, I'm galloping around like a crazed pony when, Kaboom! I plowed right into; you guessed it, Monsieur Vureclaire. I bounced off him tumbling onto the schoolyard dirt in a cloud of dust. I scraped my knees and hands.

As he grabbed me by my shirt collar and dragged me to my feet I recall him yelling, "when are you going to behave like a civilized person, you stupid little foreigner"? I don't remember which caught me off guard more, the words or his nasty backhand as it bounced off of my face. I hadn't been fast enough to fend it off. The next thing: stars and a bloody nose.

All of a sudden, the whole yard came to a screeching halt.

I could see that even the other teachers had been taken aback by his actions as they covered they mouths with their hands, especially the nuns. I think even they might have been afraid of him. Then, to add insult to injury, he sent me to stand in the corner of the yard, by the stairs right there where everyone would be marching back up to class. The rest of the afternoon seemed to drag on for me as I could hardly wait to get out of there. After school, the kids that I had known since Chemin des Dames patted me on the back and offered kind words and sympathy. However, all being nine years old, there wasn't much any of them could actually do.

"*Il est un espece de saligo,*" they had said, meaning something like "he's a dirt bag". They also used other colorful, profanity laden epithets which need not be translated. Amazing what a well-developed and expressive vocabulary those little kids had at nine years of age.

That day, the three kilometers walk home seemed ten times longer. Although my buddies kept reassuring me that everything would be alright, I dreaded going home; and then, I dreaded going back to school the next day. By the time I turned into number 6, Rue de Londres, our street, I was more in fear of what my mother and father were going to say and how I would explain the blood spots on my shirt; shirts were expensive. To my surprise and amazement, my father said something to the effect of "that sonofabitch, I'm going to see him tomorrow and rearrange his face, the bastard…" all of this in Hungarian of course, which was even more colorful than English. Go apuka!

I loved my father and appreciated the fact he wanted to take hands-on retribution against my tormentor, but as I explained to him "Apuka, if you go there tomorrow and what you said you wanted to do, it would probably get you in trouble with the gendarmes".

"But, I am not going to allow that pompous, jackass to punish you in this fashion without some action" he replied.

"And again, it would embarrass me."

"Alright then," he said. "Let me look into moving you to a different teacher or maybe to a different school altogether."

Vureclaire taught my grade, and even if I went to the fourth grade the following year, I would run into him in the hallway or at assemblies. My life seemed to be over!

Then, a few days later, my father came home with a smile on his lips. "Next year for the fourth grade we're having you transferred to the Ecole Mixte. Your problem is solved," he announced.

"That's the school where all the protestant kids go to and the retards (apologies; politically correct rules had not yet been established)" replied the all-knowing *moi*.

"Son, you are a protestant yourself," he replied patiently.

"No! I'm a Calvinist," I replied. I guess NOT listening really well in all those religion classes had just bitten me in the kiester.

"Son, Calvinists *are* Protestants," he explained patiently. And right there and then I got a two-hour refresher course on what Catholicism was and how it wasn't that different from Protestantism, except for minor details here and there. What and why John Calvin and Martin Luther protested against the Church of Rome and how and why I had gotten baptized a Calvinist. Of course, I had heard it all before, but you know, in one ear and out the other. This time around, I was sort of force-fed so that I wouldn't forget.

The next couple months I had to bide my time and stay out of trouble. I had to stay on the good side of Monsieur Vureclaire although I seriously doubted that he had a good side. He had already decided that my grades would be wanting, so there wasn't much I could do about that. My father told me to play calmly in the schoolyard, which I did, abandoning Napoleon and his horse. I was relegated to watching the other kids getting swatted and slapped and did my best to not give Vureclaire any reason whatsoever to even have to raise his voice at me. Right now, is the right place to let me segue to a related little story wherein my stupid actions would come back to bite me.

• • •

As I wrote above, I was baptized Calvinist, but attended both my mother's and father's church. I also started school in Algrange at Chemin des Dames mostly because it was only about a kilometer from where we lived, well actually, you could see the school from our back window and all kids from this end of town went there regardless of faith.

The natural progression at the time had been to advance to Saint Jean Baptiste for the higher grades. Therein lays the crux of the matter. In the third and fourth grades, we started learning about the history of the Catholic Church, because teaching in public schools in France, at the time, fell in the domain of the Catholic

Church. The topic of the Reformation and of course its influence on the masses came up in catechism and naturally it was presented in a rather unfavorable light, especially to the minds of the impressionable; that would have been us at ten years of age.

So, one day, a bunch of us newly indoctrinated true believers decided to wreak vengeance on those dirty revolting Protestants from that stupid Ecole Mixte a mile down the road; a sort of mini holy war, if you will. Six or seven of us formed a posse and came up with a plan to ambush some of the boys on their way home after school; we weren't going to touch the girls; there were boundaries we weren't about to cross even in a religious war. Our plan was not only stupid but we also didn't carry it out too well. I guess the rest of the boys realized how misguided the whole affair was and were smart enough not to go along. They also had friends who weren't Catholic; as a matter of fact, so did I, had I given it thought.

Ecole Saint Jean Baptiste was at the top of the rise of Avenue Maréchal Foch, so for us, the road went downhill. This was very favorable to our plan of attack. As the kids from Ecole Mixte were trudging up Avenue Maréchal Foch on their way home, they were totally unaware that a sneak attack was awaiting them. We all started galloping downhill and upon spotting them coming up the hill, we went after them arms flailing and actually lending a few hits. One kid in particular we all landed a punch on retaliated and caught one of our guys, right on the chin sending him flying into a trash container. Luckily, it was only his pride that was bruised. The rest of us had already galloped by and were out of sight. Our motto was 'If we get to run away, we may fight another day' or something to the effect.

This silliness went on for a few days until the kids from the other school started walking home in groups and retaliating. That took the wind out of our sails. They caught a couple of ours but instead of beating on them they just issued a stern warning to the effect of "If you guys want a fight, we'll give you a real one, down at the fairgrounds!" Gulp! We settled on an informal truce. Besides, the whole thing got rather passé by then. Our attentions had drifted to other mischief.

Still, as we would pass each on the way home, we made a point of walking on opposite sides of the street so as not to get into each other's way or to give them any ideas. There was one kid in particular that I whacked a couple of times too many, he always followed me with his squinty eyes all the way from across the street, and I knew that he would never forget.

On a serious note; we had all gotten it into our heads that we were somehow wreaking some kind of vengeance on those we believed had transgressed against the Church of Rome through their protestations. So here I was, running around like some kind of crazed avenger while I, myself was one of those very same protestors. How ironic. Then again, at ten years of age I don't believe I knew what the heck irony meant nor for that matter, what the Reformation was really all about. Just a bunch of over energized knuckleheads is what we were…

And I just knew that someday these transgressions would come back to chomp on my derriere…

My 1st grade class photo at Ecole Chemin des Dames, with my first friends in Algrange and Monsieur Redt, our teacher, towering above us all. I'm in the front row, second from the left - (Author's archives)

16

ECOLE MIXTE

As promised, in the fall of 1953, my father withdrew me from Ecole San Jean Baptiste at about the time that it took on the new name of Ecole (President) Wilson. At eleven years and five months of age, he then enrolled me at Ecole Mixte which was actually the Protestant School in Algrange and changed names a couple years later to Ecole Protestante and was located just across the street from the Protestant Church.

The moniker Mixte had been given the school because it welcomed children of other faiths to attend, as well as having no classes in religion required in the curriculum. The Protestant kids went to Sunday school across the street. The other kids did on their own what their religion required of them. We in fact had a couple Greek Orthodox kids attending as well as Jewish boy and even a little Muslim girl, Fatima, from Algeria.

The very first day of school I showed up and right off the top I became aware of all the suspicious eyes directed at me. The boys in line were smiling at me rather maliciously and grinding their right fists into their left palms to indicate that trouble might be on the horizon.

During summer vacation, I had completely forgotten the past and had just realized that they hadn't. And although I was certain that I had not swatted at all of them, I did recognize the faces of those that I had managed to hit, just the year prior as I and my misguided buddies had attempted to avenge the grief brought upon the mother church by those in the Protestant movement. I especially recognized the one that had looked at me sideways with his squinty eyes every time I had passed him on the way home; noting mentally my transgressions.

"Ah merde (oh crap!)," I said to myself. "I finally escape the school where the teacher used me as a punching bag, just to start a school where the kids are going to use me as a punching bag."

"Salut (Hello!), Va bien? (Going well?)" old squinty eyes came up to me and put his arm around my shoulder, very friendly like, as I stood very last in line, just in case a quick getaway was needed.

"My name is Georges Krischke. Do you remember who I am?" He asked.

"Gulp," I swallowed. "Oui, I might have seen you around town once or twice." I replied.

How could he have remembered those incidents when a whole year had passed since they had occurred?

"You remember how you used to sneak up on me and punch me on the arm on my way home and then take off?" he continued.

I noticed as he was talking to me that four or five other boys had broken rank and were now surrounding me, blocking my escape route. Of course, with my father's big-ass briefcase dangling from my right hand, I wouldn't have gotten very far anyway. Why did apuka have to make me carry that stupid briefcase anyway?

"Do you remember me Catholic boy?" asked Albain, another kid.

"What are you doing here in our Protestant school?" asked a third.

"Well," I replied. "I'm actually one of you, oui? I'm a Calvinist and that's protestant, right?"

Then somebody hit me in the back and another shoved me, then another.

"Allez, lessez le! (Go-on, leave him be)" yelled Georges Krischke. "We just wanted to remind him of what he did and not kill him on his first day here."

"Well, I want to kill him," said this one big kid about a head taller, in a deep nasal voice like he had a constant sinus leakage running down his throat.

How old was this kid anyway and what was he doing with these smaller kids? Maybe he was repeating this class. Maybe he was a smoker? Wait, I had been told that smoking would stunt your growth; and here was this big kid. How would they have explained that one? Somebody had to have been lying; but I'd have to worry about that later. Besides, I had never had any desire to smoke myself, to this point. And now in my periphery, I was starting to notice that even the girls were all turning around and the really small kids way over in front of the long line wrapped half way around the school were breaking rank and venturing curiously forward as well.

Since this had been the very first day back to school after summer vacation, there was going to be a formal roll call. This was the reason why they had all been standing in line in the first place. Now I had the guy who was originally going to teach me a lesson, standing up for me against the big slacker.

"Stop immediately!" I yelled, in French of course holding up my right hand. "Messieurs, your quarrel is with me, not with each other." They all stopped and broke out in laughter. At the time, I didn't think it had been that funny until I remembered where that line had popped into my head from.

"The three musketeers," they were saying. "The little Calvinist goes to the movies. He got that line from D'Artagnon in that film". I always liked quoting from the movies...

They must have seen the same movie over the summer and also remembered that particular line. They began patting me on the back for my cleverness except of course for the big, slow nasal kid who just kept snorting real close to my face. I was hoping I wouldn't have to sit next to him in class; yuck! The ranks of the roll-call line had broken up completely and all the kids were now standing around in bunches to see what would happen next. The older girls had not apparently given it much attention, yet they were huddled a few feet away giggling and pointing at us, specifically at me: the new dummy in school.

The entire ruckus of course had finally alerted the teachers that all may not be well. There were five or six classrooms and a couple small offices downstairs at this two-story schoolhouse which was located right next to the *Mairie* and the *Gendarmerie* (City Hall/Police Department).

As I had arrived, the teachers were inside, probably counting chalk and pencils; getting the classrooms ready. One of them must have originally come out to instruct the kids to line up and then had gone back inside; or else, the kids were already familiar with the first day routine. It was my very first day here and I had not yet been exposed to the new procedures. As the noise level had risen, some of the teachers became concerned and had rushed back out to return some semblance of order to the lineup, especially of the little kids who were now running around yelling like crazed chipmunks, having completely forgotten why they were here in the first place.

The women began clapping their hands like teachers had always done to restore order while a male teacher limped down the steps shaking his cane. I eventually found out that he had been in the military and had gotten injured in the war. "Let's get back in line," they were all yelling. The man finally blew on a whistle with all his might and the little kiddies stopped in their tracks and scurried back in line and finally quieted down. We older kids took our own sweet time sauntering back in line, when yet another male teacher emerged through the front entrance.

"Well, what in heaven's name is going on out here?" he asked, with a very slight lisp. "Is the circus in town?"

The smaller kids all pointed in our direction, murmuring something to the effect that we had been fighting, which had not been totally accurate. You know how little kids tend to exaggerate. This teacher was a tall, straight backed, angular fellow with a square jaw, dark hair combed straight back and bespectacled, wearing a tweed jacket and slacks and a neatly Winsor-tied tie around his neck.

"That's the *directeur* (Principal), Monsieur Lapsien" Georges Krischke explained in a whisper. "We had better get in line." We managed this promptly, just as he got to our end of the line.

"What was the cause of all this commotion?" he asked as he towered above us with hands crossed behind his back like an army sergeant major would and a very serious scowl on his face.

"Summer vacation wasn't long enough for all you hooligans,

hmmm? You are fighting already and it is only the first day back to school? I hope this does not become a routine for the whole year because it will be very painful for all of you."

Subconsciously, we all immediately grabbed our behinds. "We were just welcoming the new transfer," Georges Krischke volunteered to a chorus of "Oui, oui, it is true!" from the rest of the boys.

"Well the only new student we are welcoming this year is a young man named Georges Kapus," said Monsieur Lapsien. "Might that be you?" he asked pointing at me, with the scowl still etched on his face.

"Oui monsieur," I replied with the most angelic of smiles I could conjure up.

"Not a very good way to start at a new school, Monsieur Kapus" he admonished (in French my name sounded something like kah-pew, and he emphasized the pew), and then, "Alright now, everybody back in line and march up the stairs. Let's demonstrate some discipline for our Monsieur Kapus here."

Well at least Monsieur Lapsien was polite, compared to Monsieur Vureclaire, even if he sounded a bit sarcastic.

And that is how my formal introduction to the whole population of Ecole Mixte in Algrange on that September morning in 1953, was made. And here I had thought that I would sneak in quietly, and sit in the back of the classroom without much fuss. Instead I ended up making a grand entrance in front of the whole school and as a reward, got to sit in the first row. You know what they say about 'best laid plans' etc....

Overall though, my situation had indeed greatly improved. The teacher, who taught the fifth grade, was a loud blustering, grumpy, old World War II veteran with wild, unruly hair like you'd see on a mad scientist, who used a cane to walk due to a serious injury to his right leg. He also used this very same cane to threaten us with and would often slam it on top of a desk to get everyone's attention and had the kids wetting their shorts, but he never actually used it to inflict any physical punishment on any of us. He figured the implied threat was enough to keep everyone in line. Mostly he would just send us to stand in the corner and contemplate our transgressions and would occasionally keep a misbehaving child after school to write one hundred times what the offense had been, on the blackboard.

"Je ne vais pas bavarder en classe (I will not chit-chat in class)," was my most frequent offense and had to on at least two occasions write the aforementioned sentence on the blackboard, one hundred times.

I did learn to spell really swell in French!

• • •

Here's a little story which did not take place in the classroom but you may find it amusing anyway. In this and the other two schools in town, all bathrooms were located outside. I suppose all these old school houses had been built in the nineteenth century and back then, everybody used outhouses during the day and pee-pots at night.

At Ecole Mixte, they were located at the back of the schoolyard, opposite all the classrooms at the back of the building. However, only from the second story classroom, could the teacher see the top of the heads of any and all bathroom occupants. And just another reminder, just like in the place where we lived, bathroom meant two foot pads and a four to five inch hole in the center of a two inch deep depression where you made your number two deposits. They also had a long urinal for boys. So naturally, you had to squat and after a while I had developed very strong calf and leg muscles. I had also developed a habit people often laugh at: I read in the bathroom. To this day, I have read more books in the can then any-where else. "It's the only place where," I used to say "you could give the written word, your full attention".

Well, there I was taking my afternoon W.C. (water closet or bathroom) break. I had stuck one of my favorite pocket books in my back pocket and raised my hand for permission to leave class. I of course had made certain that all my class notes had been writ-ten and I would be ready to go when the teacher would start the next subject in about twenty minutes.

Monsieur Lapsien said: "Oui! Go on and hurry back." I was holding my stomach with one hand for added effect. I rocketed down the stairs and before you could have said *ou-la-la,* I was squatting over the target. I was really getting into the story and had completely forgotten about the time, when all of a sudden, I heard from somewhere above, "Monsieur Kapus do you think you might return to class before it is time to go home?" That was Mr. Lapsien yelling out the classroom window. Crap! To add insult to injury, the whole class was lined up in front of the window and I could hear them having a good laugh at my expense.

I cut my business short and was still buttoning up the straps to my pants as I ran out of the bathroom, when I noticed that both of the classrooms on the first floor were also lined up at the window. As I came out, the little kids let loose. I guess at first, they didn't know what Monsieur Lapsien who as I said was also the principal, was yelling about. When I walked out into the afternoon sunshine, it all became evident. I was mortified. I could hear their laughter following me all the way up the stairs.

On top of it all, in my haste to get back to class, I had left my favorite book in the bathroom on top of the shelf where the toilet paper was kept. The next kid in there would almost certainly get it. I couldn't go back. It was too late.

As it turned out, one of my buddies found it and with my name inside the front cover, he knew who it belonged to. It took me quite a negotiation and a bribe to get it back. The reason I mention this at all is even back then one of these little books was expensive. They were akin to the 'Little Big Books' and cost about a hundred Francs. That was about 32 cents American; still quite a sum of change for an eleven-year-old.

My 6th grade class photo at Ecole Mixte with our teacher Monsieur Lapsien, Lydia and my buddies (Author's archives)

Ecole Mixte in 2008 – Looked just the same when I left in 1956, except for a new paint job (GK photo)

That's me in front of the map of Africa, for our in-dividual class photo – 1955 (Author's archives)

17

THE BULLY

This chapter deals with bullying; not in general, but me personally. Now, I don't condone bullying nor do I deny that it exists today. But try to remember, I'm talking 1953, which was practically in the Stone Age and bullying had not yet been so clearly defined, quantified and classified as some sort of a social ill, nor had it reached the proportions and severity of today's bullying epidemic. We also dealt with it differently. We had to take matters in our own hands to deal with it. That was the way of the world back then.

Today it is magnified by the advent of electronic media, social networking and digital cameras in every cell phone. Back then, it was simply a part of growing up and not some sort of social disease. If you were on the receiving end, at times it made you cry. It made you mad. Eventually, it made you fight back!

Metaphorically speaking, they weren't raising snowflakes way back then.

The second point I'd like to make is that in 1953, in this little corner of the world, there was no epidemic of obesity. Fat people were simply overweight and mostly old. The kid who was my nemesis in the following tale was not only bigger and taller than me; he was in fact a lot fatter…

His name was Manfredt Dauber and I have written about him earlier. This however has to do with a time period right around when I first met him. He was really big for his age. He was a full head taller than me and about three times wider. I mean, he was big and rotund. I must say that his body had grown proportionally with his head which definitely matched his whole body well. He had two big bulging malicious eyes above a rather small nose and a not so big mouth. That was my perception of him anyway, at the time. For me, my perception was reality. In contrast, I was somewhat of a normal sized kid of eleven; quite diminutive by comparison to Manfredt. Alright, so I was petite and skinny as a rail.

I met Manfredt a few months earlier after having transferred over from the Ecole Wilson which about 70% of the kids in town who happened to be Catholic attended, to a new, much smaller school: Ecole Mixte where the rest of the kids went. The name Mixte literally translates to Mixed, aptly defining the religious and ethnic composition of this little school, although the class picture's caption reads: Algrange, Ecole Protestante (Protestant School). That was mainly because the year after I got there, it was actually renamed to **Ecole Protestante**. We also happened to be located across the street from the protestant church of Algrange. All the protestant kids attended this school, although we actually had a Muslim, Russian Orthodox, Episcopal and Jewish kids as well. In other words, all the children in town of religions other than Catholic attended Ecole Mixte. But I digress…

While most of the kids at this new school had received me well enough, especially the girls, Manfredt hadn't. The rest of the kids didn't care one way or the other.

Manfredt disliked me from the get go. No actually the words I should use would be despise or even hate. He took great pleasure in beating up on me and torturing me when no one was looking, like "Oops, how'd the sandwich get all over your face? Did you fall on it? Ha, ha, ha!" and when I looked up, he'd trip me. It seemed like every dastardly deed that he perpetrated on my person, made him laugh. I personally thought the kid just wasn't right. The word was that he had been dropped as a baby. Somewhat later on, I had found out that his family had moved from another town and that he had been a troublemaker at his last school. So I guess, he had to keep the appearances of a tough guy.

I never did figure out why I had become the number one target of his aggression.

I would go home with bruised knees from tripping, an occasional black eye, black and blue knuckle imprints on my arms and serious damage to my hair. I guess I was lucky I didn't wear glasses. This wanton torture went on for most of the first year I attended Ecole Mixte. Some of the other kids sided with me but Manfredt swatted them aside like flies. They were all eleven or twelve-year-old and scrawny like me. Even my best friend Georges Krischke got into it with the bloated beast to get him to back off. He occasionally succeeded. But, we lived at opposite ends of town and Manfredt lived in the middle, right behind the school. There was only so much that Georges could do to protect me. He went home bruised himself, on occasion. I was at Manfredt's mercy. If a change in our relationship were to materialize, it would have to be up to me to make it happen. Have I mentioned that this kid was three times my size? As he pushed me around the schoolyard, he would blot out the sun.

Worse than that, as I had mentioned earlier, the school had outdoor toilets, at the back of the schoolyard. The small little doors just barely gave you enough privacy. You see, if you spent too much time down there, the teacher could actually look out the classroom window and yell down at you to cut your business short. So, you understand, the school had been built along the main street and sat on a rise of about fifteen feet supported by a major retaining structure. This meant that if your teacher yelled down at you, the kids in the classrooms on both first and second floors would immediately swarm to the windows to see what was happening. At the next break, your best bet was to go into hiding; otherwise you would never hear the end of it.

The logistics of the bathrooms didn't go unnoticed by Manfredt. During a particular activity break, I was sitting quietly contemplating my exit strategy when suddenly I heard some kid yelling that a beehive had fallen out of the big tree in the middle of the schoolyard. I could hear a chorus of screaming and screeching.

"They're heading for the bathrooms," someone else yelled.

Then, something dropped behind me on the floor. What a sap. I fell for it. I thought someone had tossed the beehive in the bathroom and I of course, without thinking, ran out with my pants down around my ankles and just barely holding on to them to the cheers and laughter of the whole yard lead by Manfredt. I stood there red faced and with bare butt, until the teacher finally told everybody to turn around and disperse while advising me: "Monsieur Kapus, shouldn't you perhaps go back in there and button up your pants?"

Back in those good old days, spanking was permitted and for once, Manfredt got his, right in front of the whole class. All the kids could hardly contain themselves. Unfortunately, it didn't help. I felt humiliated and Manfredt smirked through the whole punishment. I didn't think he felt a thing. Besides, the next time he had the chance, he would repay me for his punishment in spades.

This torture went on for almost the whole school year, until one day I'd had enough.

Manfredt had been using me as a punching bag at morning recess, and then tripped me going up the stairs. I managed to elude him at lunchtime by sneaking out the back gate and running home. This of course caused me to return to class a few minutes late and got me a scolding by the teacher, in front of the whole class, to a chorus of laughter. All the laughing finally started my kettle boiling. A somber mood came over me. I was a bit distracted that afternoon in class with a half a mind on a plot to get even. No plan however materialized and I was obliged to answer the teacher's questions between gritted teeth.

When afternoon recess came around, I stayed back and was last to get to the schoolyard. All the other kids avoided me as I sat in the corner of the yard, by myself. Even Lydia Schoentgen, the girl of my dreams, left me alone; but not Manfredt. Nope, the behemoth sauntered over nonchalantly; breathing heavily and his big round eyes rolling around wildly in his big round head, and kicked my feet. I almost jumped up but instead I just pulled my knees in and wrapped my arms around them as I growled: "Get lost you big toad!"

My comment didn't sit too well with him. He just sneered, and looking around and seeing the other kids otherwise occupied, he quickly turned and sat his big fat derriere on top of my folded arms, knocking me sideways and sending me to the ground. As I lay there, he bent down and let out the foulest sauerkraut laced fart I had ever smelled. Did I mention that Manfredt was of German descent and Wiener schnitzel and sauerkraut was one of his favorite staples? I must admit I actually liked that stuff myself; although, lying there on the ground writhing in pain and gasping for air, eating that dish was the furthest thing from my mind. But again, I digress.

I was starting to get weepy-eyed until suddenly the thought of revenge hit me upside the head. Actually, it was Manfredt playfully slapping me as he was rolling over me and pinning me down with his big belly. It took all the effort I could muster to keep from attempting a convincing defense. Then again, no way in heck would I have been able to throw him off me. The whole time, he was laughing his fool head off, looking like one of those laughing mechanical fat ladies at amusement parks, as he kept rolling on top of me with a quick succession of foul blasts exploding that would have made a weaker kid faint. At this point, I was far from passing out. Revenge kept flashing red in my mind.

Finally, Monsieur Lapsien our teacher heard the ruckus and came over to investigate. With great effort even for a man his size, he was able to drag Manfredt off of me.

"What is going on here?" Monsieur Lapsien demanded, exasperated.

"The dirty little étranger (foreigner) tripped me," Manfredt declared with the straightest face he could muster. "I was just walking by to throw some trash in the garbage can and he tripped me".

My attempts at denial were totally derailed by my vain attempts to suck some fresh air into my lungs. To Monsieur Lapsien, this whole scene appeared to be nothing more than a concoction on my part; that's what I said, on my part. Thus, my failure to communicate properly due to lack of oxygen going to my brain resulted in an early return to the classroom where I was ordered to write on the blackboard until the rest of the kids returned: "I will not trip my classmates in the schoolyard." Needless to say, my kettle had not only reached the boiling point, it was getting dangerously close to exploding. On a positive side-note, I became a very good speller; first in my class.

When the class finally returned from recess, the teacher told me to stop writing and to sit down. As Manfredt walked by, he stepped on my foot. "Excusez-moi," he muttered, then under his breath "I'm gonna get shoo after school." To which I responded by jumping up and shoving him. Well actually, it wasn't a shove. Manfredt was after all an immovable object and I just bounced off of him like a soccer ball. My act of retaliation had been determined to actually be an act of aggression and did not go unnoticed by Monsieur Lapsien.

"Monsieur Kapus," he yelled, "you will be staying after school!"

"Oui Monsieur," I practically screamed as steam might have been irrupting from all of my facial orifices, or so had I imagined. I repeated my reply in a more civil tone, with a 'pardoner moi' added with a forced, toothy smile. I had to use my head and not be forced to spend the whole night in school. I also knew that whatever time I was to walk in that front door of ours, my father would have things to discuss with me. The longer I stayed in school, the longer that conversation with my father would take.

On the other hand, this also meant that my plans at retribution probably had been derailed for the time being.

Since Manfredt would have been at home by the time of my exit, feeding his chubby cheeks, I would have to set aside my plans: as of yet unformulated. All in all, maybe the fickle finger of faith had dealt me a reprieve. By the morrow, I would probably be able to come up with some sort of a plan for my revenge.

Of course, you know what they say regarding the Best Laid Plans of Mice and Men. Maybe they should have included chickens in that saying. Even had I come up with a plan, I was not certain I would be able to go through with it. I was always worried about consequences; what if I actually followed through? I would probably end up being the one punished, for whatever happened.

In the meantime, everyone had long gone home when Monsieur Lapsien finally got up from his desk and grabbed his overcoat from the coat rack, stuck his grey Fedora on top of his head and picked up his briefcase. Looking right at me, he pointed to the door. "My dinner is probably cold, so you had better be on your way and no more tripping classmates in the schoolyard," he said with a totally serious look on his face.

But as I acknowledged him with my eyes partially lowered, I couldn't help but spy what clearly appeared to be a minuscule, barely noticeable muscle twitch, almost like a smile curling the corners of his mouth ever so slightly. As I looked back again, any vestiges of what I thought I had seen had vanished. His lips were pulled in a straight line. It had been my imagination again.

The sun was slowly retreating behind the hill by the Old Catholic church. The whole sky at the top of Maréchal Foch was turning a burnished copper as I exited the school's front gate and began my trek home; perhaps a forewarning of things to come. I would have to pick up my pace to cover the kilometer and a half or so to get to my house in as short a time as possible or I would have a lot more explaining to do. Even as I considered my temporary reprieve, I felt like I had already lost. At least, I wouldn't have to deal with Manfredt; not today anyway.

That's what I was mulling over as I passed the Gendarmerie (Police Department) next door to our school and I started picking up my pace, when I felt a sudden jolt.

I got yanked by the collar and slung around like a rag doll and the next thing; I found myself sprawled face down in the dirt right in the middle of the empty lot between the Gendarmerie and the next house over. The nice briefcase my dad had given me at the start of the school year was now lying in the muck, flipped open and with most of the contents dumped in the dirt. One of Manfredt's toadies was kicking the briefcase while another was stomping on my homework papers which were flying all over the place. The third snot nosed little weasel shoved me back down on the ground as I vainly tried to get up. He was being extremely brave with Manfredt and his other little buddies to back him up.

For the time being, all the big doofus was doing was just standing at the edge of the lot, his face all red, glaring and grunting like a water buffalo ready to stampede.

His three little grungy sycophants were jumping around howling like a herd of deranged hyenas. They must have thought this whole affair was a real hoot and they appeared to be thoroughly enjoying it. Those little jackals, they didn't even go to our school and where did that third little misfit come from anyway? There were usually only two of them hanging around Manfredt. Since they were a lot smaller than he was he must have figured that a third one was needed to make tonight's event a real success for him; three witnesses to the little foreigner's demise.

The three sneering twerps grabbed me and tried to keep me down until Manfredt waved them off and they finally let me go. I desperately looked around to see if there was a quick escape route, but those miserable little buttheads, had me boxed in. I was a pretty fast runner, but there didn't seem anyway out, without a fight; and there were four of them. One each was guarding the corner of the Gendarmerie and the house at the other end of the lot while the third one was watching the stairs that led down to the street below the lot. I was surrounded!

As I finally pulled myself up and was standing in the middle of the lot, I was still quite a bit shaken. I was trying to dust myself off. I was deluding myself into believing that somehow the ordeal had come to an end when Manfredt waddled over to me, eyes bulging, blathering something between his teeth, waving his fists like Bluto in the Popeye cartoons; except this wasn't funny. At first, I was so shocked that I couldn't even understand what the heck he was saying. Even my ears were in shock I thought.

In previous encounters, he would just have punched or shoved me, then laugh it off like the whole thing had been a big joke at my expense. But this time, the smirk was gone. I saw real malice in those eyes. It was no longer going to be a big joke. This was going to be for keeps. One thing was certain: this whole mess was going to be settled in that place, on that evening. How, I wasn't totally clear on, at that very moment. My first reaction was to start bawling. Hey, what do you want? I was only eleven, those were part of the rules of engagement; you hit a kid. He cries. You run away. You get him the next time and the cycle repeats itself. It had worked for me before. As I swiped my soiled hands across eyes, the dirt mixed in with some tears and turned into a mucky smear. This of course brought on another chorus of laughter from Manfredt and his minions. They were truly enjoying the torture.

It was getting way too embarrassing. On top of everything, I'd have to go home and explain my ripped clothing, scratched up briefcase, my missing homework and school supplies; oh yes, and whatever damage and injuries this brute was going to inflict on my delicate countenance. In other words, this wouldn't be over by a long shot even if I escaped. I would have a whole lot of explaining to do when I got home.

Suddenly, all I could see were Manfredt's bulging eyes and his twisted lips moving in a slow and hideous wave as he started lumbering over in my direction. He sort of reminded me of Boris Karloff in the movie Frankenstein going after the villagers; which by the way we had all seen very recently in the movie theater.

By now even the toadies were looking at each other like maybe old Manfredt had completely lost his marbles. Still, with a nervous shake of the shoulders, they stood around expectantly. They definitely wanted to be around for the big finale.

He was now just a couple feet away, his face contorted with anger, when suddenly he appeared to hesitate and stopped momentarily as if he were uncertain. His eyes seemed to cross as he started to cough. He coughed and coughed and after the fourth or fifth try, he hocked the biggest, nastiest loogie which he then swished around in his mouth several times over and aiming it in my direction, with a disgusting slurping sound, he expelled and hit both my shoes. Now I had green slime covering my shoes. However, I felt lucky because all indications were that he was actually trying to hit my face. He had just miscalculated the trajectory. His eyes grew even bigger, as if that were possible as he let out a roaring bellow and his gang of three went "Nyak, nyak, nyak, nyak, nyak, nyak!" like a bunch of crazed chipmunks.

I thought I was going to wet my shorts.

However, there was no time to worry about that. Further emboldened by the clamor from his minions, Manfredt appeared to swell up in size, looking like malevolence personified; he was suddenly towering over me. I mean, he was right there in front of my face; a giant, immovable object. I tended to exaggerate back then, so let's just say that he was really, really big.

I tried retreating a few steps but he just kept coming. So, I tried moving side to side like I had seen Errol Flynn do in the movie Gentleman Jim (about a famous pugilist of the early 1900s).

"Hey why you jumping around like a stupid little grasshopper?" he sneered.

"What do you expect?" I yelled. "If I stop, you'll hit me."

"No!" he said. "I'm going to squash you like the little bug you are."

"That's not very nice," I yelled back.

So, he hit me.

Well actually, he missed his mark and I sort of wobbled out of the way.

"Stand still you little merde (excrement)," he yelled. "You know the sooner I give you your beating, the sooner you get to go home and cry to your mama."

"Ah, salaud," I yelled, meaning something in the order of dirt bag.

"Why you little merde (remember this one?)," he came after me with his rather large hands curled into really big fists.

I made a real effort to curl my hands into fists and Manfredt laughed even harder. Well actually, as a child, I had small delicate hands which did not translate into scary fists. They had been meant for art and music; not for street fighting. I rather thought of myself as a negotiator rather than a fighter. Obviously, that hadn't worked out so well in my current circumstances. While trying to avoid further bodily harm, I suddenly tripped and fell on my butt. Somehow, something this time, made me jump up at the ready in a flash. It must have been some involuntary reaction the source of which I simply couldn't explain at the time. This action actually caught me by surprise. It was like I was operating in autopilot. I must add that in that very instant, I also let out a blood curdling roar which further surprised both Manfredt and me. What was happening to me

I wondered?

This sequence of events stopped Manfredt dead in his tracks, but only momentarily.

"Merde," he swore; as explained earlier, excrement. He really liked using that expletive.

He looked dumbfounded as he stopped. My actions had gotten him confused and then I thought maybe, even scared.

For me there was no stopping. I covered the short distance between us in a couple leaps, catching him totally off-guard by my speed; in retrospect, surprising myself as well. He put his fists up but only halfheartedly. As he tried to slowly retreat, his foot somehow got caught on a big tree root poking out of the dry dirt of the lot. Did I mention that there was a large oak tree on the other side of the sidewalk whose roots extended under it, splitting it and extending all the way to the other side and on into the empty lot? I had never noticed it myself before; perhaps it had been Karma?

As he lost his balance and started to fall with his arms now flailing, I rammed my head and shoulder into his midsection. This knocked the wind out of him. His knees buckled under him and he fell to the ground with a giant thud and a big cloud of dust. His hooligan sidekicks let out a collective "EEK!" and appeared for a brief moment to consider rescuing him but changed their minds as they saw my smutty face, wild eyes and possibly even foam emanating from between my lips; they appeared to change their collective minds and disappeared in a flash.

Sitting on his belly, I started pummeling him, left and right, right and left to the nose, to the chin and wherever he was unable to cover up. He was flailing at me without much success and his chubby hands weren't fast enough to ward off any of my lightning blows. My skinny little fists were landing punch after punch; like I'd seen in old boxing movies. I don't believe that all my punches hit their intended targets although a couple actually did. However, this barrage simply overwhelmed him and more than anything scared the bejesus out of him; I mean literally. I believe he pooped in his shorts.

Under normal circumstances, he could have flicked me off his chest like swatting a gnat. But having been caught totally off-guard as he was, he had been unable to react. As he tried to cover his face in vain, I noticed a trickle of blood seeping between his fingers. In most previous altercations, that would have been my blood. This time, it was Manfredt's proboscis that was doing the bleeding.

My arms finally tired and I saw that Manfredt, the big, bad bully was all of a sudden in such dire straits that his hands simply stopped fending my punches off. He was just barely able to cover his face. Under the grime mixed with the sweat and the blood from his nose smearing all over his face, he started to whimper. I had expected him to let out some angry outburst like a wounded growl at the sight of his own blood, but instead he went into a full-fledged, hysterical bawling fit. Those big, angry eyes turned into big, sad, puppy eyes and I almost started feeling sorry for him.

As I said, his cowardly little toadies had totally abandoned him, except for the one who had stopped off at the Gendarmerie to report "some kind of fight" before running off. Of course, by then, all the racket had also attracted the occupants of a couple of nearby houses and they were now standing around on the sidewalk observing the show. We must have made quite a ruckus to have dragged all these people out of their houses. You could tell some of them had left their dinner tables as they had napkins stuck into their collars. Considering that we were a couple of eleven-year-olds, I found it strange that nobody made any attempt at separating us...

"The Gendarmes are coming," somebody finally warned.

"It's just a couple of stupid kids fighting," yelled another as he did an about face to return to his plate of escargots.

We both now looked up at the commotion on the sidewalk to which we had been totally oblivious and yelled in unison: "merde, we are in trouble!"

We knew we'd get dragged into the Gendarmerie and after a good talking-to by the captain, one of the gendarmes would be ordered to escort each of us home, where we'd get a lot more severe talking-to from our papa and maman. Then again, with our imaginations in overdrive, we decided that we might possibly get tossed into a jail cell and would have to spend the night there until our folks would spring us.

"Come on, you big dummy," I yelled. "Give me your hand!"

"Uhm?" mumbled Manfredt.

"Come on, the flics (coppers) are coming, we gotta getouta here!"

"Eh, you're not gonna hit me again, are you?" he whimpered.

"No!" I said, "not today, anyway."

As I somehow hoisted up this kid that weighed at least two and half times more than moi, I almost fell over him. But, I did get him in an upright position. I grabbed as much as I could of the contents of my briefcase and shoved it back in there, and then took off for the back stairs leading down to the street below, just as the gendarmes arrived on the scene. They did not appear to have been in any hurry to get involved in whatever had been reported to them; maybe they'd been on their dinner breaks too.

"What is happening here?" they asked. As some of the by-standers tried to explain the situation, I was already flying down the stairs and hitting the street below.

Without even looking back, I could hear Manfredt huffing down the street in the opposite direction. I ran all the way home without ever looking back. I didn't even want to know if the Gen-darmes had actually tried to follow either of us; and they hadn't.

Before I walked into our apartment, I tried to dust myself off as best as I could and finger-combed my hair. I wiped the briefcase off with my shirtsleeve and somewhat organized the content, be-cause I just knew that as observant as my father was, he would have noticed that something was amiss. I actually believed that I could pull it off. Then, I dusted off my pants and without thinking wiped the dirt off my shoes with my handkerchief. I still wasn't thinking clearly. The scratches on my arms and one on my face, I would have to try to come up with a good story later, unless of course I was able to sneak into my little corner of our one-room apartment, without either papa or maman noticing anything. Un-fortunately, the torn strap of my pants and the rip in my shirt, well that would have to be another story; and mind you, clothing was expensive back then.

As soon as my mother saw me, she began lobbying for a good spanking and at this point, she didn't even suspect that I had been in a fight. All she saw was the damage to my clothes.

You see, back in those days, spankings were pretty common-place as a means of attitude adjustment, and in hindsight they did not cause me or for that matter, any of the kids I knew, any great physical or mental harm. It was all part of growing up; you did something wrong, you got spanked, especially if you committed a major trespass.

OK now, moving the story right along. As my mother returned to her dinner duties, my father began questioning me about the cause for my late arrival, the damage to my clothes and the notice-able bruises all over me. As I began my explanation, he laid me on his lap to start the punishment phase of my lesson, but I didn't feel any pain right away. "Now, you did say that that this all happened as a result of defending yourself," he said. "You didn't start this fight, right?"

"Nem, apuka (no daddy), I didn't" I whimpered. "And besides, there were four of them against me."

"And you fought them all?" he said, but still his hand had not come down on my derriere.

"Well actually, three of them just pushed me around a bit then ran off. I only had to deal with Manfredt, you know, the kid I told you about; the one that's three times bigger than me."

"That's that big kid that had given you trouble before, right?" Phew, if that wasn't an understatement, how about living hell papa, which of course I did not articulate.

"Igen, apuka, (yes daddy)" I replied.

"But why didn't you just leave him there?"

"Well, the gendarmes were coming…" I explained.

"The gendarmes?" he said, his eyes opening wide.

I had apparently skipped over that part of my tale. Gulp, now I had to explain that as I hung there on papa's knees, in a very un-comfortable position and still in fearful expectation of a heavy hand coming down on my very sensitive backside. I waited for what seemed to stretch forever and still no pain.

"Now Georgie, when I hit you, yell really loud," my father whispered "to make anyuka (momma) believe that you are getting what's coming to you."

Well, I expected the worse, but the old man barely touched me and I went "Ouch!"

"Louder," he said "make it believable. So I did. Until my momma poked her head out saying "You're torturing the poor child. That's enough!" It wasn't until years later that my mother confessed that she had figured out the collusion between my father and me regarding the meting out of punishment in regards to my perceived transgressions. Of course, as far as I am concerned, I believe she knew it from the get go.

I slid off my father's knees and when I turned around, the old man winked.

"Not too bad for a Kapus," he said. I couldn't help the tight little smile that curled the corner of my lips.

I slept pretty well that night, but when the alarm sounded the next morning and my father had already left for work, I got this nervous twitch in my stomach. I had helped Manfredt out of a bad situation the previous night. The question was how was he going to repay me?

I started for school a bit earlier than usual mainly because I was anxious. If anything unforetold were to happen, I wanted it over with quickly. I was walking at a quick pace down Rue de Gaulle passing the little kids going to kindergarten. I passed my friend Michel Zinghoff who lived across the street, walking his little sister to school. "Hey George, what's the hurry?" he asked as I almost ran past them. "There's plenty of time!"

"I've got stuff to do..." I replied.

I passed the bakery with its door open and the fragrance of freshly baked breads and brioches, my favorite, wafting all the way to my nostrils from across the street. On occasion, even if I had been late, I would run in there and grab a croissant or a brioche. This day, I hurried right past, practically running downhill by the old barbershop and the hospital until I could see down the street, the red, white and blue flag on top of the Gendarmerie next door to the school.

I kept running and I didn't know why. I just had to get there. I was all revved up, expecting the worst. As I walked through the wrought iron gate at the front of the little school house, there were only a few kids there and none of the ones I used to hang around with. Of course Manfredt was nowhere to be seen. I didn't know if I should have been relieved or what. Slowly everybody was starting to arrive. My friend Georges Krischke and Michel Zinghoff with his little sister had finally gotten there as well. Some of the kids who lived close to the school, from Manfredt's neighborhood were starting to show up. I noticed they were talking animatedly about something, occasionally pointing in my direction. Georges Krischke and Michel Zinghoff walked over to them to see what the buzz was all about.

They both walked back to where I was leaning against the fence. "Those guys are saying that you gave Manfredt a beating last night and the flics (coppers) were even called," they reported breathlessly, trying to beat each other with the announcement.

"It wasn't anything like that," I blushed. "I just got lucky."

"They're saying you knocked him on his butt and gave him a pounding!" They replied, "Yeah, they said quite a pounding in fact."

"No, it was nothing, really."

Others came by and patted me on the back. "You got the big salaud!" they were saying.

Pretty soon, it must have gotten to my head because I was beginning to agree with their assessment of the big knockdown. In the back of my mind though, I was still worried that I hadn't seen Manfredt and the possibility of another showdown at the first recess was looming in the back of my mind. After a while, the teachers came out of the school and directed their respective classes to form a line before marching into class. As our bunch was starting to form our line, Monsieur Lapsien came over and started to count the number of kids in his line.

"Hello Monsieur Kapus," he said to me. "You must have lost

these homework papers on the way home yesterday evening," and he handed me several sheets of paper in varying forms of distress. "A very nice neighbor next door to the Gendarmerie brought them over before he went to work earlier this morning. You might want to go and thank him after school."

Yikes, I thought. I was hoping that he hadn't mentioned anything about my altercation with Manfredt. Actually, I was afraid that Monsieur Lapsien might actually have been leaving school just about that time. I was dearly hoping, not.

"Oui Monsieur," I replied and thanked him and on we marched into class.

We were starting to open our briefcases and setting up our desks when Manfredt finally slithered in. He was trying to sneak in unnoticed, but he was huffing and puffing so hard from having run all the way to school and on up the stairs that he wasn't succeeding. His usually red and puffy face was redder and puffier, if that were possible. He plopped down at his desk with a thud after apologizing to Monsieur Lapsien for being late and went about getting ready for class, almost in slow motion. He looked rather contained and didn't appear to be his usual blustery self, pretty much keeping his head down and looking at his schoolwork.

As was my habit, at the first recess I stayed behind to be last out of the class. At the bottom of the stairs I half expected Manfredt to be waiting for me with some devious form of retaliation; perhaps tripping. But nothing happened. Nothing happened in the schoolyard during recess, where he kept to himself in one corner, away from everybody. Eventually though, we found out through the schoolyard grapevine that Manfredt got punished for getting home late.

"They're saying that his old man clobbered him last night," said Georges.

"Yeah, but I don't think it was about getting home late," added Michel

"Yeah," added Jean-Marie "his old man is kind of a big bully himself and when he found out that Manfredt got clobbered by a kid half his size, he really lost it."

"You guys know me," I told them. "I don't like fighting. My father doesn't like me to fight either, but he wants me to be able to defend myself. So I did".

"Bien sure (Naturally)," they agreed.

"Now, it's all over," I declared.

And the fact was, as far as I was concerned, I wasn't going to be getting into anymore scuffles. I would just as soon negotiate my way out of trouble, and was going to try my new approach the moment a disagreement materialized. So, I walked over to the corner of the yard where Manfredt had retreated to as a whole group of my buddies and other curious kids began following. "Hey you guys," I said, turning around. "Nobody needs to come with me. This is my concern only".

I left them and walked over to Manfredt. I could still feel them following me, somewhat further behind though. Interestingly enough, I believed I could still see fear in Manfredt's eyes. I could also still clearly see the imprint of a hand on his chubby red face. Of course, that could not have been one of my lucky hits landing last night; who am I kidding? The handprint was almost three times the size of mine. Regardless, I felt sorry for the kid. After all, the way I figured, once I had a chance to think about it, he was just a little kid in a huge body. He had somehow figured that if he bullied enough other kids around, he would get more friends, especially little sadists like the three toadies that hung around him and egged him on for fear that if they didn't, he'd go after them.

I also discovered that being of German heritage; they in fact ate a lot of pork, sausage and sauerkraut and a lot of other fatty foods which they could afford because his father was some big mucky-muck mine engineer. The whole family in fact was shall we say, on the corpulent side. I suppose if we could have afforded it, I might have turned out chubbier myself. Then again, being of smaller stature, I would have been short and fat; still no match for Manfredt.

"Are we even?" I said as I stuck out my open hand.

He seemed to hesitate for a long moment as though my open hand would suddenly turn into a fist and start pummeling his face again; the way he would have normally operated. When he saw my hand still there, he reached out his much bigger hand and gave it a very gentle squeeze. "Is that all you got?" I said as I squeezed a bit harder. He then responded.

"Ouch!" I said, "Not that hard," when he applied considerably more pressure. When we finally released our clasp, I started to laugh and he joined in. It was about the first that I saw a difference in his eyes. They looked like he was genuinely happy.

The rest of the guys surrounded us patting us both on the back while showering us with congratulatory praises. The long running feud seemed to have come to an end. After that incident, Manfredt and I became friends and once or twice when some big kids from the other school had had me cornered, he had come to my rescue, to my relief and delight. I had apparently negotiated a mutually beneficial truce.

Had we not emigrated to the U.S., I would have had my confirmation with the boys and girls from the class of 1956, in Algrange, Moselle France. They sent me a photo of all of them with Pastor Michel from the Protestant Church across the street. Monsieur Lapsien was there as well. The kids were all there, Georges, Michel, Lydia, Monique and Manfredt, and a few whose name I can no longer remember, although their faces are as familiar as if I just spoken to them a few days ago; the kids who had been my friends all those early years in Algrange, smiling at me from 5740 miles away. I was the only one missing from the photograph.Just a little side note: when I moved away from Algrange, I was about as tall as Manfredt, though I still only weighed about eighty pounds.

Manfredt sent me flying (GK Drawing)

18

LITTLE LIFE LESSONS

The following are some little episodes that have to do with my time at Ecole Mixte, although these stories are related to school sanctioned activities, they are not necessarily educational in terms of classroom or book learning, rather more like life lessons.

Lesson 1 – JoJo Les Chatons

We had to come up with all sorts of fund raising schemes at Ecole Mixte. Because most of the state funds went to the Catholic middle school, our little school was sort of last in line for after school activities handout. In the period of 1952 to 1953, my first year there as I was attending the fourth grade, the students of the four upper classes, that would be fourth, fifth, sixth and seventh, all sixty-three of us, decided that for our big annual outing we would go visit some WWII battle sites somewhere near Metz. The following year, we would try for Bastogne, another major WWII battle site made famous by General Patton. All outings cost some extra money; however, this one would cost a bit more because the school needed to hire a bus and have money left over to feed the kids' lunch. It was decided that we would sell bouquets of Catkins, since this was just before Easter and the people in the area carried Catkins to Easter services. If you don't know what Catkins are, they grow all over Pussy-Willow trees in the spring.

We all loved this project because we got a whole class hour every day to cut up large willow branches and tie them together into small bouquets. Then after school, we went about trying to sell them to the town folks. Making up the little bouquets was all manual work and all the kids enjoyed the process; however, the

selling part, we were somewhat ambivalent about. Monsieur Lapsien told us to try our selling ability on our parents and neighbors
first. From there we could then spread out to friends and eventually to knocking on strangers' doors. I was eleven. What the heck
did I know about selling? I went home with my shopping bag full
of Catkin bouquets at twenty-five Francs a bouquet. That was
about seven and a half cents US.

I whined and stressed as I told my parents what I had to do. I
wanted my dad to buy the whole bag's worth so I wouldn't have
to even try selling to anybody else. My dad, being the wise man
that he was said: "Go next door and sell some to Berci (Bert), Karcsi
(Charley) and Feri (Frank). If you sell to all three, mother and I will
buy one each. You will have sold half of your bouquets. Alright I
thought, that can't be too difficult. It wasn't difficult. It was worse.
All the guys had had bad days at work. Go figure. They made me
work for my money. I was about to beg and then as a last resort,
tried crying. Before I got to tears, they each bought a bouquet.
Karcsi actually bought two or three. He went to church a lot, so I
figured he needed more than the other two. I marched home triumphantly, showing my parents all the money I had made. They
in turn, bought two more. I think I only had three or four left when
I went to school the next day. So as a reward, I got another full bag.
Here's a thought: don't show them how well you're doing because
they'll have you do even more. Show them you're struggling and
you get to do less!

OK, I know you want me to get to the punch line.

The following Sunday, there was a dinner get-together at our
place. A fair amount of cheap French wine was consumed by all
after dinner, except me of course. I sold my whole stock of Catkins.
I think I had mentioned before that if you approached adults in the
afterglow of good food and wine, they were more receptive to your
sales pitch.

As I was counting my profits, one of the overly happy adults
looked at me and said: "You know those things grow all along the
creek. Go and cut them and tie ribbons around them, then sell them
for your own profit. You do the work. You should reap the

rewards." After all, I wasn't to sell the ones from school. I was selling my own products.

All this sounded essentially reasonable and logical to an eleven-year-old, even though the older fellow hiccupped uncontrollably as he was giving his advice. Nonetheless, after school the next day, I went to work on the new project; making my own money that is. Let me tell you, I was raking in the dough. I went down one side of a street and back up the other side. I of course kept the money from my private enterprise separate from my school project. This meant that all of a sudden, my school sales suffered. I wasn't turning in as much money as I had before. When I was asked, I sheepishly said that people weren't buying the Catkins like before. However, at break time, I let it out that I was making good profits on the side. I explained to a couple of buddies that they could do likewise for their own profits. Like they say, loose lips sink ships. Now mind you, I wasn't taking the money from the sales for our outing. I was simply using the same sales pitch to sell my own product.

I soon learned the error of my way.

Somehow, it got to Monsieur Lapsien's ears and I was summoned in front of the class. "I have heard that you've gone into business for yourself and shirked your responsibility to help with the fundraising for our class outing," he stated, matter-of-factly.

"I ehr, was just trying to make a few extra Francs for pocket change, for the trip, you know," I offered.

"As I see it Monsieur Kapus, or perhaps we should call you JoJo Les Chatons (JoJo Catkins), you have let down your fellow classmates by your action and it has been decided that you would not be coming along on our outing."

A whole chorus of JoJo Les Chatons went up from the class, until Monsieur Lapsien told everybody to quiet down. Then, he sent me to sit in the back of the class.

"Ah Zut," I thought as I covered my head with both hands. I was humiliated and on the verge of tears. I had been outed by one of my buddies, I thought. There were thirty-two kids in this class. They weren't all friends with me, just like anywhere else. Some of them didn't like me at all, and they were only too happy that I had gotten into trouble. After school, they pursued me, tauntingly yelling JoJo Les Chatons. "Let them have their fun," I thought. "I'll show them." The problem was, I didn't have the vaguest idea how or what I was going to do.

When I got home, I told my mom what had happened in school. "Oh my," she just said. "You had better tell your father." So, I waited until he got home from work and told him the whole story all over again.

"The first thing my son," he said, "You should never listen to an old drunk like Joska (Joe). The second thing is, technically you didn't do anything wrong so long as you didn't take any money from the school sales. However, ethically, you shouldn't have gone into business for yourself using the same sales pitch and in fact shorting your trip funds. You blurred the lines between your two enterprises."

"Uh ha," I replied. "I didn't have a clue what he had just said. Technically and ethically were not yet in my vocabulary. I think I got the thing about blurring the lines. But it all sounded like I hadn't really done anything wrong technically, but I really did? Observing my confusion, he simply asked "Do you want to go on that trip, and what would you do to get to go?"

"Turn in all the money I made, period and try to sell some more for the trip," I replied.

"Then I guess you have learned a good lesson."

For the next few days I suffered the name calling, mostly in the school yard. Even the teacher finally dropped part of new moniker and just called on me as JoJo in class. At recess, I ignored everybody until Georges Krischke came over to tell me that it was not him that had spilled the beans about my private enterprise. He thought it might have been Manfredt. That fat kid had always had it in for me. Meanwhile, after school I was hitting the pavement and selling Catkin bouquets like a madman. I was determined to get back some respect and make it to the school outing. After the initial incident, Monsieur Lapsien didn't even ask for a status report from me. I had officially turned in my bag with the leftover Catkins and whatever money I still owed.

About a week or so before the trip was to take place, Monsieur Lapsien had everyone turn in all the money they had made for the final count. When everybody in the class was done, I finally got up and went to the teacher with a paper bag that held all the profits that I had made throughout this whole ordeal. On my own I had sold somewhere near one hundred and seventy-five little bouquets of Catkins for a grand total of 4375 Francs, or about twelve dollars and thirty-three cents. Let's just say that it was more than anybody else. Monsieur Lapsien was amazed. After a brief apology for having gone astray, I was reinstated for the trip and the moniker JoJo Les Chatons or Pussy Willow Joe was retired.

"I was just starting to like my new name JoJo Les Chatons," I said.

"Oh, sit down Monsieur Kapus," said the teacher as my classmates howled.

Lesson 2 – The Devil's in the Details

In the spring of the following year, 1954, the powers to be started a campaign warning people of the evils of Carnaval (Carnival) and asked all the kids at Ecole Mixte to create a design; something which would illustrate the concept. It was believed that during this time period, people drank way too much and behaved in a shameful manner. They were also intimating that that there were a lot of ignoble activities going on, even of a sexual nature. Carnaval was celebrated in spring, with a culmination of parades and parties on Mardis-Gras in early March where even nudity was acceptable. This campaign was sponsored by the Algrange Protestant Church. The belief there was that the Devil was behind these deviant and disgraceful celebrations and good Christians should not participate. I was surprised that the local Catholic Church supported all the celebrating, but it did mean more money in their coffers.

My design won, and somewhere in one of the boxes in our garage, there may actually be a sample of that 1954 design. It showed a smiling face mask with the Devil behind it. I believe that about five hundred of these, one and a quarter by one and three-quarter inch stamps were printed. All the kids in our schools got a sheet and we all went about plastering them all over the display windows of stores, restaurants and pubs, which really pissed the owners off. The Protestant Church had made its point. The rest of the town went on and celebrated Carnaval anyway. The town council admonished the revelers to behave and hold in check all the drinking and there would be no nudity on display in public. No one observed anything different from the previous years' celebrations, but perhaps some of the people had heeded the message and behaved in a more civil fashion. This all sounded like very old Puritanical times.

• • •

Recently I discovered that Algrange now even celebrates Halloween since 2010. Go figure!

• • •

The lesson here was, all the stamps in the world preaching abstinence from booze and sex won't keep people from celebrating Carnival. Also, I learned not to judge…

Lesson 3 – Escargots are Snails, even in France

The same year, 1954 in the fall, we decided to go collecting Escargots to sell to local restaurants. Like with everything else, all the kids turned the whole snail collecting thing into a big competition. There were places where they grew in abundance and places where you just couldn't find any.

A chart had been created and hung on the wall with everyone's name on it and columns to show who had collected how many snails. We were going to get something like five to six Centimes per snail; that's less than a penny American at that time. The first few days, no matter how hard I tried I couldn't find more than a handful or so and they were rather small and unfit for the Cuisine.

Snails are peculiar. When we wanted to grow some vegetables, we couldn't get rid of them; the more we killed, the more showed up the next day. This project took place in the fall and snails had all but disappeared from our vegetable garden. I was starting to get desperate. Some of the kids were bringing in fifty, sixty slimy creators. Like I said, the most I got was a dozen to a dozen and a half.

I was talking to one of my buddies, Armand and we somehow came up with this idea we thought was thoroughly logical.

The next day after school, we waited for the rest of our snail hunting buddies to take off for their secret hunting grounds before we took off. We hiked up one of the steepest streets in Algrange; the one that led to the cemetery. There was all sort of vegetation growing up and around the cemetery wall, pretty much all the way around the whole cemetery; there were blackberry and boysenberry bushes and thick green ferns growing several feet thick.

We started poking in and around the thick undergrowth. It smelled of wet, decomposing vegetation. It appeared that it never actually got dried which is why the snails flourished in this environment. Anyway, soon we hit the base of the wall and were picking the biggest, fattest, slimiest Helix Aspersae off the old stone wall and depositing them into our buckets. Snails appeared to be everywhere. Before we got done with just a small section of the wall, we each had around a hundred snails. We had managed this by actually leaving all the smaller, skinnier ones behind. We actually didn't have any space left in our buckets and snails were starting to slither out. We shoved them back in and tied our handkerchiefs on top to keep the escargots from escarping; sorry escaping.

We brought our buckets to class the next morning and the teacher and the rest of the class were amazed at the number, sizes and quality of our collection. Our lines on the chart immediately jumped higher than the other kids'. Of course, everyone wanted to know where we got our Escargot harvest. Both Armand and I refused to divulge our secret hunting location. The next day after school, we noticed that everybody was hanging around in front of the school, kicking soccer balls around, waiting to see where we were going to go; so, we skipped the collection and went home.

The following day, as Armand and I were plotting our next snailing expedition in the school-yard during recess, we both had this strange idea; what if there was something wrong with snails picked around cemeteries; Gulp! We didn't have a clue as to what those humongous snails were feeding on; we had seen too many scary movies. At twelve, we also had quite an imagination.

"What if they feed on human brains or something," suggested Armand.

"Maybe we had better ask Monsieur Lapsien if those snails are alright to eat," I replied. So, we did. "Your Escargots are perfectly alright to eat. There is absolutely nothing wrong with them, in fact, both restaurants want more; they were so pleased with the size and quality. Where did you boys get them?"

We told him. He thought that we had come up with a brilliant idea there.

As we skipped and hopped our way to recess, the other kids wanted to know as well. So, we finally gave up the location of the secret Escargot hunting grounds. Everybody was happy. Our teacher was happy because he wouldn't have to supplant the trip with a lot of his own money. Our classmates were happy because they had run out of places to look. Our class in fact, had such a huge harvest that our teacher was able to supply a couple of additional restaurants. Needless to say, our fundraiser had been a complete success and paid for a trip to Verdun, a famous WWI site.

Finally, I learned about sharing…

But wait a minute; here's a little side dish to go along with the main course. My friend Armand, thinking that I was really into snails, invited me over for dinner after school soon after our project was over. I don't remember the whole menu but the main course was Escargots. My parents had always taught me to be polite, so I sat down with the family as they served up a large platter of Escargots in a butter sauce with Garlic and other spices. I got served three or four which I chewed on as hard as I could. The flavor wasn't bad, but the fried snails had the consistency of strips of rubber tires. It had given my jaws a royal workout but I ate everything my friend's mother had served me and thanked her profusely, making smacking sounds and telling her "Très délicieux!"

To this day, I have never eaten another snail.

By the way, just because restaurants over here call it *Escargot*, doesn't mean that they're not the same slimy little crawlers that devastate your vegetable garden; just saying…

• • •

With all those extracurricular activities at Ecole Mixte, I'm surprised I ever got any school work done. But the fact is I studied my butt off and actually learned quite a bit. In addition, I was getting reasonably good grades as opposed to previous years at Ecole Wilson. My butt and my face were no longer in danger of physical abuse. We had to keep a workbook for every subject the teacher taught. I still have a couple of them stashed away in some box out in the garage. By the 4th Grade, we had to study World Geography, World History, French History, Literature, Grammar, Vocabulary, Geometry, Arithmetic, Science and even Poetry. We were given at least two hours' worth of homework every night: sometimes three.

What was also interesting was that public school went as far as the seventh grade, this for both the Catholic and the Ecole Mixte schools. In late fall of 1955 as we started in the sixth grade, we were all directed to take a government mandated test to see which of us would be lucky enough to go on to higher education and which would end up going to one of the regional vocational schools.

I, along with all the sixth graders took the state test and believe it or not, I came in second among boys. The top three boys and girls got to go to the Lycee which was the name for the schools from Junior High to High School in the US (from the Latin Lyceum).

Our parents were called in individually to be advised of the results. My friends Georges Krischke and Michel Zinghoff were the other two in addition to yours truly that had qualified among the boys. Among the girls Lydia Schoentgen and two others I no longer remember, qualified for the Lycee in Thionville for the fall of 1956.

When my father came in to have the conference with Monsieur Lapsien, he had to finally let the cat out of the bag and reveal that we had applied for entry to the United States as emigrants and that our request had been accepted. We would be leaving sometime in February of 1956. Monsieur Lapsien was greatly surprised and actually very saddened by the news as he had taken a liking to me even with all my misadventures. He was sorry to see me leave, he said. He also admitted to my dad that my grades had been high enough to have qualified me as number one student in his class, not the number three as he had been forced to rate me. You see over there in the 1950s, you were graded on a scale of 1 to 10, ten being the highest. Not only that but, you were graded both for content and quality of penmanship. At the end of every month, we got a report card with the total numerical grade and our position in the class against all other children. Monsieur Lapsien confessed to my dad that the school board had mandated that no foreign child be rated as number one, ahead of a French child, so I had to accept third place graciously; believe it or not.

He told my dad something to the effect of, perhaps when the war had been totally forgotten, the school board might reassess that particular unwritten policy. I'm hoping they have.

Of course, upon being informed that I was out of the running for the third spot to the Lycee, Monsieur Lapsien was able to promote one of the other kids in my stead; the one who came in fourth. The lucky one turned out to be none other than my one-time nemesis Manfredt Dauber. He of course was relieved. One thing Manfredt wasn't too crazy about was manual labor and having to go to a vocational school meant doing stuff with your hands in addition to using your head. I saved him from all that; as well as the punishment which would have been meted out by his father's giant meaty paws.

19

THE CHRISTMAS PLAY

As I wrote somewhere earlier, even though Ecole Mixte operated in conjunction with the Protestant Church of Algrange, there were no religious studies in school. Everyone who wished could attend Sunday school to learn about the Bible and the Protestant religion, and most of us did. There were other activities that kids could participate in at the church such as choir, scouts (called Éclaireurs de France) and field trips.

You may not believe this, but on one such field trip; back in 1954, we were all marched down to the city auditorium one Saturday evening to watch a movie of a young evangelist, I believe preaching in Paris to an enormous crowd. The presentation lasted over two hours. And of course, there was a French interpreter off-camera, translating to the mostly French crowd the words of the young evangelist who just happened to be an American named Billy Graham (the French pronounced it Billi Gram); believe or don't.

In addition to the usual Sunday school activities, every year, there was the production of the Christmas play. In 1954, the play's title was 'A Christmas Present for Hansel'. It had been originally written in German and translated into French. Years prior, many of the kids I was going to school with had taken part in the Christmas play. A couple months before Christmas, right after Sunday school, they assembled all the kids in the auditorium so they could volunteer for the year's play. We were all sitting quietly listening to the director, Mademoiselle Beauchamp describing the different parts for kids. This year, there happened to be only two main parts, one for a girl and one for a boy, as well as two adult parts. As she was asking for the two volunteers, no hands were going up. As she kept scanning the crowd without success, Michel Zinghoff, sitting in the chair directly behind me poked me with a pencil, right in the touché. Naturally, I jumped up in pain.

"Merci," Mademoiselle Beauchamp immediately thanked me for volunteering.

She obviously must not have heard me when I tried to explain what had happened. Instead, everybody started clapping. Michel was cracking up and the others were laughing their butts off; at my expense. In that moment, I might have threatened them with bodily injury.

As the applause kept going, I couldn't help feeling rather elated and just kept bowing that is, until I realized that they were in fact clapping for someone behind me. I turned to see this cute little girl, about my age, who had gotten up and had actually volunteered for the role of Hansel's somewhat older sister: my co-star. She had pretty blue eyes curly blonde hair and a perky personality; she also attended a private school. My ego was deflated. The sister's name in the play was of course Heidi and not Gretel. And yes, all the clapping had been for Marie-Claire. She had been in several plays over the past couple years. I of course had other things to do and hadn't even seen any of these Christmas productions. So here I was, having to act alongside a stage veteran...

To my dismay, not only was I in the play, I would get to play the main character of the title, Hansel since there were no other parts for boys. This was a little three act play which lasted about an hour with a couple intermissions in between acts for cookies and Christmas punch.

I of course had never acted in a play. I had acted up in class and at home, but that didn't count. I mean on occasions, my parents had me recite poems at Hungarian celebrations, along with other kids, and of course if I recited fast enough, I was off the stage in a matter of a couple minutes. I would actually recite faster and faster because I was so afraid I'd forget the line; that is until a stern look from my father set me back to the proper speed. I was trying to explain as much to Mademoiselle Beauchamp and I was pretty certain that if I whined convincingly enough, I might just get out of the whole mess. It didn't work. She reassured me that I would do just fine. "Everyone needs such a challenge," she said. My only question was "why?"

She was a very peppy and positive person. She handed me the script with my part underlined. And my part seemed to go on and on, page after page after page. That was also when I realized that there were only the two kid parts; Marie-Claire and mine. The other characters in the play were adults. And, did I mention that I had a hard time memorizing lines from all those poems I had to recite…

"That was very brave of you to volunteer for the play," my father praised me when I got home Sunday afternoon.

"You don't understand," I replied. "Michel poked me in the butt and I jumped up and the next thing I know, I'm in the Christmas play."

"You should have explained to the director" he said.

"And you don't think I tried?" I replied. "Mademoiselle Beauchamp was persistent. She said I would do just fine. All I had to do was learn a few lines. She has a very positive approach to her task."

"Well son," my father said, "I'll help you with your lines".

That didn't reassure me all that much. If you had to find anybody more positive than the director, that would have been my father; he made speeches and never forgot his lines. Yikes!

I read and reread my lines for days on end in preparation for our first rehearsal. Now, Mademoiselle Beauchamp had given us a synopsis of the play so we'd have an idea of what we were supposed to do while we recited our clever little lines. I might as well tell you what it was about. This kid Hansel, writes a letter to, in this case, Pere Noel (Father Christmas a.k.a. Santa Claus, man with long, white beard and a red suit), asking for a whole bunch of presents, mostly expensive toys. Come Christmas Eve, he doesn't get what he asked for. If I told you any more, you wouldn't want to read on any further.

We had our first rehearsal and considering that I was just a rookie, I had thought that I'd pulled it off rather well. The second rehearsal went even better. The play was now only a couple weeks away. The final rehearsal took place a couple days before opening night. The whole production staff was there as well as the girl's parents, stage hands, the minister and some board members. And of course, I flubbed some of my lines. I choked! That caused me to panic. I was really glad my parents weren't there. But, they would be there for sure opening night…

I went home and studied my lines to the point where I could recite them in my sleep. There was no way that I could go up there on that stage and let everyone in the production down. In those days in the fifties, we got the week of Christmas off. I didn't even worry about what I was going to get that year. All I was worried about was, not forgetting my lines.

The big day finally came. We had to get to the church auditorium a couple of hours early to get the set ready and get everyone in costume; you know, work out the final kinks. I was to wear short pants with suspenders and a nice short sleeve shirt like kids in Germany might wear, or in France; in other words, pretty much the clothes I wore to school every day. I believe I have mentioned previously that boys back in those days, in Algrange, even during the cold of winter, wore short pants with long socks and big warm jackets. So, that's what I wore, almost. They made me wear lederhosen, you know, short leather pants with suspenders.

Of course, cute little Marie-Claire, who played opposite me, had a touch of makeup applied and her hair for her role was braided into pigtails by the makeup people: her mother and older sister. For me, they slicked my hair down. That was it. The adults had more makeup and hair work done and we were almost ready for the curtains to go up. I peaked. The little auditorium was packed. By that I mean, there were around seventy to eighty people there and about half way down the aisle, I spotted my mother and father, and that made me feel good. Unfortunately, it also added to my stress level. What if I flubbed my lines? That would embarrass them.

I started to sweat. I would have said perspire, however under great stress, the flood gates went wide open.

After several tense minutes of positioning us on the stage, the curtain rose and everyone started clapping. Before I could speak my first line, I gulped and almost choked on the saliva, but finally the brain connected with the vocal delivery system and my lines started pouring forth. I was going along reasonably well. The scene was a discussion between my somewhat older sister Heidi played by Marie-Claire and me, playing Hansel, about writing a letter to Pere Noel and what we were each going to ask for Christmas presents.

Heidi was telling Hansel (me) not to ask for too much because Pere Noel has a lot of children to worry about and it would not be nice to be greedy, especially at Christmas; the little miss goodie two-shoes. She flashed a beautiful toothy smile and her eyelashes fluttered like a pro's. However, Hansel was just not getting the message. He was old enough to know where exactly the presents would be coming from. He also just happened to be going through a selfish faze. I must interject that I wasn't like that at all. Moving right along, Heidi and Hansel finish their letters and walk off stage to mail them. The curtain comes down; end of act one. So far, everything went just right. The audience gave a hardy but polite round of applause.

Act two has to do with the parents discussing how they could get the children what they had asked for, considering the financial situation. They noticed that Heidi had not asked for very much so they would try to satisfy her request. On the other hand, Hansel was being inconsiderate and deserved to be taught a lesson; end of scene two and more hardy applause.

Scene three begins with the children getting up and coming on stage rubbing sleep from their eyes to see what Pere Noel has brought them. This whole third act was a discussion between the brother and sister about the meaning of Christmas and being grateful for what you received. Heidi opened her package and was indeed very happy as she had received every item she had requested.

"I got everything that I asked for," Heidi said again flashing a brilliant smile, eyes sparkling.

"Is that all you wanted, a stupid doll and some doll clothes?"

asked Hansel.

"Yes, that is all I asked for," she replied with her sweet and angelic and in Hansel's opinion, condescending smile.

"Ah, that's stupid," counters Hansel as he starts opening his big, wrapped gift.

So here, I had to say my lines as I desperately tried to open my package. Of course, someone had decided to wrap and tape the gift box so securely that I would actually have needed a big kitchen knife to cut the darn thing open. Naturally, I was starting to sweat more. I was ripping at the wrapping, but the packaging just wouldn't give. I must say that under normal conditions, I was very good at unwrapping gifts; so good in fact that you could reuse the wrapping paper; not this time, no!

By now, the audience was perplexed, they weren't sure if this was part of the act, or that I was actually losing it. They were applauding tentatively as some actually started to chuckle. I kept ripping at the package, tearing and tossing small shreds of wrapping papers all over the set. I peeked stage right and I could see Mademoiselle Beauchamp staring in my direction with a perplexed expression on her face.

Since there was supposed to be a dialog going on between brother and sister, nobody was going to rescue me. At this point, we had run out of our practiced dialog. Me, I just kept grunting and ripping, while looking at the audience and trying to smile. By now, even Heidi was getting giddy. Finally, I got the ribbon off and ripped the remainder of the wrapping paper off the box. I (Hansel) reached in and pulled out an orange. That's of course all there was supposed to be in the box; of course, I was supposed to know that. For some reason fiction and reality intermingled.

"A stupid orange," I heard Hansel scream in frustration. Now I was really feeling my role. "Is that all I get?" The audience saw the emotion that was emanating from my on-stage persona and took it for good acting; nay, great acting...

At this point in the scene, to show his displeasure, Hansel was to swipe the orange off the table so it would roll away behind the curtain. Instead, as I swung, I missed the target. On the return swing, I finally hit the orange which then rolled off the table and hit one of the chairs which sent it rolling to the wrong side of the stage. People in the audience started to snicker and I could hear them whispering. This got me really flustered. My lines were coming out in spurts: lines I wasn't sure were actually in the play, as though someone was punching me the gut. Again, the audience believing that it was being done in character, started to crack up. Nobody ever told me what I had uttered during those frustrating moments.

So, as the orange lay there, wobbling side to side, in frustration I took aim and kicked it clear off the stage, bouncing in the direction of the audience and down the middle of the isle as I fell on my kiester. Applause irrupted and I got a standing ovation. I got up and dusted myself like it was part of the act. Then, as if on cue, the whole cast and the director ran on stage. We all took several bows. The curtains came down. The audience kept clapping, so we took another bow.

I had ad-libbed from the point where I missed the orange. I was supposed to read the note explaining why Hansel only got the orange. I had basically chopped off a couple minutes of dialog from the production by forgetting that small part of mine for which I more than made up by my slapstick antics by taking an inordinate amount of time struggling to unwrap my package and kicking the orange off the stage.

The audience, having no clue that my little scene of frustration had not been planned, had apparently appreciated my creative ending and never did realize that there should have been additional dialog. Fortunately for me, my mishap instead turned into a very successful impromptu routine amidst the chaos of laughter and cheer.

My parents were very proud of me.

Mademoiselle Beauchamp came over after the play and complimented me on how cleverly I had covered for a prospective disaster, and then asked me to be in the following year's Christmas production.

"You were so wonderful and funny," she said. "You are a natural. Next year, we will write you an even longer part and have Marie-Claire as your co-star."

Meanwhile Marie-Claire was at the other end of the room, soaking in the praises of her adoring fans but she turned in my direction and threw me a kiss as she waived regally. Her entourage followed her lead and smiled and waved in my direction as well.

And I was thinking: "Frankly my dear Marie-Claire, I don't give a damn. We won't be on stage together again!"

"I'll give it some thought," I told the Mademoiselle Beauchamp as I smiled because I didn't want to hurt her feelings and tell her how I really felt about show business in general and Christmas plays in particular.

She organized many other events at the church at major holidays and I heard from my wise guy buddies that she often inquired about me. I literally hid from her and avoided being seen by her lest she decided that there were other roles for me in one of her plays.

Little did I know at the time, just how close we would be moving to the place made famous for all things to do with acting, Hollywood; just a skip and a hop from San Francisco.

The Protestant Church of Algrange, from an old 1950's photo (GK Drawing)

20

FRENCH FRIED SAUCER

"… On a vu une soucoupe volante, la haut sur le plateau." The boy was yelling excitedly as he came running down the street that came out of the mine-housing complex on the side of the hill. "We all saw a flying saucer up there on top of the Plateau," he was yelling this (in French of course), as he was animatedly pointing up toward the top of the hill behind him.

My friend Lucien and I had just left Ecole Mixte. It was late in March of 1954. School let out at four o'clock in the afternoon, every day, unless you had been caught chit-chatting in class. My friend and I were taking our sweet time, goofing off as we made our way home. We were kicking a soccer ball around along the street that like every other little town in France, had been named after the famous WWII General De Gaulle. Algrange was a small town of about seventy-five hundred to eight thousand people and most folks did not own a car. Some rode motorcycles or Vespas (scooters), but there was no heavy traffic to speak of except for a rare city bus or commercial vehicle; so, we did our kicking right down the middle of the street.

We had just reached the corner where my friend would normally turn left to get to his house, when that other kid had come running toward us. At this point, I still had a kilometer or more to get home. Lucien grabbed the soccer ball and we both ran across the street. The kid was now bending over, and huffing and puffing, completely out of breath. "What were you yelling there, a minute ago," we both asked. "You saw a flying cabbage?" we laughed.

"No!" he said. He looked at us totally exasperated. "A flying saucer, a flying saucer," he repeated excitedly.

"You mean one of those things like in 'The Man from Planet X' movie?" we asked. It had finally gotten to our town, some three years after it had been made. "Those things aren't for real, you big goof. They're only in the movies," Lucien told him.

The kid went on the defense. He was adamant. His name was Guillaume. Neither of us had seen him before. He went to the other school uptown, Ecole Wilson (Yes, the one I had attended before my father had me transferred to Ecole Mixte).

"I swear," He said, "there was a bunch of us playing on the *plateau* by the old *Maginot bunker* when we saw it. It was real bright and spinning slowly, very low to the ground. It looked like it was about to land," he spat out.

"Are you sure you didn't just make up the whole thing? You're just telling us a Munchausen (in the USA it would have been a Pinocchio) aren't you?" we said.

"No, no, absolutely not; go see for yourself." he replied. "I'm going home to tell my parents."

That thing about telling his parents got us thinking and we were almost convinced. His grimy little face looked sincere and all as he was definitely out of breath. If it was an act, he was doing a great job. Then again, how silly would we have looked after we'd found out the whole thing had been a big joke all along? As we were mulling the situation over, Guillome suddenly turned and took off, running up the street, back in the direction he had just come from. "I am going to tell my parents," he kept yelling.

We slung our briefcases over our shoulders and Lucien with the soccer ball under his arm, we took off after Guillome. He was pretty fast for a scrawny little kid who had been out of breath just a couple of minutes ago. He was almost all the way up to the housing complex by the time we made up our minds to actually follow him. My friend and I looked at each other as if we still were not totally one hundred percent convinced by this kid that his story was on the level. As we slowed down and contemplated turning around, we heard his voice again. "Keep going. It's on top of the plateau," he yelled. "As soon as I get my parents, I will bring them too."

We were intrigued. What if it was all true…

We kept on climbing the steep road at a quick pace and soon the road ended and turned into a dirt trail. Some of Guy's (it's pronounced Gee as in Geek) friends fell in line to follow us at a reasonable distance, and this reassured us somewhat. Why? We didn't know, maybe safety in numbers. We thought about it. What if we had just been suckered into an ambush? What if, these kids from the other school were going to jump us and beat the crap out of us, or something? Well, it was too late to change our minds. They were behind us, cutting off our escape route. We picked up our pace. We would look back every once in a while, to see if they were still following us. They were right there alright, but for some reason, they did keep their distance. OK, we decided, maybe they're not here to beat us up, but then why were they picking up stones? Soon though, we made it to the edge of the plateau.

They called it *le Plateau* because it was a reasonably flat expanse, though somewhat of an undulating stretch of real estate a couple hundred feet wide running about a mile in both directions, except for occasional mounds here and there. The eastern slope of the hill was bordered by a rather sizable forest, which extended down and into the next county. The western slope was mostly treeless and dropped down toward town. As we reached the top, we came out of a small gully and did not yet have a very clear view in either direction. We turned around to check on our pursuers. They had stopped just short of the edge and did not appear to have any desire to close the gap between us.

"We don't see anything up here," Lucien yelled back at them. "This was just a big stupid joke, non? (French for, right?) Espece de fils de chien (son of a dog)."

The kids just ignored the insult. It was a very somber bunch. "It was over there to your right. Keep going. You'll see it soon" yelled one of them.

"Why aren't you coming?" I asked.

"We've already seen it," another kid replied "it was very strange." We will wait for you, here," said another. "When Guy's parents show up, we will follow you. We promise!"

"Right!" both Lucien and I replied.

We took a few more steps forward. For some reason, we both turned around. The spot formerly occupied by our brave pursuers was now empty except for a cloud of dust. "It was a joke, sacrébleu! (A very common French expression)" we both yelled, though neither of us laughed. A gentle breeze caressed the grasses. It wasn't cold. We took a few more steps and the breeze suddenly subsided. The air felt eerily calm and the silence suddenly deafening.

We took a few more steps, past some small divots, and there it was. In all its shimmering radiance, there was the flying saucer.

Neither of us knew what we were getting into at that moment. At about a quarter mile to our right, was a large mound, about eight to ten feet high. Somewhat behind it and a bit to its right, there was this bright object which appeared to be floating just off the ground. It appeared to have been made of some luminescent material several feet taller than the mound. About the middle of it, a ring made of the same luminescent material, extending out several feet encircled the object. At that distance, it had the appearance of an upside-down plate or saucer, with an upside-down bowl resting on top. From where we were standing, we could not see if it was actually resting on the ground or just floating above it. It was emitting yellow, red, blue and green lights through what appeared to be portholes in the top portion of it. The whole object glowed in an eerie pearlescent white beneath the colors.

Neither of us said a word. Our mouths fell open. We were awestruck.

Slowly, we began advancing in the direction of the lights. I do not remember how close we actually got. We had possibly advanced to about half of the original distance. It was a mesmerizing sight that kept drawing us closer. While we had made our climb, dusk had slowly enveloped the Plateau. The sparsely clouded sky was slowly turning shades of magenta and gray. The sun was well on its way to setting, somewhere way to our right, just above the tree line. The plateau looked desolate in all directions, except for the glowing, pulsating thing in front of us. The air was still. There were none of the familiar sounds emanating from the forest below.

The kids, who had followed us for part of the way, were nowhere to be seen. They had totally abandoned us. They were probably at home trying to sell their stories to disbelieving parents. So, what in the heck was I doing, up here on this dark and dusky stretch of real estate? I was certain Lucien was asking the same question. For whatever reason, we just kept stumbling forward, like we were hypnotized.

I forgot to mention earlier that the plateau was not totally devoid of vegetation. There was a loose sprinkling of small scrub brushes here and there. They grew to two to three feet tall. Under normal circumstances, we would have recognized them for what they were: little bushes. On this particular strange and darkening twilight however, to us they suddenly took on the appearance of mobile, living and breathing entities, perhaps not from this world. And, we thought that they were actually moving slowly toward us. The closer we got to the light display, the more we both believed that in fact the occupants of that Flying Saucer were coming to get us. The little scrubs seemed to be closing in on us; and they might actually have.

Just as we hit the midpoint to our intended destination, we looked at each other and almost in unison we yelled: "The Martians are coming to get us! (In those days, we believed that Mars would be the point of origin of any interstellar visitation, just like in the old movies.)"

Without much debate, we turned tail and took off running. We ran as hard as we could back in the direction we had come from. We stumbled a few of times, but never looked back to check if in fact the **Martians** were getting any closer. And who knows, they might actually have gotten closer. But for certain, we outran them.

We hit the dirt road at full gallop, sending gravel and dirt flying. Lucien dropped his soccer ball which took off bounding along the dirt road and kept bouncing all the way down the hill and across Rue De Gaulle. Only when we also got there, did we glimpse back uphill to see if anybody had perchance followed us. To our surprise, we couldn't see anybody or anything back up the hill; no group of kids with their parents, and no Martians. That did not stop Lucien from speeding across the intersection and keep on running in the direction of his house just barely slowing down to scoop up his soccer ball. He never turned to even say ciao. That was my cue.

I turned right and just took off running for home. I had a little over a kilometer to go, lots of it uphill. Running as fast as only a skinny seventy-five pound twelve-year-old could run, I made it home in record time, though still late by my father's watch. I also noticed that the twilight had gotten considerably darker.

My mother was waiting for me at our apartment door. She looked worried. "Your father wants to have a talk with you," is all she said in greeting. No explanation was necessary. I was over an hour and a half late. Only then did I finally stop to take a deep breath.

"Where have you been, young man?" he asked, with a scowl. "Your mother and I have been worried." He was a man of few words.

My vocal floodgates opened and I blurted out everything that had just happened at about a hundred miles an hour. Adrenalin, emotion and a lot of excited gesticulating probably helped convince him of the story's veracity. He also recognized the signs that, something truly out of the ordinary had taken place, as exhibited by my agitation and wildly rolling eyeballs. He figured, I must indeed be telling the truth or this was the biggest whopper I ever laid in his lap. He asked a number of key questions, the kinds only my father could come up with. I answered them all as truthfully as I knew how. When he was satisfied that I could not possibly have made this absurd story up, he told me what I should do.

"First thing in the morning, when you get to school, tell the principal. Ask what he recommends you do. Maybe he will tell you to speak with the gendarmes," he advised sincerely. Algrange was a very small town and the **Gendarmerie** (Police Station) was more than likely closed for business by this hour. There just weren't any criminals to chase at night…

"Besides," he said, "that thing you saw is probably already gone."

The next morning, I got to school unusually early. Lucien got there only seconds after me. His father had given him pretty much the same admonition as mine had given me. Apparently, all level-headed fathers operated in the same mode.

The principal who also happened to teach the grade both Lucien and I were in, was just entering the schoolyard as we got there. As best as we could, we retold our story just as our father had admonished us to do at about the same speed.

"Slow down, boys," he would cut in occasionally.

Our excited demeanor helped to convince the educator of the legitimacy of our incredible tale. He finally put his hand up, saying: "Hold on boys, you'll need to tell your story one more time."

"Let me speak to the Gendarmes," he said as he walked over to the Gendarmerie next door.

In no less than five minutes, the principal was returning, a uniformed gendarme in tow. He motioned us over. Before we even had a chance to tell our schoolmates of our adventure, the gendarmes summoned us.

As we walked into the station house, a police captain greeted us. In a very serious and even manner, he told us that he understood we had had an unusual experience. "You have seen a flying saucer," he stated. We both responded with an emphatic "Oui, absolument!" meaning "absolutely, yes!" in French. He looked at us with no visible emotion except a twitch in his left eyed. He waved us down the hall to an office. Inside, two of his officers were waiting. Lucien and I looked at each other as if saying: "We should have kept our traps shut. What did we get ourselves into, now?"

We both blinked as each of the officers walked us into two separate interrogation rooms (I think they may have been the only two interrogation rooms in the whole station). We were separated to test the veracity of our tales. "Pretty clever of those Frenchmen," I thought (since I am not French).

I spent about an hour in the room, giving the very stoic gendarme all of the details from the night before that I could remember. I tried to keep my imagination in check and did not mention the thing about being pursued by the Martians. The officer took copious notes in his notebook and asked many questions, which I answered truthfully. Just as the hour was about to end as indicated by the big clock on the wall, a knock on the door interrupted our little tete-a-tete (that's French for interrogation). The captain poked his head in and asked if the officer was done. "Oui!" replied the gendarme. I was motioned to follow him into the hallway where Lucien was already waiting nervously with his escort.

The captain informed us that we were to take the officer, Jadeau by name, to the location of our sighting.

Within five minutes' time, our little column of Lucien and myself, the gendarme and a very big police dog (the French did not call them German Shepherds, as this was too soon after WWII and they still had a bone to pick with the Boches), was ready for the trek back up to the plateau. We tried to stay way ahead of the big growling dog as it kept trying to sniff our 'derrieres' (That's also French!).

It took us a good half an hour to get to the location of our sighting. We of course did not mind since this little promenade would keep us out of class for some time. We took the same exact route we had taken the day before. We did stop a couple of times to let the dog relieve himself and sniff the greenery, and also to catch our breath.

We retold our story to the gendarme as we retraced our steps, all the way to the point of our retreat, the previous night. This time though, we kept going. Lucien gave me funny looks as we passed the scattered scrubs, whispering: "Les Martians?" "Ah oui," I replied, "but, yesterday, there seemed to be more of them and they looked like they were coming after us." By this time, we both felt a little giddy about the whole experience, or maybe it was just the climb using up our oxygen.

We finally got to the spot, right next to the big mound. On the ground, just a few feet past it, there appeared to be a giant circle of yellow, wilted grass. You have to remember, to a couple of scrawny twelve-year olds, that circle seemed huge. It turned out to be about ten to twelve meters in diameter, which would make it roughly thirty to thirty-five feet across. Officer Jadeau stopped, but his stoic gaze could not completely mask his astonishment. His eyes twitched and he kept tugging nervously at his little black mustache as he scratched the thinning hair under his pillbox hat (Quite a task, considering that he was also holding on to the big police dog...).

He walked around and inside the circular patch of limp grass, several times. He then scribbled profuse notes. Pulling out a big measuring tape with a hand-crank on it from his leather pouch, he asked one of us to hold the end. He then proceeded to take measurements of everything. All the figures went into his notebook. "What do you think it was?" I asked with an angelic smile, as Lucien added a sweetly questioning look.

"It looks like someone had a very big campfire," the gendarme replied screwing up his nose while practically ripping the little black mustache right off of his face.

"Where is all the burnt wood and ashes, hmm?" Lucien asked innocently. We were both in the Boy Scouts and were fairly well acquainted with campfires big and small.

"Why, it looks like they cleaned it all up very well, and perhaps buried the ashes somewhere" the Gendarme replied. "They didn't want to start a forest fire."

"When pigs fly," we wanted to say, but the expression had not yet been crafted so instead, we just politely said "Ah, oui!" which would translate to something to the effect of "You've got to be kidding right? Do you think we're some kind of petit imbeciles?"

No way in heck, had this been a campfire or a bonfire, or a fire of any kind. "Can you say 'qu'est çe qui çe passe, mon ami," Which would be the equivalent of "who're you kidding monsewer?" We might have been twelve, but no way were we sitting in the back of the class with the slackers. Lucien agreed with my assessment as indicated by the look on his face and roll of his eyeballs.

Neither of us of course questioned the venerable Jadeau. All the while, this conversation was taking place, the police dog kept trotting around the big wilted circle of grass, actually avoiding stepping on it. Every time he got close, he would put his nose to the ground and just sniff near the edge of the yellowed patch, whine, and bark loudly and run off. "Why is your police dog running around like that?" I asked the gendarme sweetly.

"Why, he is happy to be out here in the great outdoors. He is just playing." The gendarme replied.

"Ah, oui" we both replied.

What could we have said about this highly trained police dog, frolicking when he was supposed to be sniffing or whatever he was supposed to do? It just didn't seem right at the time. It took me years to get real answers to the dog's mysterious behavior.

When he had taken sufficient notes about the big *bonfire*, gendarme Jadeau slowly walked us back to school while mulling over what he had just seen. We never heard another *official* thing from the Gendarmerie of Algrange, Moselle, France. The Case of the Mysterious Glowing Object was closed.

However, a couple of weeks after the incident, a kid from another class at the school, not involved with our original sighting, brought an interesting newspaper clipping to school. It was from a town about ten miles south of Algrange.

In part, the article read something to the effect of: "…On that night of (I don't remember the exact date) at about 6PM, several citizens of our town observed a luminous object rising from the hills above Algrange. The object shone with a yellowish white glow and multi-colored lights flashed all around its rim. It was visible for several minutes, as it rose from the plateau, then floating above the hills it took off at a great speed and disappeared in the night sky. There were a dozen citizens who had witnessed this event. This corroborates the story given by the two boys from Algrange, claiming to have observed a landed, luminous object on the plateau, etc., etc., etc.…"

We felt vindicated.

Lucien and I didn't broach the subject of the flying whatever incident after that. We both knew we had seen something out of the ordinary. We just didn't know what for sure. Over the years however, I was often asked to tell my tale of the flying saucer around the dinner table especially to guests. Some would throw strange glances in my direction at the time of my telling as though my parents had raised an *odd child*.

For years, I did feel a bit 'odd' for having had this strange experience. To this day, people are still fascinated by the tale, although I no longer get the strange looks. I only have one regret; had we gotten just a little closer to that thing, that night, the 'Martians' might just have taken us on the wildest ride of our lives.

Moving to the States in 1956, I lost touch with Lucien and still wonder how the incident might have affected his life, or not.

Some Final Observations:

1) The gendarmes initially concluded that we had actually seen the setting sun, after they had decided that it couldn't have been a campfire. However, we could clearly see the sun going down behind the trees, at about arm's length to our right, making it further west. The object was a good thirty degrees, back in the opposite direction of the sun and was actually sitting on the ground or floating close to the ground.

2) There was nothing near the mound or in front of it that would have had the capability of reflecting the setting sun which by that time was going down way behind the tree line. This object was facing us, and the trees were behind it. It also appeared to be shimmering...

3) The thirty-foot diameter patch of yellowed, wilted grass was not the result of any campfire. The grass did not look scorched or blackened. There were no charred pieces of wood nor was there any ash left behind. The grass was wilted and limp NOT burned.

3b) About thirty or so years later, someone explained to me the effects of electro-magnetic discharges on vegetation. I was informed that it would have caused wilting and yellowing of healthy green vegetation. It was also possible that radioactivity caused the wilting. I don't remember the gendarme carrying a Geiger counter, nor would I have recognized one at the time.

3c) The police dog stayed away from the wilted circle of grass the whole time we were there. The gendarme could not even drag him unto the circle. I was told that because of his nose being so close to the ground, it would detect the acrid, acidy smell given off by whatever chemical discharge that the ground had absorbed.

4) The shape, luminescence and colored lights given off by the object my friend and I saw, fit the description of literally hundreds, maybe thousands of sightings of similar objects of which I became aware many years later.

5) Although neither my friend nor I fell for the bonfire story, neither of us 12-year olds had enough technical knowledge to have made up the more scientific details of this event. Also, remember that, two different gendarmes, in two different rooms, interviewed us separately. The captain must have believed sufficient aspects of our story, to warrant sending one of his officers to the sight to take measurements and write detailed notes. Too bad that crime scene analyzing had not yet been developed to its current sophistication, or maybe we just weren't informed of the complete results. Also, some kids told us later in the week that they had actually seen a couple of gendarmes climb back up to the plateau for another look. What would have been the justification for another trek up the hill? Was it just curiosity or something else?

6) Then, there was that pesky newspaper report we both read with just about all the kids in the schoolyard. Several people in that other town saw something as well. I wish I knew who eventually ended up with the article or was it just filed in the circular file? It was unfortunate that I didn't know how or where to get a hold of a Xerox machine in Algrange, Moselle, France in 1954. As a matter of fact, I don't think I had ever heard of a Xerox machine in 1954.

Finally-To this day, I stand on what I have described in the above story. Everything happened exactly the way I have described it. Whether that luminous object was from Mars, Orion's Belt or some secret government laboratory like Los Alamos or maybe left over from Hitler's experiments, it was real. It was three-dimensional, solid and emitted all those lights and left a definite imprint on the grassy surface of the Plateau. I have actually written to a French UFO organization a couple times without a satisfactory reply. They apparently didn't keep reports that far back.

They should have…

Look, the flying saucer is over there, like those kids said (GK Drawing)

21

WE'RE OFF TO SEE THE WIZARD

Yes, back in those ancient times of the 1950s, refugees in France had to actually travel to the Consulate of the United States of America located in Paris; it might as well have been the Wizard. You were required to apply in person, for entry to the United States and to become a resident of the country. The reason for having to go on this quest to the US Consulate in person was so that they could take our fingerprints and have a little chat with us regarding our intentions for immigrating. We had also been instructed to bring along the required photos taken beforehand, for our passports and a variety of other identifying documents such as birth certificates, marriage licenses and immigration documents issued to us when we had relocated in France. It wasn't that easy to get into the States back then…

Once all your paperwork was filed and checked, you were issued a Green Card prior to departure. Not only that, but before we were even accepted for entry to the US, we also had to find someone already here and was already a legal resident who would be willing to sponsor us. Sponsoring meant that this individual (or family) was vouching for the veracity of the information that we had provided to the consulate and would be willing to house and feed us for a minimum of three months should either my father and/or mother be unable to find employment. Luckily, my father had already taken care of the connection.

Now, all we had to do was to get to Paris and fill out the proverbial boatload of papers.

We were going to make the trip during the summer of 1954, mostly so that I wouldn't have to explain to anybody why we would be going to Paris; on a trip we could hardly afford. Then explain to everyone why we would want to leave France. So, just in case the whole thing didn't work out again, we wouldn't have to further explain. Well actually, it was so that my father and our friend Bert didn't have to tell their employer that they were thinking of leaving. They both took a week's vacation. We also believed at the time that we would be able to leave in the spring of 1955. It usually took anywhere from six months to a year to process all the paperwork and wait for all the background checks that the US officials would go through before accepting us into the program. However, due to a quota system in place at the time, there was a limit on the number of refugees accepted annually. If I remember correctly, that number was 2000. Unfortunately for us, there were only two spots left for that year. Thus, our departure had to be moved to the spring of 1956 when we would actually get onboard that ship.

In the meantime, I had been admonished by my father not to say anything to anybody about our leaving Algrange. This was due partially to the fact that there were actually individuals in the Hungarian community who would have been all too happy, shall we say to torpedo our exit. These were individuals with dubious backgrounds who had not been able to get into the program. So, if they weren't able to, no one else should be either.

My father also didn't want somebody to blab it at the plant where he wanted to work until the last possible minute. Life in Algrange was rather cheap, but you still needed a good job and steady income to feed your family and be able to save a Franc or two.

My father also didn't want me to say anything in school, just in case our move did actually fall through and it might have undermined my chances to get into the Lycee (High School). I swore an oath to keep my trap shut. Of course, sometime during the course of our wait, I am certain I had blabbed it to a couple of friends who luckily forgot about it or perhaps thought that I was just making it up. I did sweat it because I was certain that one of them would let the cat out of the bag at school and the next day, everybody would have known and eventually the whole town.

Truth be told, I all but forgot about our eminent exit myself because on the rare occasions that I would ask about it, my father would say that there were no news and nothing would be certain until we were standing at the train station with our suitcases.

• • •

My father had wanted us all to go by train from Thionville to Paris, via Strasbourg, however Bert, you know the guy who was immigrating with us, had an old motorcycle that he had fixed up and had decided that he was going to save some big money by riding it all the way to Paris, rather than spending it on train tickets. And of course, that sounded like so much more fun than sitting on a train for ten to twelve hours that I asked if I could ride along with him. Initially my father looked at my mother shaking her head with downcast eyes and said

"Not only no, but never in a million years..."

Alright, I would have to work on that. It took me days of nagging, begging and a heavy dose of whining along with a downright ornery demeanor at the dinner table before the effect slowly broke through my parents' resistance. They finally consented and began to accept the fact that I was going to be a willfully miserable child lest I be permitted to ride to Paris on the back of Bert's motorcycle.

I had declared with arms crossed, legs apart and with a sullen downcast look that I wasn't going to move to America with them, no sir, so I had no need to go to Paris and they couldn't make me; well my father could have, if he wanted to. I was going to stay right there in our one room home and he and my mother could move to America without me. I must admit, I was stubborn as a mule once I had made my mind up. This had always been one of my fortes. The only options left for dear old dad was to either give me a swift kick in the pants to adjust my attitude or to relent and allow me to ride with Bert. "Besides Apuka, you'll save all that money on not having to buy my train ticket," I declared. This round, I had won.

Let me tell you though, riding some four hundred plus kilometers on what was the equivalent in size to a piece of two by four with very thin padding, taught me a good lesson. The 'two by four' I'm referring to was the passenger seat on this 1939 BMW motorcycle. In actuality, it was a metal frame with some horse hair padding, wrapped in leather. In retrospect, I would have been crazy to ride around the block on the back of this thing; which I should have done just to see how uncomfortable it would be on a long haul. It was! When we walked around Paris, I clearly walked bowlegged because the discomfort I felt in my undercarriage.

Not only that but I had thought this thing would literally fly us to our destination. I was wrong. We weren't able to go faster than 75 Kilometer per hour (around 45 to 46 miles per hour). Even in those days that wasn't very fast; main reason had to do with narrow two-lane roads most of the way. There were no freeways in those days in France. Even the highways weren't very wide by American standards.

We left very early Saturday morning and actually had to stop half way there and spend the night in a haystack by the side of the road, out in the country because we could only go so fast and it had gotten dark and Bert didn't want to ride in the dark, with me on the back seat where I practically had fallen asleep and almost fell off the back when he hit some bumps. Bert only realized that I was about to go night-night when he felt my hands loosen their grip from around his waist.

So, while my mom and dad rode in reasonable comfort and had nice sandwiches to eat in a nice, warm compartment, we slept with the livestock. As a matter of fact, the folks had already gotten there well ahead of us and were all settled in at the hotel when we finally arrived on the following late afternoon.

My father told us that it had taken them about sixteen hours to get to Paris, with a couple transfers while Bert and I made it thirty.

Both my mother and father had been worried sick that something had happened to us and regretted immensely the whole decision of letting me ride all the way to Paris on the back of that motorcycle. At this point, I had regrets myself.

There were even some harsh words exchanged between my father and Bert regarding the whole idea. That was a rather uncomfortable feeling for me, as we were taking this big step all together and now, we had a blowup. So, besides the pain in my touché, I was also upset and starving.

We had luckily arrived on a Sunday evening and were able to rest up a bit for our interview on Monday morning. After our appointment, we had a chance to take some strolls down a number of avenues. I actually remember walking by the Follies Bergere and admiring some of the artwork by Toulouse de Lautrec. Even at twelve, I could appreciate the female form, though my father kept urging me to move along when he realized that I was in fact fascinated by the scantily clad waitresses I could see through the smoky windows, serving drinks to some very happy patrons.

• • •

I have to do some more explaining here, so let me backtrack again. The whole idea of immigrating to the US had started almost as soon as we had arrived at Algrange. My folks had kept in touch with some of our friends from the camp in Austria, especially with a man named Victor Egry. At some point, about two years after we had left the camp, Victor had gotten married and now had a little girl Victoria. They had been part of the first wave of refugees to depart the camp and move directly to the United States.

Schmitzberg camp administration had however forwarded my father's letter to Victor. He had replied almost immediately that, had we waited just another six months, we could have been part of that very first wave ourselves.

Unfortunately, due to the thousands upon thousands of requests from WWII refugees, the US Immigration and Naturalization Services were so overwhelmed that an annual quota had been established for each country. Hence, for the years 1950 through at least 1956 that I am aware of, the quota was two thousand from France.

Then again, had we stayed in Austria and then relocate to the US from there; I wouldn't have much to write about.

• • •

When we travelled to the US Consulate in Paris in the summer of 1954, there were only two openings left on that year's quota. The very nice man at the consulate, perhaps the first African-American I had ever spoken to, in French no less, who just happened to be from California, suggested that my father and our friend Bert could go ahead in 1955 and find work and that my mother and I could follow them a year later. He told us that we would be first on the following year's quota (1956) list.

My father thanked him but told him that we had stuck together through thick and thin since we had left Budapest and we would not to be separated one from another, for even one year. The man at the consulate smiled at us and said, "I can understand that. I wouldn't want to leave my family behind either".

Now Bert could have gone to America on his own in 1955 as he didn't have any family and our friend in San Francisco had been able to get him a sponsor of his own, but he felt that since we had all come to the decision to leave together, he had insisted on waiting with us until the following year.

You have probably guessed that my father nixed the whole idea of my return trip on the back of Bert's motorcycle and then, even Bert had a change of heart and ended up on the train with us and his bike rode in the back in one of the freight cars.

So thankfully, instead of bouncing along on my sore derriere and sucking in road fumes while spitting out flying insects, I was able to snooze peacefully to the soothing clickety-clack of the railroad track as the train rhythmically rolled along the French countryside, with occasional squeals of the wheels on the old worn *French Chemin de Fer* all the way to Thionville.

• • •

The man from the Consulate had promised that he would put us on the top of the list for entry to the US for the year 1956 and that we would be notified via a letter as soon as possible, when we could start packing for our journey. The letter from the consulate did arrive, in December 1955. What a Christmas present!

• • •

Christmas 1955 was a 'low-budget' Christmas since at this point we needed every Franc we had for our journey to the Promised Land. We also started sorting through our meager possessions, giving away most everything we couldn't pack into the three suitcases we were to carry. My mother had sewn on an old Singer sewing machine a one-foot high comforter, stuffed with goose down that had kept us warm all the cold winter nights for at least six of the seven years we lived in Algrange. The very happy recipient of that comforter was an older Hungarian couple that had befriended us upon our arrival there and remained good friends until the end. The woman had always admired my mother's sewing handiwork and she had been thrilled with the big comforter.

The Bodognis got our Blaupunkt radio, my mother's old sewing machine, some dishes and the Bodogni kids got all of my toys. After all, I was now going to be fourteen. I no longer had need for children's toys, like the lead French and German armies and vehicles or the erector set that I received for Christmas from my father's employer. The only things I packed outside of my clothes were my collection of *Bibliotheque Verte* (Green Library - all books were bound in green cloth) and *Bibliotheque Rouge Et Or* (Red and Gold Library – bound in those colors and a little more expensive) a total of twenty books and of course, twelve volumes of Tintin. I was not willing to abandon these treasured tomes that had been my companions on all those long, dark and dreary winter nights and helped me learn the French language; by the way, I do still read them occasionally now and then just to remind myself of their timeless value.

The single guys next door, Frank Bajor and Charles Springer split up and one of them moved into our apartment and inherited whatever furnishings we had left, living there until we heard he had gotten married.

We had arrived at Algrange with practically nothing, packed into two beat up suitcases and we were leaving yet again, with practically nothing but the clothes on our backs and the contents of our three suitcases.

Of course, as we went to Paris in 1954 and our trip got rescheduled from 1955 to 1956; a few events took place in Algrange such the arrival of **Le Cirque des Frères Romanoff**, or The Brothers Romanoff Circus, as well as my trip to the Alps for the Camporee of 1955.

This also meant that I would stay at Ecole Mixte for another year and a few months and I would have to not let it slip at school or in church, for that matter at the bakery and butcher shop that we would be immigrating to the United States. Algrange was a small town and one slip of the tongue in any store and a day later, everybody in town would know. Why were we so secretive about our voyage, you ask? My folks still held to the belief that there were still vengeful individuals, shall we say, who would have been all too happy to derail our plan. After which, they would have said to us with a saddened look in their eyes "I am so sorry your plan didn't work out; what a shame!"

We didn't want to give them that chance.

With the circus coming to town and the Camporee the following year, they would be a couple of good distractions to keep me from thinking about our eminent departure and filing away for future reference our big plan.

That's Bert Bartha, me and my mom in front of Bert's motorcycle, the one we rode to the US Consulate in Paris, in 1954 (Photo by my dad with Bert's camera. Author's archives)

Dad's photo, required by the United States Consulate in Paris,
taken in 1954 - (Author's archives)

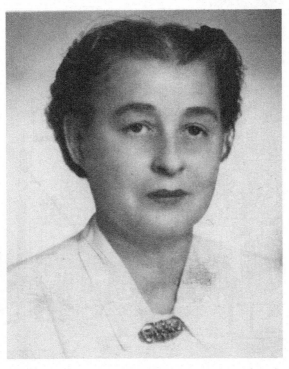

Mom's photo, required by the United States Consulate in Paris,
taken in 1954 - (Author's archives)

George Jr.' photo, required by the United States Consulate in Paris, taken in 1954 - (Author's archives)

Notre Dame de Paris in 1956 – (GK-Photo converted with FotoSketcher Program to simulate a pen-and-ink drawing)

22

NINOUTCHKA

The summer of 1954 had finally arrived in Algrange. The weather had warmed up to what we considered warm, about 27 degrees Celsius (80 degrees Fahrenheit) and we could finally run around all day long in shorts with t-shirts or without. Well actually, we wore short pants almost all year round going to school, even in the winter. I had only one pair of what was considered long pants. They actually looked like golfers' pants (Knickers) and were Navy blue in color. I wore those for church on Sunday, and for an occasional wedding, funeral or some patriotic event. When we would get home, the pants were hung back up in the closet neatly folded along the creases. They were too expensive to wear all the time and risk getting them dirty or torn. So, to make up for the short length of the pant legs, we just wore long woolen socks up to and over our knees and right under the pant legs, in winter.

Anyway, school was finally out. There would be no more school clothes, no more books, no more late hours of homework for the next three months or so. Life was good.

And then, the circus came to town. Life got even better.

A couple months before school would end there would be posters pasted up all over the display windows of town's businesses advertising the circus' arrival.

'Le Cirque des Frères Romanoff' or The Brothers Romanoff Circus, rolled into town with great fanfare to the shrieks of joy of all the kids in town, young and old. I wasn't a shrieker myself, although I was happy to see it coming down the streets of our little town.

Actually, as Algrange was a rather small town, we didn't have a railroad station, so the circus with all the trucks, trailers and wagons and cages had to unload in the town of Hayange, a few kilometers down the road. And that's exactly where it had been set up the week prior. After they had packed up all the gear and animals and gathered all the performers, they marched into our town like a conquering army.

There was a loud brass band with giant bass drums leading the colorful caravan into Algrange, followed by jugglers, Cossack horsemen from the steppes of Russia, acrobats and of course a bunch of clowns running around doing silly clown things like packing into tiny cars that would drive round and round on the verge of flipping over, but never did. Behind them came the elephants pulling cages with tigers and bears and screeching monkeys. And riding on the elephants were pretty women in tights with tutus, ou-la-la!

It was quite a sight. Pretty much the whole town came out to line the Avenue Maréchal Foch and watch the spectacle. The parade marched along until the street came to a rather steep rise about a mile from where I lived. This was actually the spot where the local bus turned around during winter months, because it couldn't grind its way up the grade. Which is also why I never took the bus to school, since from this spot, it was just a mile or so to get there.

This was the point where the parade made a left turn and marched straight on down to the fairgrounds along the mine's railroad yard. There they set up the Big Top and the circus village overnight and were ready for the public the next day. They were to stay for a whole week.

On Saturday, my parents gave me enough money to pay for the ticket and still have change left over for snacks and lemonade. Cokes and Seven Ups hadn't made it to this corner of the world at this point and for some reason, the French didn't make popcorn. When we asked why, they said "Corn is for peegs" with a sneer.

I was going with a friend named Marcello, who came from Italy and whom we had nicknamed Mouchi or Housefly because he was a real pesky little kid who buzzed around all the time annoying the heck out of everyone. Still, he wasn't a bad kid as long as you could keep his chatter to a minimum and away from sugar. Also, as he was getting older, the buzzing slowed down but the nickname stuck.

We had actually become friends after a rough and tumble in the schoolyard where he had been especially annoying and I had taken exception; imagine me the peaceful one. After rolling around in the dirt and punching and kicking without a whole lot of damage, the principal grabbed us both by the ears and dragged us into the classroom. When class resumed, we received ten whacks on our derrieres in front of all the kids. For giggling during the administration of the punishment, we received a bonus of five extra whacks from Monsieur Lapsien. Having gone through such an embarrassing ordeal together, you just knew we would become friends, lest the ordeal would repeat itself.

As advertised and as unbelievable as it all sounded, it really was a three-ring circus. As we walked into the gigantic tent, a new and magical wonderland opened up in front of our eyes. Even by today's standards, the tent would have been big, but for the two of us at around five feet tall, well it was gigantic. The trapeze artists flew about in the main ring while Cossack horsemen rode around in the next ring over and a dozen clowns tumbled out of their tiny cars in the third to the cheers and delight of the packed tent. Then a tumbling act took over for the horsemen and fifty dogs replaced the clowns while a high wire act took over the center ring. The show went on for almost two hours and Mouchi and I definitely got our money's, well our parent's money's worth.

Oh, before I forget, while we were wondering about, checking out the exhibits, games and the goodies booths before the show started, we got to talking with this very cute girl who appeared out of nowhere and looked to be about our age. She kept looking in our direction with the bluest baby blue eyes and when we finally took notice of her, she smiled at us and her cute eyelashes fluttered in our direction. At first, we weren't certain that she was actually directing her gaze at us. We turned around to see if perhaps she knew someone sitting behind us. Nope, she was really eying us.

We just didn't know why.

"Mouchi," I said "do you know her?"

"Never seen her before," Mouchi replied. "She sure is cute!"

"Well, I don't know her either."

After a while, she disappeared. As we were ready to enter the big tent, we noticed a number of circus posters on display by the entrance illustrating various famous circus acts. One of them happened to picture a tumbling act by the name of the **Magnificent Karamatzoffs** if I remember correctly. And none other than a pretty little blonde by the name of Ninoutchka, wearing a tutu no less, who happened to look a lot like the little girl that had smiled our way, was balancing on her hands atop a pyramid made up of what must have been the other members of the Karamatzoffs.

We obviously watched the acrobatic performance of the Karamatzoffs with great interest now that we were aware that Ninoutchka was, in our minds, starring. Both Mouchi and I sat with our mouths wide open in amazement by what an incredibly flexible acrobat she was. When the act was over, they all waved to the cheers of the crowd and as they ran out the big side curtain. Ninoutchka, to our surprise, threw a kiss in our direction, we thought. That wasn't all. As a new act came to life in the ring right before us, we were both caught off guard when suddenly I felt a hand sliding around my shoulder and realized that it wasn't Mouchi but Ninoutchka and she was sidling in between us on the bench seat, with a big smile on her pretty pink lips. Up close, I could tell that she was wearing lipstick and some makeup: interesting, I thought.

Mouchi and I just looked at each other and I could see his face turning various shades of red and the silliest of grins twisted his lips. I had a feeling I must have looked just about as goofy. Some of kids we knew from school sitting just a couple rows away stood up one at a time and looked in our direction pointing like we had just grown some gigantic horns on top of our heads. Ninoutchka sat there with us for about a half an hour when she finally left. We were a bit puzzled and even mystified, especially when she whispered:

"Come find me when the show is over," as she slipped her arms from around our shoulders.

After the show, we walked around, looking for her and caught up with her as she was heading toward a circus trailer we thought she might be living in. She was still wearing her little tumbling tights and tutu which we thought looked a bit too-too big for her, with a pink satin cape over her shoulder. We cut through the crowd, bumping into angry grownups and kids alike as if we were on a mission. We wanted to catch up to her and when she saw us; she turned around and gracefully jogged in our direction; taking what almost looked like ballet steps.

We started talking as we strolled along. Very adroitly, she had gotten a hold of my hand as it hung by my side and the next thing I knew, we were strolling hand in hand. Did I mention that she was extremely cute? This was of course the first time in my life that I had noticed how soft and warm a girl's hand could be and how much makeup can make a difference in a woman's appearance. I also must admit that this is probably the very first time that I had held hands with a girl that wasn't the daughter of a friend of my parents'.

I soon became aware that her other hand, was tightly wrapped around Mouchi's. So, we were now walking hand in hand in hand. I began to seriously question my bright idea of bringing my friend along in the first place. Suddenly the French expression *Femme Fatale* acquired a clearer meaning. Then again, I thought, if I would have been by myself, would she have noticed just moi?

"Would you come back to see the show tomorrow?" she asked.

"Ah oui," I said, before I realized that I had a shortage of Francs for this kind of extravagance. I mean, you went to the circus once a summer, period, unless you were the mine director's kid.

"Certainement," Mouchi said. He of course seemed to have money all the time and I had no idea how he was acquiring all this moolah: maybe his family was connected?

"Come as early as possible, so that we can spend the whole day together until it will be time for my performance," she told us, "and don't worry," she added, "I will get both of you in to see the show *gratis* (that's free in case you didn't know)."

Hey, this was 1954. Remember, there was no TV to speak of, not in this part of the world anyway. Well actually, to be perfectly truthful, one local dispensary of adult beverages and local cuisine had a working television set. It was called **Le Cochon Bourre** or The Stuffed Pig; in the local parlance, it could also mean The Drunken Pig. And don't even ask how they came up with that name. The set was of course black and white or to be more precise, light grey and dark grey, and through the snow and haze it actually displayed some images broadcast by possibly the only TV channel in the region or perhaps the whole of France, on a fifteen inch or so, almost round picture tube. On some Sunday afternoon, you would have observed some old guys with a tall Belgian (beer) staring at test patterns for hours. It turned out to be a great marketing tool for the owner, although I never understood.

Needless to say, the circus was a very big deal; it was life size, lively and in full color. On top of it all, it was going to be free. So naturally we both said: "Oui, oui!"

As we kept strolling along, Ninoutchka suggested we go behind the trailers and sit for a while by their unit as her next appearance would not be for quite a while. There were some packing crates about and a couple old folding chairs, so Mouchi flopped in one of the folding chairs and I perched on one of the crates while she went into the trailer. She returned a couple minutes later with a bottle and clutching something in her other hand. It was a pack of cigarettes. She offered us one and took one herself. She adroitly snapped a lighter on and lit ours and then lit her own.

Up to this point, I had never tried smoking cigarettes. As a matter of fact, when my folks smoked after dinner or at parties with their friends, I always held my nose and fanned the smoke away. Of course, I didn't want the other two to know, so I took a long drag and just about chocked. Mouchi cracked up and Ninoutchka laughed so hard she almost fell out of her chair and then proceeded to inhale and blow smoke rings like a pro. I'm certain I blushed profusely but did as the other two all the while thinking what a yucky taste I had in my mouth and hoping I wouldn't throw up.

"Would you like a drink?" she asked as she handed the bottle of clear liquid to Mouchi.

"Sure, why not," he replied and took a big gulp. His eyes rolled to the top of his brows and he almost choked. It had gone down the wrong way, I thought.

"You, showoff," I said as I laughed along with Ninoutchka.

"Here, you have some," Mouchi said as he handed me the bottle. All this time I was thinking, it's only cool, clear water. So naturally like a big showoff, I grabbed the bottle and took an equally big gulp. My eyes felt like they were going to pop right out of my head and my throat burned like I had just swallowed some Hungarian red-hot cherry peppers. It wasn't water. I had obviously been wrong.

"Vodka," Ninoutchka giggled, "My papa's favorite drink after work. I better go and put it back on the shelf before he comes back". She corked the bottle and quickly took it back inside the trailer. She returned with a handful of German chocolate candies.

Mouchi and Ninoutchka finished their cigarettes and I feigned doing the same. She gave us some of the chocolates which helped to soothe my throat and chased away the yucky cigarette taste. We lounged around for a bit longer, chatting and laughing about this and that, until she finally got up and said it was time for her to get ready for her next performance. We said goodbye and she kissed us on the cheek to our delight and total embarrassment. Up to this point in my life, I had not been kissed by a girl in quite this fashion, really.

"Au revoir until tomorrow," she said, "Come early oui?"

"Oui, oui!" we both replied and took off our separate ways.

When I finally got home from the circus that Saturday afternoon, I told my father that I wanted to go back the next day, Sunday, perhaps right after church since the circus was set up just a few blocks away. He asked me if I had any money to pay for this extravagance. I mean, you went to the circus once a summer and certainly not two days in a row. I told him that most of my allowance was gone but, "this nice girl we met, she said she would get us in free," I said.

"Her name is Ninoutchka!"

"Nothing in life is free, my son," he said. "Those circus people are shady and sneaky Gypsies."

"I believe they're Russians," I said.

"Well, they're sneaky Russian Gypsies, is what they are," he said as he waggled his finger at me.

"But apuka (daddy)," I protested, "She speaks perfect French."

"Well, they're French speaking sneaky Russian Gypsies," my dad growled, "and, they steal children."

"Steal children, you say? You're kidding, right?" I squealed, quite incredulously.

"When you go back there tomorrow," he went on, with both eyes squinting. "They will most certainly steal you away and lock you up in the monkey cage. You'll be stuck in the circus for the rest of your life, probably cleaning up elephant poop and feeding bananas to your cage mates! You'll never see your poor mother or me, ever."

How sinister, I thought! At the time, I still wasn't quite sure if the old man was serious or just pulling my leg. One eye still squinting, he delivered that last proclamation and took a sip of very dry cheap red wine.

"Maybe he's kidding" I thought. But, I wasn't certain.

To be safe, I discarded any notion of returning to the circus the following day and pretty much hung around in very close proximity to the house. I was unsure as to how far the sneaky Russian Gypsy circus people would go to steal a kid to clean up after the elephants and feed the monkeys.

We didn't have a telephone in those days and come to think of it, neither did my friend. So, Monday morning as we were standing in line, waiting to march into our classroom, I told him that I had gotten sick from all the cotton candy and junk we had eaten at the circus.

"C'est domage (that's French for: "Ha, ha, ha, sucker!)," he told me. "Ninoutchka was very disappointed that you didn't show up."

Then he proceeded to really rub it in by detailing what a nice time he had had holding her hand, and how she kissed him on the lips and he kissed her back.

"You kissed her on the lips?" I said.

"Oui!" he said with a goofy grin that I felt like slapping away.

"Salaud Cochon (translated dirty pig, pig being the operative word)," Is all I said.

"And, next year when the circus returns to town, she wants me to visit her again."

He didn't have to say it, but he was most certainly thinking that they would kiss the next time they met. And my name had not even come up as far as next year went.

And he kissed her, that little cochon (swine)!

How nice! And then the little gears inside my head started grinding, "Ninoutchka, that's probably not even her name," I mumbled. "It's a name they made-up for a circus performer and she probably isn't even Russian".

Maybe she had actually been stolen when she was a baby by those shady Gypsies and sold to the circus. Besides, what if the circus didn't return the following year, and what if she had not really kissed him on the lips and he had made the whole darn thing up just to make me jealous? Well he was most certainly succeeding. And what about all that makeup she was wearing? It looked a bit too much for a twelve-year-old girl. Now I was fuming. However, the thing that bugged me the most was the way Mouchi kept on smirking. Now I was positive that they had kissed.

As it turned out, none of it would matter anyway.

The following year we were to leave Algrange in France for the San Francisco Bay in America we thought. However, as fate would have it, we would actually have to wait a whole nother year for our big move, which would happen two years later than planned because of the quota of 2000 for refugees immigrating to the United States from France, which had been met for the year 1955.

This was quite a confusing time for a twelve-year-old who one minute was packing a suitcase for a long voyage and the next, to unpack and put everything back on shelves and hangers, and wait another year. However, I survived the whole mess and after a couple months, I had almost forgotten about the whole moving thing.

Now, the other conundrum I never quite figured out nor even thought about and I'm sure that Mouchi hadn't either, was why we had been so lucky at becoming friends with such a cute girl as Ninoutchka. Come to think of it, in 1954 I couldn't have been able to spell conundrum, nor would I have known what in the heck it meant.

It wasn't until a few years later that I realized, she had actually picked us, me and Mouchi to be her friend. That's exactly what she did. But why would she have, you ask? Here is my own deduction; it looked to me like the whole Circus Romanoff community was made up mostly of grownups. Both her sisters and brothers were a few years older, as in seventeen or eighteen and up. She worked with these grownups and did the work of a grownup. She ate with them and interacted with them on a daily basis. So, she desperately needed and wanted to be with kids her own age, for just a little while, maybe a couple days or even just for a few hours to just feel like a little kid. In retrospect, I realized that with her sunny, outgoing personality, she probably made friends in every locality the circus set the big top up. She had discovered a great way of coping with having to operate in a grownup world at such an early age.

And now, as they say, here's the rest of the story.

The Romanoff Brothers Circus did in fact return to Algrange in the summer of 1955. And, as she had promised, Ninoutchka was there too. Mouchi and I of course had remained friends even after the kissing incident and we eagerly awaited her return. When she saw us, she looked genuinely happy and came over and kissed us both on the cheek, just like old times.

But something had changed, because she definitely looked different.

She practically had to bend down a bit to kiss us; well, not really. But she had grown a couple of centimeters. She also had on makeup that actually looked good on her and made her appear more mature. Her blonde hair was thick and wavy. Gone was last year's ponytail. She had grown up alright. But she wasn't just a

year older like Mouchi and me. She really looked very grown up.
She had not only gotten a bit taller than the two of us but her legs
appeared to have gotten noticeably longer and shapelier; and she
had boobies. That right there had made quite an impression on us.
The girls we went to school with hadn't yet blossomed as they
would say, to even the training bra stage.

Yes, the changes were immensely noticeable. Mouchi and I, well
we had maybe stretched a couple centimeters but we still looked
more like a couple dorky twelve or thirteen-year olds. Whereas Ninoutchka, well she looked more like a young woman. After I had
time to think about it, even the year before, she might have been
more like thirteen or fourteen, just sort of smallish for her age. Well,
she had definitely made up for it in the past twelve months. Then
again, like my anyuka had told me on many occasions, girls ma-
tured faster than boys. I suddenly realized what she had meant,
when I saw the evidence right in front of my eyes.

As we strolled along the three of us, like old friends, Ninoutchka told us about all the wonderful places she had been to
with the circus and how she had looked forward to seeing us again
and tell us all about it. We strolled along by the trailers and tents
where the performers lived and practiced their acts, she pointed
out how the circus now had grown by two elephants, making a
total of five, and how they had acquired newer trucks and a bigger
pipe organ.

However, the biggest surprise she had for us was when she
pointed to a high-wire practice setup.

"We have a new high-wire walker," she said.

She pointed to an older, good looking young man, to us, of
about seventeen or eighteen who was balancing a long pole in front
of himself with two muscular arms, carefully sliding his feet along,
feeling the cable underneath his feet, stretched out about eight feet
above the ground. Ninoutchka waved in his direction and then
threw him a kiss. He smiled back a big toothy smile and almost
dropped his pole while trying to recover his balance. As she covered her mouth she could barely suppress her laughter. I saw him
blushing.

"That's Grigori," she finally said, "mon bon-ami (my boyfriend)!"

My balloon deflated. At that moment, I would have felt totally devastated, had I not remembered Lydia Schoentgen. Ah yes, Lydia, she would be coming home from her auntie's, at the end of summer. By then, she'd be missing me. But that's aother story.

Ninoutchka, offering what we both thought was water (GK drawing)

23

LYDIA

Following my initial introduction at Ecole Mixte, way back in September 1953, I eventually became friends with most of the boys and even many of the girls. Although the little girl I really liked, wouldn't come along until 1954, or perhaps, it was not until then that I would actually notice her.

She was an unassuming, quiet, sweet and an all-around nice little girl but until 1954, I didn't know she even existed; not because I was such a hot item, I was just more interested in hanging out with guys and doing goofy guy stuff. Lydia always sat at the other side of the classroom and hung around with the other little girls. I of course hung around with the boys. I was eleven. At that point in my life, girls just didn't interest me a whole lot. The next year however I started noticing the opposite sex.

Lydia had a cute, oval face with a celestial or small slightly up-turned nose and pale blue-grey eyes. I would say she had smiling eyes. Her hair was the color of light brown honey nearing blonde and her mother had it cut in what way back then, in France was called *garçonniaire* which meant tomboy style; very similar to a Dutch Boy cut over here. But she was anything but a tomboy. She was all-girl.

The last picture I have of her was sent to me by one of my friends from the confirmation class of 1956 at the Protestant Church of which I would have been part of, had I stayed in Algrange. In that picture, Lydia had been given a permanent and with her new confirmation dress on she looked like a very mature, attractive young woman. In just six months' time she seemed to have grown up; and I was still just a fourteen-year-old goofy kid. When I had opened the letter containing that picture, I remember wishing very hard that I could have been back there with them all; especially Lydia...

Of course, Lydia and I didn't become friends right away; far from it. When I first started in the fourth grade our teacher was Monsieur Uhl. I didn't know Lydia even existed. As a matter of fact, as a result of some rather unkind behavior on my part and my cohorts the following year, she actually disliked me. Let me correct that statement; she actually despised me. Hard to believe, isn't it; sweet little moi?

• • •

Again, to show how immature boys can be, we started picking on this poor girl who came from a rather large family. She had also been mostly invisible to me until we needed someone to torment. In class, none of us guys wanted to sit next to her. We would pinch our noses and claimed that she smelled bad. Even Monsieur Lapsien was getting annoyed at us holding our noses and making sour faces. But what can I say, she did smell different and I wanted to be accepted.

Up to this point in our immigration, I had never come across someone who was truly poor. I mean, everybody in this little town worked for one of the mines or one of the foundries and other supporting industry or working in the stores around town. It didn't appear that many were unemployed, perhaps none. The streets were always clean. Garbage was picked up regularly and everyone took care of their property. There were trees lining the streets and flowered borders in front of even the mine housing projects. But many of the families had a lot of kids. Not having television might have had something to do with this trend. Raising a lot of kids cost more than raising one or two. My folks were lucky; they only had one. This is however where some larger families ran into trouble even though there was government assistance.

As far back as I could remember, although we could have been considered poor ourselves, mainly because we didn't own a lot of *stuff*, we never smelled poor. Whatever it took, if it was with cheap hand soap, my mother would wash our clothes with it over and over if she had to, just so we wouldn't smell of the stale odor of hand-me-downs initially given to us to get started. She also insisted that I did the same thing with my own body. "Wash with soap," she would say, "Twice if you have to." She didn't want any of us to carry the odor that abject poverty gave off.

If you have ever come across real poverty, it does have a unique stench all its own. Subconsciously I really knew it. I had had sufficient occasion to smell it. Perhaps the idea of it emanating from me repulsed me. But somehow, I chose to carry on with the rest of the knuckleheads.

It went on like that for several weeks when one day, out of nowhere, Lydia got in our faces and read us the riot act. Yes, they had those in France too. She caught us in the middle of the schoolyard and in front of the girl and the rest of the kids, with hands on hips; she gave us a sound lecture about treating others the way we wanted to be treated.

"You boys ought to be ashamed of yourselves for the way you are treating poor Nadia," she scolded us. We all looked at her. What the heck was she talking about? Stinky people were fair game.

"Nadia smells bad," One of us said. I don't believe it was me. It might have been Michel; yeah, that's who it was.

"She actually stinks," said another. I can't remember who that was.

"Her family is very poor," Lydia said. "They all have to wear hand me down clothes."

"Well, they should wash them first," maybe I said that.

Then again, I was the prince of hand-me-downs.

Since Austria, I got my wardrobe from Care packages or the International Refugee Assistance Program, or something like that. But I knew that my mother washed and ironed every item of clothing I ever put on; I mean really wash things, sometimes twice to get the old stale mothball smell out of them. When I would put them on, they looked like they were store-bought. Maybe other people couldn't do that or they had gotten used to the smells.

Come to think of it, my mother did tend to overdo the clean thing, especially after seeing all the filth and unsanitary conditions along the road to freedom.

"Well, her papa works very hard, because she has three little brothers and two little sisters," Lydia went on. "They all have to eat first and then comes soap for washing."

"Well, we didn't know that," we replied, begrudgingly.

"Well, think about it the next time you want to hurt her feelings," Lydia said. "Can't you Nigauds (knuckleheads) find something constructive to do?"

"You are absolutely right," I said to her. "Come on guys; this is not right. How would you feel if somebody did this to you?"

"I actually do," said Georges Krischke. "Did you forget already about the sneak attacks you inflicted on us, way back when you thought you were Catholic?"

"I did that in error," I said. "Remember, I was confused. I had an identity crisis. Besides, this is different, she's a girl. My father always said; always do what your heart says is right. This isn't right. " It took me awhile to realize that.

"Oui, oui, très bien," they all begrudgingly agreed. "Still, don't girls just take all the fun out of everything," they mumbled as we headed over to the schoolyard to kick a soccer ball around. However, from that day forward, we put out great effort to stop harassing that poor girl. And I, well I believed I had scored some points with Lydia; but not right away, mind you.

Just two Sundays before the edict from Lydia had come, down Pastor Daniel Michel of the Protestant Church across the street from the school had preached a sermon about caring for the poor and opening your heart to them and helping them any way you could.

Of course, we had all sat in church, near the front and heard most of his words. In fact, we had probably all half-consciously agreed with him to the point where all of the one hundred Francs my father had given me for the collection basket had actually gone into it. I usually tried to keep a tithe for my expenses, especially if it wasn't' a single one hundred Franc bill. The girl herself was sitting in the pews across the aisle from us. Perhaps, it had been a voice from above speaking through Pastor Michel who had actually planted a seed in our little brains about mending our errant ways. Otherwise, you know as well as I do that we wouldn't have given in to Lydia's mandate so easily.

But, I did mention about scoring points with Lydia, right?

After our encounter in the schoolyard, Lydia would smile at me sometimes. And she did have the most radiant smile. After a while, she actually spoke to me without using the words idiot or imbecile to preface every sentence. And of course, not missing a beat, my cohorts started to tease me. "Georges a une Bonne Amie" meaning "George has a girlfriend." And yes, Georges is the French spelling for George, without the s at the end. I know it can be confusing.

Of course, the only ones who didn't know this fact, were Mr. and Mrs. Kapus. My father had on many occasions told me of all the problems the female gender had brought down upon the heads of men, throughout history in fact. He had indicated seriously that it would be very advisable if I wouldn't think about girls until I was in my twenties and had a job; maybe I could even wait until I was in my thirties, like he did. At the time, it sounded reasonable, however, there was Lydia. Remember, they were old-fashioned and this was the 1950's. Of course, I had to say "Igen apuka, persze!" meaning "Yes father, of course!"

Moving right along, Lydia and I fast became good friends and hung around together at class breaks and of course I got to see her in Sunday school. A bunch of us, including Lydia, would climb up to the top of the hill that we called **Le Plateau** to play hide-n-seek and explore the old German bunkers in the surrounding woods. We caught an occasional movie at the Odeon or Sax cinemas, sharing ice cream in the dark. We might have even shared a piece of pastry at **Schmouk's** Pastry shop just across the street from school on occasion. Mostly it was just a good feeling to have a friend of the female persuasion who actually liked me.

However, after we had been friends for about six months, our relationship ground to a screeching halt.

From one day to the next, Lydia didn't want to speak to me any-

more. When I asked her about the cold shoulder, she wouldn't answer; she'd just simply turn her back and walk away. She had actually moved from her desk next to mine, all the way across the
classroom. Even Monsieur Lapsien noticed the wall of ice that had
materialized between Lydia and I. Georges Krischke and my other
buddies asked what was going on. "Je ne sais pas," I replied, meaning I don't know.

"Did you hurt her feelings," they asked. "We know you sometimes think you're funny when you're not."

"Moi," I said. "I would never do such a thing. We said au-revoir
yesterday after school and today she won't speak to me."

"Well, why don't you find out what's going on," Georges
asked.

"Ah sacrebleu," I said. "She won't answer my questions. She
walks away from me. How can I find out?"

"Well, we'll have to do some reconnoitering and ask around to
see what's going on," promised Georges Krischke. "Maybe she has
a new Bon-Ami (boy-friend)!"

"Ah oui. C'est rigolo ça" meaning "Right, that's really funny!"

This went on for a couple weeks. I felt guilty like I had really
done something wrong, and I just didn't know what. And, I could-
n't go to either of my parents and cry about it. Nonetheless, it was
really upsetting me. This went on to the point where Lydia would
miss Sunday school just so as not to run into me. I was about to
give up when fate stepped in. More specifically, it was Lydia's
friend Nadia who now liked me since the time I had mended my
ways and put an end to being a jackass.

"I will find out what is bothering Lydia, and if she will tell me,
I will tell you tomorrow, why she has been acting the way she has,"
Nadia reassured me after class one day.

"Merci bien Nadia," I said. "You are a good friend." Of course,
the way she said it, I had this strange feeling that she already knew.

The following day, Nadia did as she had promised. At the
morning break, she called me over to a corner of the yard and first
she told me that Lydia was ill and wouldn't be in school that day.
"She is very sad herself about how she has been behaving with

you," she started out. "Her mother has basically forbidden her to speak with you."

"Why?" I gasped. "What did I do?"

"You didn't do anything. But, her father who was in the French Army was killed in the war, by the Germans."

"But, I'm not German," I replied. "I am Hungarian."

"Her mother said that you all fought on the same side."

"But I was only three years old when we left Budapest," I protested. "I never went to war and never fought on anybody's side. Even my father never fought the French. As a matter of fact, he actually likes the French; especially some of their authors like Alexander Dumas and Edmond Rostand and of course their wine, Mouton Cadet. My papa actually fought the Russians."

"She is still very sad over losing her husband," Nadia explained. "To her, any enemy of France is an enemy to her husband and now to her."

"C'est incroyable," I said. That means incredible. "I had nothing to do with the war. As you can tell, we had to escape from Hungary because of the war and now we have to live here in France."

"I know," she said. "We had to do the same. We came from Poland."

"So now what," I asked. "Is she never going to speak to me again? Maybe, I should talk to her mother."

"That would not be a good idea right now," Nadia advised. "I think when she gets well, Lydia will speak with you. She kind of promised me."

The bell rang and break was over, so was our tete-a-tete. Lydia didn't get back to school until the following week. And, she did speak to me. As a matter of fact, we had a nice talk. She in fact told me that she had been urging her mother to not hold anything against a little kid who had nothing to do with her father's death. "She is a good mother to me and she works very hard," Lydia explained. "Without a man in the house it is very difficult."

"I understand," I said. "My father works very hard and even my mother cooks occasionally for our single guy neighbors to help with the grocery money."

"It is not very easy going for anybody these days," she said.

"I know. I see why you stood up for Nadia," I said. "Her family is really struggling, with all those kids."

"Yes, there are six of them. Nadia is the oldest."

"I am sorry about your papa," I told her. "My mother and I would be very sad if anything happened to my papa."

"Well, that isn't all," she said. "My father was a French citizen, although our name Schoentgen is German. When the war broke out, my mother didn't like the fact that we had a German name. She was so French, that she was upset with my father for having that name. And then, he went to war and got killed by the Germans. Now, she feels angry and hurt and sorry for the way she acted with my father…" And tears started to roll down Lydia's cheeks.

"I am so sorry Lydia," I tried stifling a sniffle myself. I could get emotional at times. "I understand. If your mother doesn't want you to be friends with me, I understand that too. I certainly don't want to add to her hurt and cause bad feelings between the two of you."

"Oh, it's not like that," she said. "My mother is slowly realizing that she shouldn't take it out on a stranger who had nothing to do with what happened to her husband."

"Oh, c 'est bien alors," I said, meaning, that all's good. "So, we can hang around together again?"

"Oui," she said. "As a matter of fact, I told her what a nice boy you were, and now she wants to meet you."

"Vraiment," I gulped; meaning really?

I had shown quite a bit of bravado when I had offered Nadia to go speak to Lydia's mother and all of a sudden, I found my bravado trying to leave town. But, Lydia was smiling at me. She then took a hold of my hand and squeezed it gently, which made me feel a lot better. We would probably have hugged we were both so happy, had hugging in the schoolyard not been embarrassing.

I was going to meet her maman after school!

I was as anxious as Lydia as Nadia and I walked toward Lydia's home which was fairly close to school. Her and her mother lived on the second floor of a stately old 19th century building. We slowly climbed the stairs to the second floor. I kept thinking that I could come up with an excuse at the last minute which would get me out of this encounter or just turn around and run like crazy. Nothing came to mind and it was too late to run as I found myself in front of Lydia's apartment and she was already knocking.

The door opened and there stood a rather youngish looking woman of about my mother's height, with light brown hair and in the eyes of a twelve-year-old, with a rather nice-looking figure, in a motherly sort of way with features very closely resembling her daughter. Lydia introduced me and her mother put her hand out in greeting. I did something which even surprised me that my father had taught me since I was about five, I took her hand and I kissed it. She was so caught off guard that as she pulled her hand away she said "that isn't necessary."

"My papa taught me to show ladies respect," I said "especially when you meet them for the first time."

"You are a very polite boy," she said.

"See, maman," Lydia said. "I told you he was a very nice boy."

"Yes, you did" her mother said with just the shadow of a smile on her lips; while I was thinking she probably thought I was just a little kiss-ass; although sincere.

"And Nadia, you can come in now," she added, seeing a shadow moving away from behind the door. Lydia's friend had stayed in the hallway stating that this meeting should only be between the parties involved; whereas I surmised that it had been more for a quick get-away in case things didn't work out well.

So, Lydia's mother offered us a wedge of *tarte de cerise*, or cherry tart and a glass of lemonade. All four of us sat around talking for almost an hour, after which I thanked Lydia's mother for her hospitality and excused myself. I hadn't felt so good in a few weeks and started jogging for home, when realization came that I would be a whole hour late and would have quite a bit of explaining to do.

What could I say to my mother who was probably worried? I was also hoping that my father hadn't gotten home from work yet because I couldn't make a story up that he would believe. I could have tried manipulating my mother in which I had been successful most of the time, but my father was like a living lie detector. As it turned out, he was late because of the irregular bus schedule but, my mother told me to hold my story until he got home. So, what could I do? I had to tell the whole truth and nothing but.

"You know you're too young to get involved with women," my father started out. As I said, I had heard this lecture a few times before.

"She's just a girl my age," I countered.

"They are all the same…" I believe I had zoned out as I could probably have repeated the whole lecture word for word. But the old man didn't seem to be that angry. He felt he needed to do his fatherly duty.

Needless to say, Lydia and I rekindled our friendship and spent more time together whenever possible. We were really just very good friends. We occasionally went to the movies together, but always in a group with the other kids. We even held hands sometimes, especially when no one was looking.

This was one of those early childhood romances that upon looking back, you knew wasn't going anywhere. But when you're just starting to look at your world in that different sort of way where girls are no longer just buddies as the boys were, it was an important period of time. It was sweet and tender and yet an innocent period of time that you end up remembering for the rest of your life.

That cold February day in 1956 when I said goodbye to the school, Monsieur Lapsien and all my little buddies, I knew that possibly it would be for the last time. Of course, I had promised that when I made it big in America, I would come back and visit, or maybe someday, they would come and visit me.

Here's a funny side note. A few weeks before our departure, I had told my friend Georges Krischke "You know, my father told me that his friend from America wrote to him that, in America everybody has a good job and many people get rich."

"Ah, oui!" Georges replied.

"When we get to America, I am going to get rich in a few years and I will come back to Algrange and maybe marry Lydia. Wouldn't that be terrific?"

"We would have a big wedding party, oui?"

"Oui!"

"How long do you think it will take for you to get rich?"

"Perhaps four of five years."

"I will be waiting anxiously..."

When it came to Lydia, that last day in school, I held her hands in mine and promised that I would return. I even jokingly suggested to her what I had told Georges, that maybe we could get married when we grew up and I became rich. What was I thinking? We of course both laughed. We hugged. She kissed me on the cheeks and I kissed her back. When it came time to finally let go of her hands and as I looked into her bright blue eyes, we both sort of knew that this would be the last time we would ever see each other.

As I turned to leave, I had a hard time suppressing a sniffle. Guys weren't supposed to cry, especially way back then.

Lydia, sweet Lydia, I must go far away
I shall miss you most of all
But I promise to return one day
When I've become rich and famous
And then, I will take you away
Was a promise I could not keep
As time so swiftly flew away
And all that was left of Lydia
Was the image of her sweet face
Forever stored in my memory
For, what was I thinking anyway?
Making a promise I couldn't keep
As a displaced kid of fourteen

I would miss Lydia the most.

Saying goodbye to Lydia was the hardest thing I had to do in February 1956 - (GK drawing)

24

THE BIG CAMPOREE OF 1955

In case you've never been a Boy Scout or Girl Scout or any kind of scout for that matter, the title Camporee refers to a regional gathering of scouts, a sort of a smaller cousin to the more expansive Jamboree, which is a gathering of scouts on a national or even an international level. As you may or may not know, a guy named Baden Powell is credited with having founded not only the Scouting Movement but this organized gathering of scouts as well with the very first Jamboree being held in 1920. These major gatherings are held about every four years and the attendance has been in the hundreds if not thousands from many countries around the world; in the past, anyway. Nowadays, with the attacks on scouting, I have no idea if any Jamborees are still being held. Back then, kids needed scouting and our Camporee was a total blast.

Our 1955 gathering included about a hundred seventy-five to two hundred participants and consisted of scout troupes from our corner of France, the Moselle region pretty much. The early days of scouting have a fascinating history; however, since this is to be my history, we'll segue right back to 1955.

In the summer of that year, the Protestant Church of Algrange sponsored my way to go to a Boy Scout Camporee in the Alps. This is something we of course couldn't have afforded without their help as unbeknownst to me; my folks had already committed every centime they had to our eventual emigration to the United States; and I mean every centime. And of course, I knew of our attempts to immigrate to the US, but I had to be quiet about it and then, it was on and off for about two years, until we actually got accepted and added to the list. But even had they not saved every centime for our eminent departure, this would have been a luxury we simply couldn't have afforded at the time.

When the decision had been made to emigrate, we started cutting back on movies and other luxuries, even vino. You see, my folks had to sign a promissory note for a loan from the Church World Service which allowed us to pay for passage on a ship and tickets for a long train ride to San Francisco that we would be obligated to pay back, at a rather reasonable pace once we had settled in the United States. Back then, there were no such things as coming in for free: but more on that later...

That year also, I had taken notice of another little girl at our school. She was very pretty and had curly auburn hair. She had striking hazel eyes and fluttery long eyelashes. She was always dressed in more stylish clothing than the rest of the girls. She also lived up on the hillside, in considerable better housing than the rest of us. Her father, instead of being a laborer, a miner, machinist or a merchant, was in fact the director of some company or other in the city of Hayange, just a few kilometers down the road. They were one of the few families in town, who actually owned an automobile, and I can tell you there weren't many and we had no parking problem in our little town because not many people owned private vehicles.

She was somewhat aloof and standoffish I thought and didn't appear to make friends easily. At first, I thought that she held her nose too high as my mother would have said of someone who thought of themselves as better than you. She pretty much spent her breaks by herself except for an occasional interaction with a couple of classmates. She was however a Girl Scout and in fact was going to be going to the very same Camporee I had been signed up for. Of course, when she found this out, it was like breaking ice. She actually approached me and we began talking about going to the Alps for a whole month. We had both discovered a common purpose that gave us an excuse to occasionally hang out together at break time. As a matter of fact, Gabrielle fast became my new best friend, sort of.

After all I had gone through with Lydia and that incident with her mother and losing Ninoutchka, sort of, I found myself in a peculiarly difficult situation. I should have listened to my father and not get involved with *women* at all. Lydia's feeling had naturally gotten hurt because I was no longer spending as much time with her. Of course, my buddies, the little rats, were merciless in all the teasing they put me through as a result of my new friendship, which only helped to exacerbate the situation with Lydia. What can I say? I was thirteen and I never had to deal with this sort of issues before; the attention of two women.

Thank goodness, summer was coming. Lydia informed me that she was going to spend most of her vacation, about two and a half months, with an aunty somewhere around Metz which was about twenty-five miles north of us. She also said something to the effect that I wasn't going to miss her anyway since I had a new best friend. I said that I would most certainly miss her, but with the date of my trip fast approaching, I started packing a whole month ahead of schedule for my big adventure in the Alps. This also helped to take my mind off of Lydia, a bit. This had also been the first time since I had gone to the sanatorium in Austria at age five that I was going to be away from my parents for an extended period of time. I was torn between excitement and reluctance; however, I was now thirteen. I tried to convince myself that I was growing up and to stop being a sissy mama's boy.

I was now a Boy Scout. I was also looking forward to the whole big adventure and especially since Gabrielle was going to be there as well; that was going to be a bonus. Besides, she had told me that she had already attended a Camporee for the past couple of years held at different locations in France. She was a veteran and I was just a greenhorn…

School let out and summer vacation began. Most of my buddies went to visit one relative or another, although I discovered that a handful was actually going to be in camp with me after all. With Gabrielle on my mind and friction with Lydia, I hadn't been paying attention to what the guys had been telling me all along; some of them were going to be there as well.

Juggling all these various relationships was clouding my thinking a bit. My life had gradually become more complicated…

On departure day, I was ready to go. My dad walked me to the Protestant Church with some final words of advice and I went to stand in line with the rest of the scouts, some of whom I knew and quite a few that I didn't. We were loaded on a bus and driven to Thionville. Here we met up with a hundred or more other scouts, twice as many boys as girls. We boarded a train that would take us through Besancon with an eventual destination in some small town at the foot of the Alps. From there, we were bussed up the mountain for the final eighteen or so kilometers to our eventual destination, the Camporee site. It was located on a large, flat, empty stretch of pasture next to a large farm, where from the edge of the tree line, we could glimpse Mont Blanc in the distance, being located a good fifty kilometers away.

Thinking back, I wish I could have had a camera. Of course, back then, I felt lucky just to have had the opportunity to go in the first place. Someone always seemed to remind me to keep those pictures in my mind; they'll never fade. And, they never have.

About two or three kilometers down the mountain from the campsite was the Northern shore of Lake Geneva. The third week of our camp, we were to actually go on a hike around the lake, or as far as we could hoof it and into Geneva. I had no real clue as to the distance involved I was so ready to go.

With all the gear offloaded from the trucks, we were told to set up camp. Set up camp? What did they mean? In my mind, I had envisioned a nice field with tents all set up in a row with bathrooms and showers and a mess hall; all we would have to do is stash our personal gear and plant our troop banners. I was wrong.

There were tents of course, all folded in the trucks. There were tools in the trucks, for digging large holes where the portable toilets were to be installed. Portable stoves and tables were to be set up in an area designated as the mess area. One large tent was set up in case eating outside would not work due to inclement weather. Luckily, the weather cooperated the whole time we were there and the tent was generally used only on cooler nights for sing-along's and talent shows. The rest of the time, we sat around campfires under the wide starry skies.

We started out by setting up our own tent so that we would have a place to sleep that first night. We were also assigned to the potty hole digging detail. That very first night we went to bed beat and slept all night until reveille early the next morning. And yes, somebody brought a bugle.

The one thing I forgot to mention is that the girls didn't share the camp with us in so far as habitation. The bus with Gabrielle and the rest of the girls on it, made a right turn at the edge of our camp and drove about another quarter mile down a narrow gravel road bordered on one side by the edges of some thick reed covered marshes that extended past the big barn where they would be staying, right next to a big farmhouse.

"Ah, Zut," we said in a chorus. "They didn't tell us the girls were staying someplace else.

We would get to see them in the evenings for games and supper; but right after, they would be marched right back to their comfortable accommodations under a solid roof. This would go on like this for the whole month, although I did get to see Gabrielle on fairly regular basis at meals and the other coed activities. Us, the boys however, were not allowed to visit the girls at the barn on our own. No siree Francois (Bob)! That was a no-no interdit, verboten, forbidden and even frowned upon.

So, almost immediately, some of us decided to remedy the situation by planning a secret night raid. To what ends, none of us had a clue. For one thing, we were curious. The only thing we were certain of was that we wanted to see where the girls were staying and maybe scare the heck out of them.

Unfortunately, our plan would not materialize until much later on and would actually not turn out as planned. The raid was to take place following the big talent show that was apparently held on the third Friday of all Camporees; in other words, almost at the end.

25

THE MIDNIGHT RAID

The plan was simple, wait until everyone in camp was fast asleep which would insure, we thought, that by the time we got to the girls' barn, they would in most likelihood be fast asleep as well. Then what? We thought that we'd sneak into the barn, whooping and hollering like a bunch of Indians: ones we'd seen in American movie Westerns. Like I said, the plan had not clearly been thought out. We would all get a big laugh out of the whole thing and then head back to our tents and there would be talk about it but no one would know who'd done it. So, we thought.

"One problem," I said to my buddies, "when the girls see us, they'll know exactly who we are. I mean, do you think for one minute that the girls will think that a bunch of savages crossed the ocean to scare them? If any of them have a problem with any one of us, they'll turn us in for sure. We'll be sent home in disgrace; our parents and the whole town will know about it. We'll be marked forever." I could be melodramatic at times. "They'll never let us go on one of these Camporees, ever again. I'll be staring at the corner of our room at home for the next six months." I was losing my enthusiasm as well as my courage for the whole stupid idea.

"Alright then, here's what we're going to do," said Armand. "We'll smear soot from the campfire and mud from the pond all over our face and our bodies and none of the girls will recognize us."

"That sounds like a clever idea," said Philippe. "Why didn't I think of that?"

"Because you are an espece de cornichon (cucumber, actually meaning a rube)," commented Gérard.

"Bien, then we will disguise ourselves with mud and soot and wrap our shirt around our head like turbans," added Etienne.

"I thought you wanted to look like les Peau Rouge of America (*American Red Skins), not like the Indians from India," I said.

Remember, this all happened some sixty years before the current 'Red Skins' naming controversy, and it was in the French Alps.

"Bien, we will tie together a couple handkerchiefs and tie that around our head," suggested Bruno. "I have seen a lot of nice bird feathers around the trees, some nice long ones like from a hawk or maybe an eagle. There are also some rooster and duck feathers around the barn."

"Bien, this afternoon on our free time, we will go on a scouting mission in the woods and around the barn and collect all the bird feathers we can find," I said. "But we mustn't let anyone see us do it, so let's bring a couple of backpacks and hide them in there until tomorrow night after the talent show."

Alright, American Indians in the French Alps, with real bird feathers stuck in their hair and painted up with mud and soot; that ought to fool just about anybody, right?

So, the afternoon of the day before the talent show, during free-time, we went out in the nearby woods to scrounge all the feathers we could find. We were then set for the raid the following night.

The following day was Friday. After breakfast, we were assigned to firewood detail. In the evening, after supper, there would be a big bonfire which we had to build to provide illumination for the evening's entertainment which would be the talent show. Each tent had to pick a group of three or more, to present a skit or a funny song, something to make everyone laugh. Those of us who would be involved in the raid, sort of sidled to the rear so we wouldn't be picked. We even hunkered down and tried to stay as invisible as possible. But, wouldn't you know, four of us got picked for a skit, especially because we had made such an effort not to participate.

Well, we had to quickly come up with some sort of entertaining act and try to work it out after lunch and make it good enough so the whole camp would laugh at it. No problem, right? So, in addition to our raid, we now had to come up with a stupid skit. We couldn't reschedule our raid for some other night or the following week because that was the week of the hike along the Lake of Geneva with an eventual destination of the city of Geneva, some thirty kilometers away. There were also some prizes involved for all the teams doing the hike and a special one for the team getting to Geneva first. No way were we rescheduling the raid, we wanted that prize. The show must go on.

The way the rules had been devised for the hike to Geneva, you had to walk at least one third of the distance, but you were allowed to hitchhike the rest of the way. We were given four days for the round trip. Our team felt that we had no worries about the competition. By the way, you could also opt out and some of the less, shall we say active kids chose to stay in camp and begin the cleanup of the camp, in preparation for our eminent departure some three days following our return from Geneva.

Just about the time supper was to begin, we had our skit all worked out. It was a very long time ago, but I can still remember that it had to do with three of us playing drunks (we were acting drunk for the sake of art) getting paid to sweep out a tavern while the fourth was to play the boss. The plot of course involved three of us feigning being inebriated and falling all over the place and each other, causing quite a bit of damage in the process of trying to clean the tavern up. We started out a bit slowly but eventually we got into the act. The audience really got into it as well. The more they roared the more we bumbled.

The fact that all the Girl Scouts were present as well encouraged our overacting even more. We all tried to out-perform each other. And of course, Gabrielle was sitting right up front. We were supposed to just bump into each other as we went about singing incoherently while sweeping the imaginary floor, but the act got the better of us and went totally out of control when we all fell down on top of each other to the roar of the crowd. They never did realize that it hadn't been planned that way. Finally, when the kid playing the boss appeared from left stage, to inspect our work and discovered all the destruction, he proceeded to chase us out of the establishment with his broom to the cheers and laughter of the audience.

They were still roaring when we came back for a second curtain call. We ended up with Second Prize. First Prize went to a group singing French show tunes or something. In our minds, we had been Numero un; that's number one in French!

And by the way, even though we were in our early teens, it was acceptable to imitate drunks. It wasn't frowned upon in those days, in France; not even in the Scouts. As a matter of fact, as I might have already stated somewhere else in my tale, our town drunk was a sixteen-year-old dropout, construction worker; though he wasn't a Scout. I would also like to state that to my knowledge, there was no age limit on alcohol consumption; at least not in our small town and in the presence of your parents, unless of course, you were sixteen. I clearly remember going to dinner with my folks to La Fourchette Du Mineur (The miner's fork) over the years and the waiter pouring me a small glass of red wine. Lucky for my parents, wine was wasted on my palette and I would ask for a glass of lemonade (akin to Seven Up) instead each time. Thinking back, had I acquired a taste for the stuff, I might have become the town drunk and they might have refused to let me in to America; the shame of it...

Now, back to the night in question, after much merriment (no alcohol was actually involved), we got to bed much later than originally planned, but before getting to our tents, we all agreed to go through with the raid, except one of the guys, Thierry. He said he was too tired. It was past eleven and way past his bedtime. We all thought he was just a big chicken. This gave us seven for our raiding party. Not always a good number.

We figured that the girls would have to march back to the big barn and get settled in, which would take a half hour, we hoped. Then, we would wait another thirty minutes or so just to make sure and meet by the turn in the road at exactly midnight. So now our ten o'clock raid just became the midnight raid.

As the time finally arrived, I was attempting to quietly slip out of my sleeping bag. My spot just happened to be next to our troop leader, who happened to be a seventeen-year-old named Fabrice who had attended Ecole Mixte and was now home for the summer from the Lycee in Thionville. He was a nice kid and we all liked him, even though he was a few years older than us. As I slowly unzipped my bag, I heard Fabrice whisper. "If you're going on your raid, put on your galoshes, the gravel road to the barn is rough on bare feet." Yikes, he knew.

"How did you know?" I asked, surprised. All along I thought the whole thing was not only a big secret but was very original.

"I did the raid three years ago," he replied. "It's a tradition with the most intrepid of us. The guy that told me about wearing shoes, he found out the hard way."

"Merci," I said.

"Be careful and don't get caught," he advised. "It can be very embarrassing.

"We won't," I said.

"Oh, and be careful in the reed," he added. "Reeds are very sharp."

I didn't know what he had meant. We were going to jog up the road, not in the marshes. When I made it to the road, all the other guys had galoshes on as well. I guess the troupe leader in their tent had also done the raid, before. And I thought we had come up with this great new idea...

Didier came with all the bird feathers. We all wrapped our neckerchiefs around our head and stuck feathers all around it. We got soot from the bonfire and mud from the marshy shore and smeared it all on our faces, chests and arms. Did I mention that we had decided to wear no undershirts (t-shirts), to make our savages look more real? That was my great idea. As we looked at each other, we thought we looked fierce.

"Like a bunch of wild Indians," whispered Bruno; yeah of course, an Italian Indian, right?

We started creeping down the gravel road to the barn. It was a good couple hundred yards, maybe even a quarter mile. At that altitude, the sky was a-sparkle with millions of stars and with a full moon just overhead, we could clearly see the shape of the big barn detaching itself from the darkness of the wooded backdrop and the mass of the farm house sitting further back. All of a sudden twin beam of lights way over to our right caught our attention. Some vehicle was barreling down the main highway, in the direction of the farm. "Quick," I yelled, "everybody in the reeds, it's probably the farmer getting home late.

"I'm not getting wet," whined Sylvain.

"Keep quiet you imbecile," Jean-Pierre whispered overly loudly.

"Well, you either get wet or you get caught," I warned.

"Ah salaud (dirt bag)," he swore, "you and your stupid ideas."

"The minute I mentioned the girls in their nighties, you were all for it," I said. "Now let's get off this road before that car gets here."

We all dropped into the water and realized it was only about a foot deep close to the road. We sloshed our way a few feet into the tall reeds, to hide. When we all felt well hidden, we parted the stalks to watch for the approaching car. It was almost at the entrance to the property when it suddenly veered left and kept on following the highway as it went past our camp and on down the mountain instead of continuing in our direction. As we splashed our way out of the mucky water, I noticed that my hand was smarting in several places with tiny little cuts. The reed indeed was sharp as razor blades. Everybody had cuts!

Back on the gravel, with our galoshes sloshing, we reprised our advance towards the barn. We finally made it to the big doors, now both shut. "Alright, on three, we open the doors and we start whooping like we planned," said Bruno.

Charlot grabbed the handle of the right-side door and Jen-Pierre, the left. We all got ready to breach the entrance. After all the whooping and yelling, we weren't quite sure what we were going to do. We were making it up as we were going along. What the heck would our reward be anyway? Would the girls be so scared that we would have to console them and then they would fling themselves into our arms? What the heck were we thinking? This whole idea was starting to feel pretty stupid but it was too late to turn back. Besides, just as I'm thinking about doing an about-face and taking off, the door slams open and the other six are rushing in, screaming like savages.

The girls start screaming. The boys keep hollering and whooping. As soon as we all get to the center of the barn, a deluge of water rains down on us from above. Instead of being asleep on the hay bales around the perimeter of the barn floor, the girls were all up in the loft, with every utensil that could hold water. We were now wet head to toes, which also meant that our war paint had mostly been washed off. They were laughing their heads off at the washed-up band of savages on the barn floor dripping muddy water. Was it possible that some of them had gone through one of these raids, or did one of our buddies spill the beans?

"We know who you are," they teased.

"Yeah, I can see Bruno Denucci," yelled one of them and cackled with delight.

"Isn't that Gérard Martin under all that mud and soot?" laughed another.

"Were you trying to look like some kind of scary savages?" giggled yet another.

It was absolutely, totally humiliating.

The laughter exploding from the loft had gotten so out of control that we couldn't help joining in. When suddenly a door in the back of the barn flew open and the female scout leaders in charge of the Girl Scout contingents stepped out with lantern in one hand and brandishing long sticks in the other.

"What in holy Hades is going on out here?" yelled out the one in the lead in a rather very deep raspy voice. The other women joined in a cacophony of screeching and actually some swearing, demanding a reason for the racket. They were wearing robes and a couple had their hair in curlers. A cloud of smoke followed them from inside the room.

We later on found out that after they had ordered lights-out for the girls, they retreated to their bunk rooms, lit up cigarettes and brought out a deck of cards and maybe even some Cognac. They went on about playing Rummy when they thought the girls were asleep. The girls told us that the matrons could be heard bickering and joking as they sometimes played into the night.

As I had been the one last in line to reach the inside, I was standing closest to the doors for a quick getaway. I also hadn't gotten as much of a shower as the rest so most of my war paint was still intact; but it wouldn't be for long. I slowly started backtracking and inching my way out of the barn, getting ready to retreat when I yelled "Let's get the heck out of here!"

We all turned tail and bolted from the premises; everyone taking off in a different direction. A couple ran down the gravel road. Another two headed for the trees on the other side of the barn. I had no idea where that road led and figured that they might eventually have to come back by the barn door if the trail didn't double back towards the camp. Bruno and I, we ran for the marshes. We jumped into the brackish water heading for the thickest clumps of reed and then started to make our way toward the middle and hoping to stay out of sight. We were working our way in the general direction of the camp road. When we had almost reached the road at the edge of the camp, we stopped and squatted down quietly in the cold water to wait and see if the rest of the guys had made it back to this spot.

Jean-Pierre with his long legs came into sight first, so we crawled out of the water and joined him. "Where are the others?" we asked.

"They got scared and hid in the trees instead of running," he replied.

"Why?" Bruno and I asked.

"They thought the old lady with the stick was coming after us," he replied.

"We don't see anybody coming down the road," I said. "The old lady probably already went back to the card game after she scared the crap out of us."

"Oui," Bruno added. "Let's get into our tents before we all get caught."

So we did, just as one of the senior leaders came out of his tent to check on the commotion, we thought. We quietly slipped into our tents; but the old guy was just going to the W.C. (toilet).

"I see you made it back in one piece," said Fabrice as soon as I got to my sleeping bag.

"I thought you'd be asleep," I said.

"With that damned racket you knuckleheads made, I'm surprised half the camp didn't hear you," he snickered good-naturedly as he zipped his bag up. "Get some sleep. Tomorrow we'll see if anybody's in trouble."

"Bonne nuit (good night)," I replied as I buried my head in the sleeping bag.

The next morning at breakfast, there was a general announcement about breaching the sanctity of the girls' sleeping quarters. Some veiled threats were made just in case some scouts decided to break the rules, again. We knew none of us had squealed. The seven of us did however believe that Thierry had spilled the beans to possibly his sister who was in the girls' camp and she had blabbed to the other girls as she was known to be a blabbermouth just like her brother. Whether it was accidental on Thierry's part or on purpose, we were never to find out. We knew Thierry couldn't keep a secret. Hello!?

Oh, and by the way, the girls weren't wearing nighties. They wore pajamas!

26

THEY SHOOT HORSES, DON'T THEY?

The Tuesday, after the Midnight Raid, we were set for the trek to Geneva along the shores of the Lake by the same name.

This was to be a sixty something kilometer round-trip hike, to be accomplished in roughly five days. We were all to meet in Geneva the following evening, spend a day in Geneva and then start hiking back to camp the day after.

Everything went according to plans, almost. This took place in the 'good' old days when people could hike along the highways and weren't worried about deranged mass-murderers who might pick you up and then no-one would ever see you again.

So, five of us took off bright and early. A few other groups had taken off before us. These were older kids who could walk a lot faster than the five of us. We later found out that some groups took off after us. But we never ran into any of them.

Thierry wanted to come along and whined when we told him he couldn't. Somehow, we had lost our trust in him. Besides, he was one of those kids who wanted to take part in everything then found a way to sabotage things by slowing down or wanting to change the rules that had been agreed upon. Anyway, we nixed him.

Then, Sylvain came down with some mysterious ailment. He was the one who was afraid to get his feet wet on the night of the midnight raid. We all thought that he was just lazy, and was happy to lie around the camp while we gallivanted around the lake. That would have actually taken some effort and energy and might have been good for him; maybe taken a couple kilograms off his touché.

With the five of us, we figured we would do a lot better and make decent time and wouldn't have to nurse along the two whiners.

We carried a very light backpack with just the bare necessities like underwear and first aid kit, a few chocolate bars and packs of crackers to sustain our energy. We rolled up our outer jacket and a light blanket and stuffed them into our backpacks. As the last and maybe the most important item on our checklist, we clipped our canteens to our belts. With our official uniforms on and wearing our everyday boots, we started down the road from the camp to the highway around the lake. That stretch of road is now called A-1 and is a divided 4 lane Highway, parts of which are toll controlled. Back in the 1950s, it was a simple two-lane highway and I can't remember what its number and designation were.

We were all thirteen except Jean-Pierre who was fourteen. He had been assigned as our leader, for this hike. The other members of our adventurous troop were, Bruno, Gérard, Charlot and yours truly. We made good time following the road downhill from the camp for a couple miles until we met up with the highway to Geneva along the shores of the lake. From there on, it was all level and we practically jogged for the first few kilometers until we realized that we had to slow it down a bit or we would crash way before our intended mid-point rest stop.

Our legs held out reasonably well, once we got in a healthy rhythm and by evening, we were just a little past midpoint.

In addition to a change of underclothing in our backpacks, we had also rolled up a blanket instead of the bulky sleeping bags which we left at camp. All we had to do was to find a cozy little spot close to the highway for the night's sleep. We went off on a side road, in search of a good resting place when we came up on rather nice-looking farmhouse. We walked right up to the gate and asked the caretaker who happened to be raking the big yard, if we might be allowed to sleep in the barn. He was a rather nice old man, but also gave us very strict instructions.

"Bien sure," he said, "as long as you make sure that the big gate by the barn is latched, before you go to sleep."

"Mais oui," we said in unison.

"Le patron, he has some very expensive horses grazing way out there by the tree line. He doesn't want any of them to get out. You understand?"

"Absolument, we understand," was our reply.

He explained that during the summer months, they allowed the horses more freedom by leaving them out in the pasture. We promised, Scout's Honor that we'd make sure the gate was secured should we have to go get water or use the facilities.

We spread our blankets on top of the hay bales in the stables. They were comfortable enough and we were glad we hadn't dragged our big, heavy sleeping bags along (Back in those days, sleeping bags were bulky and heavy.).

We ate one of our chocolate bars with some crackers and drank from our canteens which we knew we could fill from the faucet outside the barn. We were all settled in and lying around on our blankets on top of hay bales and were having fun talking about what we were going to do when we got home. We exchanged addresses and promised to send each other postcards. Back then, very few people could afford telephones, so, there was no exchanging telephone numbers. We were telling jokes and having great fun bonding. One of us got up to shut off the only overhead light and we all slowly went to sleep.

The sun was just starting to peek over the tall Alpine ridges when we were awakened by some movement and intelligible shouting outside. We could hear people running around and the gate getting slammed and clearly lots of yelling.

"What the heck is going on?" asked Jean-Pierre of no one in particular.

"Where the heck are we?" asked somebody else. It could have been me.

"It's only half past five," yawned Charlot. "I wanted to sleep a little longer. We got a long hike ahead of us, today."

"We had better find out what is going on out there," said Jean-Pierre. "Let's pack our gear and see what is happening."

We all did as Jean-Pierre suggested. With our backpacks on, we slowly emerged from the big stable. People were in fact running, towards the highway, a couple hundred meters down the road. We ran into the old man that had allowed us to sleep in the stable. He looked a bit out of sorts.

"What has happened?" we all asked.

"Someone had left the main gate open last night, and one of the thoroughbred horses escaped," he said.

We looked at each other. "What the heck is a thoroughbred?" we asked.

"It is a very expensive horse," the man explained impatiently, "a racing horse".

"We didn't let him out," we all protested. "We closed the gate and kept the barn door closed and nobody even went out after dark." There was a toilet inside and there would have been no reason for anyone to go outside. While we were having the dialog with the caretaker, one of the farm workers returned with some bad news.

"The horse was hit by a car and is lying in the ditch by the side of the road," he reported.

"How bad is he hurt?" the old man asked.

"We don't know," said the worker, "but he is unable to get up and there is some blood on his front quarter. He might have a broken leg."

"Merde!" yelled the old man. "You boys better get going," he told us. "When the patron gets a wind of what has happened, he will not be very happy and might blame you."

"But Monsieur, we really didn't do anything wrong," protested Jean-Pierre.

"I am sure you didn't," replied the old man. "But, he will want to blame somebody for the accident to his race horse."

That was the end of our dialog. The old caretaker took off after the worker at a quick pace. Nobody even had a chance to pee. We took off at a trot, hoping to get to the highway before the owner had been informed and would come out himself to find out what had happened to his horse. We had it in our heads that this guy might come after us and put us in jail or something. The figure the old man had painted about the value of the horse had more zeros in a row than all of our fathers' paychecks together.

As we jogged closer to the corner where the side road met the highway, we actually considered turning left and beating a hasty retreat back to the safety of our camp. We figured that since we told the old man at the ranch that we were hiking our way to Geneva, they would never figure we had gone in the opposite direction. Wasn't that brilliant?

Unfortunately, as we got to the corner however, we were forced to rethink our plan, for you see, a couple hundred meters down the other side of the highway, a crowd had gathered. There were obviously some of the farm workers as well as civilians milling around excitedly over the writhing brown shape of the horse desperately trying to get up and out of the ditch. Several vehicles had pulled over to the side of the road; perhaps the culprit as well as some witnesses. Since our escape route was cut off, we turned right and kept on jogging for over half of a kilometer until a bend in the roadway finally blocked us from sight.

We kept marching at a quick-step until our legs ached.

I must admit that after this incident, the rest of the hike turned out to be rather uneventful. However, until we would finally got back to camp three days down the road, we were still under the illusion or perhaps delusion that somehow, somewhere, the horse's owner would pop up and believing that we had in fact been responsible for the injury to his horse, he would in some fashion want to prosecute and punish us.

"That poor horse," said Jean-Pierre. "I wonder if they fix his leg."

"Don't they shoot horses with broken legs?" I replied. "You guys have seen those cowboy movies where a horse breakes a leg and John Wayne has to shoot it."

"That's in American cowboy movies," said Charlot. "That stuff happened a hundred years ago."

"Maybe they no longer shoot them," said Jean-Pierre. "But how can you race a horse that broke his leg, even if it heals?"

No-one had an answer for that. We really didn't know that much about horse medicine.

We made it to Geneva by late afternoon. Our legs had carried us onward as though we were possessed and the Devil was hot on our tails.

At the onset of this hike, we had been instructed to locate a YMCA youth Hostel and spend the night there. We were all given sufficient funds for the small fee such places charged; about the equivalent to a quarter. Finding the hostel had been fairly easy. We just wandered around until someone pointed us in the right direction. After all, the Swiss do speak the same language we spoke, French; in addition to German and Italian, depending on which side of Switzerland they happen to live.

We at least got to spend the night indoors with a bunch of other kids, some of them older than us; and many of them backpacking around the lake like us while some took the same route on bicycles. The following morning, we asked for directions to 'Le Musé d'Histoire Naturelle de Suisse' or the Museum of Natural History which was supposed to be famous. That's what we had been told anyway.

Along the way, we discovered Yogurt. Back then, it wasn't as popular as it is today, unless you were Swiss. As matter of fact, none of us, coming from the north-east of France had ever heard of the stuff; well maybe we'd heard of it but never tasted it. I personally felt sort of neutral about yogurt; sort of like the Swiss. It was almost like eating sour cream that had gone sourer; as if that were possible. A couple of the kids wanted their Centimes back saying the stuff was spoiled. "It is supposed to taste that way," the old woman behind the counter told them. They grimaced their way through the little cartons and took a big swig of water to chase away the taste; yummy!

We finally got to the museum by midday. Being as we were Boy Scouts, we got in free. It was about the most interesting museum any of us had ever been in. As a matter of fact, it was a first. I wish I could recall everything I saw in there, unfortunately, the only thing I can still remember was in this one section on animal reproduction. There were all these jars which contained the embryos of a whole slew of animals, in various stages of development and lots of animal skeletons. All those jars, we thought were really gross while at the same time, we were so fascinated that it may actually have been the only section we visited before we decided that it was time to get going.

Unbeknownst to us, the Girl Scouts had not been permitted to do the hike; however, they took them all to Geneva in a bus. Well actually, they had probably announced it, but whoever listened to official camp announcements and remembered any of them anyway? That's usually what got us into trouble...

The way we found out about the bus or rather reminded of and all was rather interesting.

We were making our way out of Geneva and decided that we should try to bypass the part of the highway that ran near the horse ranch by taking another route back to camp. The specter of the angry owner had really given us the heebie-jeebies. We had also heard that although the Swiss were neutral, as far as participating in wars, they were allowed to own guns, for hunting and defense. So, the specter of the patron wielding a big gun, gave us the heebie-jeebies squared.

So, we had decided on a particular little detour that we were certain would accomplish our intended goal. We were going to take this little side road that would bypass the area of the ranch way on the other side of the hill that was behind it. Of course, none of us geniuses figured on the fact that it would add a few extra kilometers to the return hike. Needless to say, when we finally met up with the lake highway, we were pooped but happy that our plan had worked. We thought!

We plopped down on the side of the road to rest under some trees. As we were lounging there trying to think of the next step in our plan, we heard some honking. What the heck, we thought. Hitchhiking was going to be our next step but we hadn't gotten up to stick our thumbs out just yet, so why in heck would anybody be honking at us?

"Yoo-hoo, you boys want a ride back to camp," a chorus of girls' giggly high-pitched voices hailed us. We all turned to see this bus pull over to the side of the road and squeak to a stop as its door clanged open. It was our Girl Scout troupe; the one we had forgotten was being taken to visit Geneva in a bus. Whoopee!

Let's just say that none of us minded the fact that we wouldn't have to find a place to sleep that night and to have another fifteen to twenty kilometers to cover the next day, to get back to camp. And what can I say? Gabrielle was on the bus; although the chaperones didn't allow us to even sit next to the girls. Proper distance had to be kept. As a matter of fact, if it had been up to the chaperones, they wouldn't have picked us up in the first place. It had been at the girls' insistence that the driver had pulled over. I think that after our midnight raid, our stock had gone up a bit; we were considered bad boys, in a good sort of way.

The chaperones made us sit in the back of the bus for our ride back to camp. At this point we didn't care. We would be back to camp in no time and sleep in our own tents. We leaned back in our seats and stared out the window, following the jagged peaks of the Alps and watching little boats peacefully cruising back and forth on the glistening clear waters of the lake, when suddenly we came upon a familiar sight. Coming around a curve in the roadway, way off on the left side of the highway, we could clearly see the horse ranch where we had spent our first night, a few hundred meters ahead. We had apparently taken the wrong bypass. Had we read the map wrong?

As we got closer to the turnoff, all five of us slowly slid down in our seats so only the top of our heads, were visible. We stayed low until we were certain that the ranch was but a dot in the bus's rearview mirror.

Thankfully, the girls had thought we had simply gone to sleep.

Early Sunday morning, we packed up the camp and after loading the gear on trucks and us back on to the busses, they took us down to the train station for our ride back to our little corner of Moselle.

• • •

The Sunday following our return from the Camporee, after the service, Gabrielle with a long, sad face announced that they were moving away again.

"Zut," I said, "pourquoi?" Meaning, "Shucks, why?"

"Papa is being transferred to America," Gabrielle replied.

"C'est domage," I said. Meaning, that's too bad and I meant it.

So fate again, had stepped in and stirred things up. This meant that I would no longer have to worry about two girls fighting over me; well they actually never really fought over me.

Little did I know at the time that fate was on the verge of dealing me a really crappy hand? But for the time being, I would have a whole heck of a lot to talk to Lydia about, and talk we did right on the first day we got back to school. We were of course friends again. As a matter of fact, even Gabrielle joined our little group for the last couple months she was there as she was no longer a threat to our relationship.

Gabrielle's Family moved away late in 1955. Before she left I had found out from my folks that we would in fact be leaving for the United States ourselves in a just a few months, this time for certain; unless of course, something unforeseen came up again…

As Gabrielle was leaving Ecole Protestante (the name had changed the previous year) for the last time I told her about us going to America as well.

"We will perhaps run into each other there," I said.

"It would be nice," she replied.

"See you in America," was my final goodbye to Gabrielle.

Little did either of us comprehend the difference between running into someone in a small town of eight thousand, like Algrange as opposed to that same happenstance materializing in of all places the United States, with a population of around 180,000,000 people (best guess) at the time. As a matter of fact, that would be the very last time that I would ever see pretty Gabrielle with the curly hair, dazzling smile and big hazel eyes; or speak to her.

Unfortunately, upon revealing our eminent departure to a place six thousand miles away, the cat was out of the proverbial bag. Lydia now knew. Georges Krischke my buddy also knew and by the afternoon, the whole school knew. In another four months or so, I would be leaving behind this whole little world of mine that I had become so familiar with and was very comfortable in. I was leaving my friends, my best buddy and Lydia, basically everyone and everything I had known for most of my life, to this point. But there were still four months left; I would try to get the most out of them that I could.

Then again, the whole trip could fall through again.

It had happened a couple times before.

By the way, as fate would have it, I never did run into Gabrielle ever again.

When we finally left, I felt like my world had ended. Perhaps, a new world would be waiting for me, beyond the Atlantic.

27

THE PERFECT STORM

We had been told that our transatlantic voyage to New York would take five to five and a half days, depending on weather. It took seven and a half and it was definitely due to the weather.

Up to this point in my life, I had never been on an ocean. I had never seen an ocean. The largest body of water I had seen was the Seine River in Paris and Lake Geneva in Switzerland. I had never been aboard a boat of any kind, not even a rowboat. Imagine my amazement climbing up the steps to the deck of the S.S. America, purported to be at the time, one of the largest ocean liners to sail the Atlantic.

The S.S. America was built differently than today's cruise ships that look more like apartment complexes on pontoons. It was 723 feet long. It had eleven decks and carried 1046 passengers and a crew of about 690. It had two gigantic stacks and featured a swimming pool on the top deck called the Sport Deck. Unfortunately for me and the other refugee kids, access was reserved for first class passengers. Did I mention that the pool was heated and we could see the swells amid the steam, enjoying a warm dip on sunny, frosty afternoons?

Just so you get a sense of the makeup of the passengers, the ship had started out in Bremerhaven, Germany. It then picked up passengers in South Hampton, England before crossing the English Channel and docking at Le Havre in France. From there, it made a last stop in Cobh, Ireland before heading out for the open sea. So, you can imagine what a cacophony of languages one would have been exposed to on any given day, on the deck or in the dining hall. Nobody really cared what language you spoke in the movie theater; all the movies were made in the U.S. to my chagrin. I didn't understand any of them but the seats were comfortable for an afternoon of napping.

The one thing that everybody enjoyed equally was the meals. There were a couple of huge dining halls where I discovered that any passenger, at any time of the day, was welcomed to eat from the buffet. This was indeed enticing. To this point in my short existence, I had never seen this much food for the taking, in one place. I gorged myself. Did I mention that there were as many desserts as there were regular dishes, if you could call them that? In fact, there was nothing regular about any of it. What I also discovered very soon after departure was that about fifteen minutes after filling my belly, I had to run up the stairs to the main deck and purge the whole load into the waves.

I was going to say barf but I thought purge would be more appropriate...

There was this one time; we should have been a day or so away from arrival when we hit a severe storm that started the big ship bucking like a wild carnival ride. Come to think of it, it just happened that it was the night of the 'Captain's Dinner'. My parents had me dressed up in my best short pants with a nice shirt and I was sporting one of my dad's best ties. I can still remember looking in the mirror and complaining "this tie is chocking me. Do I need to wear it? How am I going to eat, with it hanging in front of my face?"

"Don't worry son. You'll do just fine and it makes you look civilized," said my father

"Yes, you look very nice," added my mother.

The captain greeted everybody and made a toast with some words in various languages. I understood the French part. I was anxiously awaiting the food that would be served on this occasion because usually my preference had been buffet style.

We had a nice Consommé Royale (fancy named French bouillon soup) and lettuce and tomato salad to start with, and the best sliced French bread this side of France.

And, the reason I remember so well what was on the menu is

because, I still have the actual menu from that Captain's Dinner, dated Sunday, February 25, 1956. The amazing part of this menu is that it contained French dishes I had never eaten in seven and half years in France. And for some reason, people seem to believe that if it has a French name, it must naturally taste better. So, in fact, these could have been American dishes with French names. I wouldn't have known one way or another as I had never eaten any American dishes either; because my mother cooked Hungarian.

The menu included but was not limited to these fancy dishes: pâté-de-foie-gras Sur Croute, Red Snapper Meuniere and Poached Filet de Sole with Sauce Mousseline and of course French dressing for the salad. There were a number of other savory dishes and there were desserts; these were printed in English with German translations; Royal Anne Cherries (Kirschen Kompott), Mocha Layer Cake (Schokolade Kuchen), French Ice Cream with Chocolate Sauce (Französische Rahmeis) and more. See what I mean? Where I came from, you either got the ice cream or the sauce; not the two together. It was all rather shishi. It made me wonder what the first-class passengers had on their menu.

My eyes couldn't believe what came on the plates. Not only that, I could ask for more or for different dishes. I was halfway through my meal, when my parents noticed that I had started turning various shades of green. Both my hands went to cover my mouth, my cheeks bulging. Some of the other people sitting at our table, looking at me also started covering their mouths. At first, I was somewhat embarrassed with everybody looking my way, like they hadn't seen a kid get seasick before.

Suddenly I took off like a crazed rabbit, rocketed up the stairs to my favorite regurgitation station right along the railing on the main deck somewhat out of sight of strolling passengers; of course, right at that time, there wasn't a single soul visible anywhere as the storm was hitting us full force. Even with the storm, the icy cold wind made me feel better although it almost did blow me overboard.

As I said, the ship was bucking and rolling with a vengeance and all around, as far as the eye could see, the ocean was roiling and churning with such a fury, that it was sending enormous whitecaps splashing right up onto the deck. I had just unloaded the wonderful meal I had gorged myself on and was wiping my mouth with my dad's soaked tie, and was desperately trying to steady myself when this monster of a wave hit the side of the ship. I was soaked and thought for sure I was going overboard, when out of nowhere this hand grabbed me and dragged me back inside the vestibule of the big Main Deck lounge.

The man in a white uniform was angrily yelling at me, not one word of which I understood; but I could tell he was really pissed off by the spray of spittle hitting my face; then again, it could have been the storm. I sort of gathered that I wasn't even supposed to have been out there on the deck in a storm. Who the heck knew? When you're about to unload a very large undigested meal, the last thing on your mind is attempting to decipher the warning sign in red letters, stuck on the wall by the door, written in five different languages. By the time I would have gotten to French, I would have unloaded right in front of or right on the glass doors; then I would have gotten yelled at for that.

All soaked, I politely tried my best to explain to him in French why I was out there.

"Stupido!" he yelled, and with that, I deduced he wasn't French, but knew what he meant.

"Hey," I said, "I was sick. I had to throw up."

"Next time," he said in the worst French I had ever heard, "use the W.C. (water closet or toilet).

He then proceeded to lock the glass doors; which by the way had not been locked when I had initially flown through them. Might have been his mistake, maybe?

"Merci," I said and as I walked back to the dining hall, for what, I don't know. Going down the stairs, I could still hear him carrying on in a language that I would eventually discover was Spanish, but at the time, I couldn't understand. Since then of course, I have learned quite a few Spanish words. Imagine that.

On the way-back to the dining hall, the smell of the food wafting into the hallway so repulsed my senses that I had to take off at a run to the nearest W.C. That night, I promised myself that I had learned my lesson; until the next meal, that is.

You notice how I started out by talking about the food aboard the S.S. America rather than the other accommodations. It goes to show, I always liked to eat. Unfortunately, there hadn't always been enough food that looked that good; even though my mother was a wonderful cook, we couldn't afford to get all the ingredients to cook like they did onboard that ship.

As I said, we were emigrants. This put us in a category below tourists, which meant: no private cabins. We actually had to share our cabin on the second to the lowest level. The rumbling of the ship's engines was what rocked me to sleep every night in my little bunk which was more like a hammock. Our cabin mates were a very nice old Rabbi going to New York and a younger guy we didn't see very much. We later found out that he had somehow finagled his way up to the next level and a lady was involved. "He found a new bunkmate" I heard somebody say, in French.

My mother had to share her cabin with the Rabbi's wife, a nice old lady and a couple of other women, none of whom could understand each other which made for some interesting staring time. Lucky for my dad and me, we both spoke German and were able to communicate with the old Rabbi. The other guy, he never seemed to be around and when he was, he was not very sociable. Then again, maybe he didn't understand any of us or he didn't want us to figure out what he was up to. For some strange reason, Bert had been assigned to yet another different cabin down the hall, but we all got together for meals.

I wasn't crazy about all the pitching, yawing, and rolling of the ship and really only felt reasonably steady when I was out on the deck, hanging around with the other kids. I never did get my 'sealegs' whatever the heck that was supposed to mean. Although we were from many different countries and cultures I understood some as they had come from Germany which is how I found out that their family was going to *Milvoki* (Milwaukee). Grownups would yell at us to slow down and behave ourselves and even occasionally curse us out. But even the best of us had to work off all the pent-up energy of being confined on this huge floating hotel.

We ran around and round the deck but beyond the railing, there was nothing but water as far as the eyes could see. It could have made anybody a bit stir-crazy, especially kids. I wanted some dirt and grass, something solid under my feet; terra firma.

As we'd been originally told, this crossing was supposed to take only five days and a half. Unfortunately, when the ship hit that big Atlantic storm that caught me at the railing feeding the fish, it delayed our arrival by two whole days; not me at the railing mind you but the storm. It also put an end to my socializing and running around on the deck with the other kids. With all that motion, I spent a lot of time in my bunk, staring at the ceiling, praying for a quick end to our voyage. I tried watching movies in the theater but in addition to all that rocking and rolling, there were technical difficulties, probably caused by all the rocking and rolling, when the projector would get jammed or shut off altogether. Back then, they used film projectors to show movies, not videos like today. The journey needed to wind down…

By the time the weather calmed down, we could almost see New York on the horizon. We were however two days late. Our late arrival had also caused a few glitches in our debarkation procedure.

One of those glitches was, instead of debarking on Ellis (now Liberty) Island, under the outstretched arm of Lady Liberty holding the torch, our ship docked at the Port of New York where we were officially welcomed by the members of Immigration and Customs. We were all very happy to be able to get off that enormous floating carnival ride and step down on to solid ground although very disappointed of not having been welcomed by Lady Liberty and the words associated with her and written by Emma Lazarus: "Give me your tired, your poor, your huddled masses yearning to breathe free, the wretched refuse of your teeming shore. Send these, the homeless, tempest-tossed to me; I lift my lamp beside the golden door!"

After some seven and a half days and being tempest-tossed for at least two, we had finally arrived in America.

Bonjour New York!

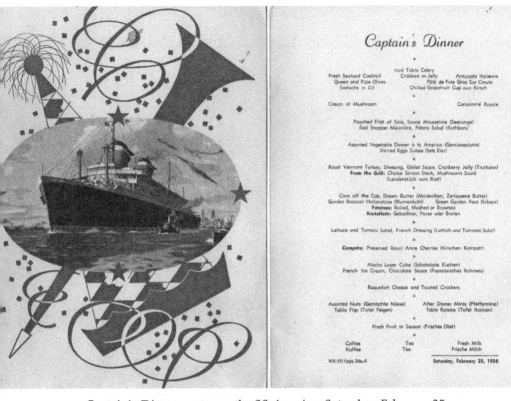

Captain's Dinner

Iced Table Celery

Fresh Seafood Cocktail   Crabben in Jelly   Antipasto Italienne
Queen and Ripe Olives   Pâté de Foie Gras Sur Croute
Seelachs in Oil   Chilled Grapefruit Cup aux Kirsch

Cream of Mushroom   Consommé Royale

Poached Filet of Sole, Sauce Mousseline (Seezunge)
Red Snapper Meunière, Potato Salad (Rothbars)

Assorted Vegetable Dinner à la America (Gemüsseplatte)
Shirred Eggs Suisse (Sets Eier)

Roast Vermont Turkey, Dressing, Giblet Sauce, Cranberry Jelly (Truthahn)
From the Grill: Choice Sirloin Steak, Mushrooms Sauté
(Lendenstück vom Rost)

Corn off the Cob, Drawn Butter (Maiskolben, Zerlassene Butter)
Garden Broccoli Hollandaise (Blumenkohl)   Green Garden Peas (Erbsen)
Potatoes: Boiled, Mashed or Browned
Kartoffeln: Gekochter, Püree oder Braten

Lettuce and Tomato Salad, French Dressing (Lattich und Tomaten Salat)

Compote: Preserved Royal Anne Cherries (Kirschen Kompott)

Mocha Layer Cake (Schokolade Kuchen)
French Ice Cream, Chocolate Sauce (Französisches Rahmeis)

Roquefort Cheese and Toasted Crackers

Assorted Nuts (Gemischte Nüsse)   After Dinner Mints (Pfefferminz)
Table Figs (Tafel Feigen)   Table Raisins (Tafel Rosinen)

Fresh Fruit in Season (Frisches Obst)

Coffee   Tea   Fresh Milk
Kaffee   Tee   Frische Milch

WB-TC Capt. Din.-T   Saturday, February 25, 1956

Captain's Dinner menu on the SS America, Saturday, February 25, 1956 - (Author's archives)

The SS America on the high seas in 1956 - (Author's archives)

28

BOY ON A TRAIN

The captain and his staff made the big announcement and welcomed us to New York over the ship's public-address system, in five languages as we sailed past Lady Liberty's torch and Ellis Island, even before we disembarked.

Unfortunately, since there was no welcoming ceremony or pictures taken, the only mementos from our arrival are the few items my parents managed to save from the ship, such as the Captain's Dinner menu, a little US flag with forty-eight stars, the passenger manifest with all of our names in it and a couple of postcards of the SS America.

We were given an abbreviated version of the official welcome.

There was no walk around Ellis Island or riding the elevator up to Lady Liberty's crown, nor did we get to read the now world-famous quote at the foot of the Statue of Liberty.

The minute we docked, all processes were sped up. We would have been able to spend a day and a half in New York City and given a tour before boarding the train that would take us to California, had we arrived on time. As it was, it was announced even before we arrived at the docks to have our luggage in hand and be ready to disembark. Without much fanfare, we were all lined up along the hallways leading to the exits as they dropped the anchor and began disembarking as soon as the gangplanks were dropped.

The very first thing that happened while going through customs, the six big oranges my dad had carefully wrapped and saved for later treats, were removed from his luggage. It was explained to him that no foreign agricultural products were permitted into the country. Everything else we had was OK, including some packets of salted crackers, since they were actually made in the United

States. Our passports and papers were speedily but carefully checked and pictures in them were matched to our faces and then stamped and re-stamped.

A man and a woman from Church World Service waving a placard with our name on it were anxiously awaiting our arrival and had as matter fact been down on Ellis Island the two days prior just to be told that we had not yet arrived. Instead of a city tour, they now had about four or five hours left to instruct us on what to do next and then to get us to Grand Central Station and aboard our train for our ride to the West Coast; more specifically Oakland, a city we had never heard of before.

We had finally arrived in the United States of America, land of the free and home of the brave; a land of opportunities unlimited. For us, even the air smelled different, maybe even a little better, here in the bastion of democracy where anybody could make it and capitalism actually worked for anybody who was willing to roll up their sleeve and work hard.

• • •

We actually, in a roundabout way, did get a sort of a tour of New York City. We were driven from New York Harbor to Grand Central Station to catch the train that would take us to the west coast.

It has been many years but I still remember the tall buildings lining the streets all the way to Manhattan and the closer we got to the heart of New York City, the taller the buildings got. As I watched them slowly rolling by, they became the walls of a concrete canyon which appeared to reach up and scrape the steel grey sky above, making it appear to actually be connected with it; giving it a feeling of being in a totally enclosed space. It was almost like travelling through an enormous cavern.

The distance between New York Harbor and Grand Central Station is about twelve and a half miles and under normal conditions today, would probably take somewhere between twenty and twenty-five minutes, depending on how fast you were going. Back in 1956, it took us almost an hour. There were no expressways built yet, so traffic moved at a much slower pace through the surface streets or else our hosts had decided to get us to Grand Central in a roundabout way to give us a glimpse of what New York City was like.

If you have never seen Grand Central Station, let me tell you, it was colossal and breathtaking. A whole book could be written about its history, architecture and functionality and probably has.

The CWS people handed us our train tickets and with them in hand, we approached a conductor who instructed us to climb aboard and lucky for us, since he spoke French, he was able to tell us exactly where we would be sitting. He explained that later on, someone would come by and tell us how to set up the sleepers for the night. Thus, began our journey out of New York City, heading for Chicago and eventually to Oakland and San Francisco. It took a good couple of hours before we were finally rolling along through the suburbs.

As it was late February, there was still snow on the ground; though you wouldn't have known, because it wasn't clean and white, the way I had remembered snow. It was soot and grime covered along the tracks and only looking into the distance could I spy any of it that was a bit cleaner and whiter.

Now, how many stops we made and through how many cities we rode, I am not certain. I do recall the train stopping periodically and passengers getting off while new ones would come aboard.

We did roll through Cleveland, Toledo, Chicago, Davenport, Des Moines, Omaha, Cheyenne, Salt Lake City, Reno, Sacramento, Oakland and finally San Francisco. Someone might actually have written a song about it.

Between Cleveland and Toledo, we glimpsed Lake Erie in the distance and rolling into Chicago, Lake Michigan extended out to the horizon. Somewhere around Davenport we crossed the mighty Mississippi. At Omaha, we rolled over the Missouri. The most surreal span of water I ever saw was the Great Salt Lake coming out of Salt Lake City, Utah and eventually morphing into the brilliantly white salt flats which went on until the outskirts to Wendover,

Nevada. Speaking of getting a lesson in the geography of the United States, this would have been it. Every kid should be required to ride the train from New York to San Francisco; or vice versa.

You just have to remember throughout my tale that I had lived a rather sheltered life in Algrange. It isn't even that at fourteen, I was immature, well maybe I was, sort of. I did have occasion to travel of course, mostly from one neighboring town to another and the farthest I had ever gotten was Switzerland to the Camporee of 1955. Now here I was, just having crossed an ocean which I had never even seen before, and was on my way to the other side of the biggest land mass I had ever read about. I was totally overwhelmed by the events of those couple weeks and found myself amazed by what I was experiencing; the sheer size of everything, like buildings, bridges, rivers and mile after mile of flat plains. Every sight, sound and taste was a new experience.

While crossing at least twelve of the forty-eight states, not only did I get a lesson in geography but a good dose of cultural anthropology and even physics; this of course I didn't realize at the time. What do you want? I was only fourteen and this whole trip had been pretty much force-fed to me. Fortunately, due to my power of observation and memory, to this day, I fondly recall the encounters I had on that three and a half days' ride with some of the very first Americans I had interacted with. Well actually, my interaction had been limited to trying to explain in French that I didn't understand English and what my situation was. I was lucky to discover that a number of other passengers spoke my language du jour, French...

Starting out in New York, many of our fellow passengers were from the Military. I of course could recognize sailors and soldiers because of the American movies we had been exposed to, even in Algrange. The men with the long whiskers and long, curly sideburns, wearing large brimmed black hats and long coats, I had to ask my father about. He explained that they were Hasidic Jews. Imagine my confusion when these people got off the train and some got on who looked the same, well almost the same. They had big, black hats and coats, but no long, curly sideburns. We had to ask, and luckily, somebody happened to have understood what we were asking when they told us that these people were Amish. They were very stoic looking individuals and at one point I thought that I had understood bits of their conversation which strangely enough, sounded like German. Of course, when I got the eye from one of them, I stopped listening and went back to staring at the ceiling or out the window and counting telephone poles.

As I said, a number of military personnel in varied uniforms got on and off the train, pretty much throughout the whole journey. One such group of guys saw me getting bored and walking up and down the aisle and asked me something, to which I of course replied "Je ne comprend pas," meaning that I didn't understand. A couple of them did just happen to understand French. So, from that point forward, I had already made friends. They gave me candy bars and chewing gum while they engaged me in a Q&A about where we came from and all. This of course was great relief to my parents because I stopped asking "are we there yet?"

All these young men although obviously older than me, couldn't have been more than in their early twenties.

Eventually, this bunch got off the train and they wished us luck, in French, as they were leaving.

One of the more interesting passengers to board our car was a cowboy, a real honest to goodness, American cowboy. I mean, I had seen guys like that in the 'Jean' (John) Wayne movies, but definitely not ever in real life. He not only had on the outfit, the boots and the wide brimmed hat but instead of luggage, he had actually brought aboard a beautiful leather saddle. I didn't see a horse anywhere. He rode along for a couple hundred miles and got off somewhere at a really small station in the middle of nowhere; a really flat and treeless landscape, where only a couple of old rundown buildings could be seen; however, there were horses grazing as far as the eye could see. Maybe, he was getting a horse he was going to ride back to where he had gotten on the train?

Later on, some Indians, yes, I know, we now call them Native Americans, came aboard. I of course knew this because fellow passengers whispered it. I don't mean they wore fringed outfits and feather headdresses, and carried tomahawks in their belts. They looked a bit different than most of the other passengers because of their totally black hair which ended in twin braided tails, and perhaps a complexion a couple shades darker than the other passengers. They wore colorful shirts and vests. Their overcoats weren't much different from what everybody else wore. They wore big ornate belt buckles inlaid with what I later discovered was turquoise, to hold up their trousers and necklaces of silver and turquoise dangled around their neck. Besides that, they looked like anybody else. They even carried suitcases.

I didn't want to stare too much but I couldn't help it. At this point, I wasn't totally sure if scalping had been outlawed. It may sound stereotypical, however, that had been my very first time to have been in the presence of a real Indian; I mean a Native American.

In addition to meeting new people, I was also introduced to American food. Nothing was stranger than the sandwich one of the soldiers bought me. He must have thought I was starving. I might have mentioned that I was a rather skinny little kid for my age and my cheek bones stuck out rather prominently and I even had dark circles around my eyes, giving the illusion of malnutrition; not that I wasn't hungry, mind you. It was the best sandwich I had ever eaten. They called it a Poor Boy; how appropriate. When I first opened the wrapper, there was all this creamy white stuff oozing out from under the lettuce leaf. "C'est Mayonnaise," (it's Mayonnaise) the soldier had explained.

To the best of my knowledge Mayonnaise was invented in France by Richelieu's chef in 1756, although there are those who want to accredit its origin to some sandwich maker from the town of Mahon in Menorca, Spain. But then, shouldn't it be called Mahonaise? Maybe Richelieu's chef lied and he had actually acquired the recipe on a trip to Spain? I'll let the French and the Spanish epicureans duel this one out; en guarde!

The only thing I remember about Mayonnaise was that this very nice woman back in Algrange had made up a bowl of the white stuff and let me taste it. She had called it Mayonnaise and served it with some steamed artichokes; and I remember the whole presentation though heartfelt, was like a slap to my taste buds. Perhaps my gastronomical curiosity hadn't yet fully developed. Anyway, the stuff on that sandwich, on the train in 1956, tasted great or maybe I was just really, really hungry. I swallowed that sandwich down like there was no tomorrow.

• • •

Rolling along through the mid-section of the country, the weather had been less than welcoming. The sun had only occasionally peeked out from behind the grey blanket of winter clouds. We were snowed on most of the time with occasional spells of rain and slush.

Upon leaving Reno, Nevada, the Sierras were blanketed in several feet of thick, fluffy white stuff. I started wondering what the heck we had gotten ourselves into. Maybe this train was heading for Alaska and not California. Our sponsor, Victor had written to my dad that the weather had been great in San Francisco. The temperature had been in the 10 to 12 degrees (Celsius) range which would have made it at around fifty to fifty-five degrees Fahrenheit; and that wouldn't have been too bad for late February.

Of course, when I stepped off the train in Reno to look around for a couple minutes, while passengers were loading and off-loading, the sun was actually visible and skies were blue, still I almost froze my tiny hiny.

It wasn't until we started our descent down the western slope of the Sierra as we were leaving the snow behind and were headed in the direction of Sacramento that the skies cleared up for good and I could actually see all the way to Mount Diablo. Of course, at the time, I didn't know what mountain I was looking at.

• • •

My father had arrived here with no expectation of getting stuff for free; certainly not money, welfare of any kind or free housing. The whole idea of living for free off of someone else's labor was not only foreign but totally repulsive to him. All he wanted was to get a job as soon as possible so he could take care of his family and wouldn't have to depend on anybody.

It didn't take him long to fall in love with this great big, beautiful country that had taken us in. Within a couple days of disembarking from the Oakland-San Francisco Ferry down at the San Francisco Ferry Building, a job had been secured for him. But, I'm getting way ahead of myself again…

Let's get to San Francisco first!

29

SAN FRANCISCO, HERE I AM!

We got off the train in Oakland, my folks and I, because at the time, the Oakland-San Francisco ferry did not transport the train across the bay; only passengers. We were to cross yet another large body of water, the San Francisco Bay on the ferry boat. On the way over from Oakland, we got to see for the first time, the longest bridge in the world (at the time): the Oakland-San Francisco Bay Bridge, or as San Franciscans like to call it, the San Francisco-Oakland Bay Bridge. Suitcase in hand, we disembarked from the big ferry boat with hundreds of harried commuters and were surprised to find that a small group of folks were there to welcome us to California.

Our welcoming committee at the Ferry Building in San Francisco consisted of our sponsors, the Egry family, Victor, his wife Elisabeth and Little Vikki all of seven and of course her grandma whom I remembered from the camp in Austria. Also present was Bert's sponsor, a Mrs. Penzes, a future friend of the family Frank Zegrean as well as an attractive middle-aged woman in a stylish white outfit, whose name I can't remember. I do however remember her hitting on Bert.

They loaded us into Frank Zegrean's 1953 Pontiac Station Wagon and Victor's 1954 Chevy for a ride to the Egry flat on Schrader Street. They occupied the whole of the first floor, right above the garages for this three-story Victorian, in what would become known as the notorious Haight-Ashbury in the 1960s, just a few blocks from Kezar Pavilion and the Stadium by the same name, where the San Francisco Forty-Niners played their games way back then.

Victor's Egry's mother-in-law served up a mouthwatering old-fashioned Hungarian dinner consisting of stuffed cabbage and veal cutlets and plenty of sour French bread, with of course Dobosh torte (8-12 layer Hungarian cake) for dessert and my folks were introduced to California jug-wine.

We were to live with the Egry family for as long as needed while my father and Bert were driven around the Bay Area by Frank Zegrean to try to find work. Within a day or two, they both had jobs on the docks in Oakland, working for a Hungarian guy's company that made and repaired shipping pallets. As it turned out, they would only work there for a couple weeks as they both moved on to better and more permanent jobs; Bert to a garage in Berkeley as a mechanic and my father to Trinity Methodist Church in Berkeley, as the caretaker. But, more on that later...

• • •

The Monday following our arrival, I was sent off to school with my new little friend Vikki whom I had mentioned, was seven and attended first grade in the little neighborhood school around the corner from their house.

So, here I was just a month and a half shy of my fourteenth birthday, having to attend school with a bunch of kids half my size; a daunting task as they were all smarter than me in so far as the English language.

The teacher and her class greeted me enthusiastically. I was the first alien they had ever seen, a legal one at that; and not from outer space. Still, they made every effort to treat me nicely although they all laughed their little butts off when I couldn't pronounce the name of the country I was in: The United States. Well actually, I did try to say it but immediately discovered that the letters that I had pronounced a certain way in France for the past seven and a half years were coming out of the mouths of the little urchins strangely contorted into a totally different sound.

By the end of the day though, I had finally succeeded in saying correctly 'hello, good morning, goodbye, how are you and of course United States' (You-knighted Staits).

The next day, by putting my right hand over my heart, I attempted to recite the Pledge of Allegiance, along with the little tots. I was mouthing what I thought the kiddies were saying, but not very loudly. Well, it didn't sound right and I had no clue as to what I was saying. Of course, the whole class tried to help the teacher help me try to recite the alphabet, again, in English and it sure sounded different than in French. Numbers one to ten sounded just as strange, but slowly, by the end of the week, I had mastered both. I had been very astute at learning a new language in both Austria which was German and of course Français. Now for English, I had to reprogram the machinations of my mouth and more specifically my tongue in addition to reprogramming my brain to forget everything I had previously known about the alphabet.

I was getting a kick out of attending class with little Vikki, however, at break time, the older kids in the higher grades looked at me like I was some kind of freak, hanging around with little kids and all: antennae might as well have been sprouting out of my head. As a matter fact, Vikki even had to stand up for me when she took offense to some of the things one of the older kids had said about me. At the time they said it, it didn't register with me. "Retard" was what I had heard. But the way he had said it, I didn't even understand the insult. Lucky for him, I just smiled and looked confused; which probably made it worse.

Through Vikki's translation, I was informed that Monday of the coming week, I would have to start attending a school more in line with my age, called a Junior High School. It was located several blocks away from the Schrader street address and would have required me to actually ride the trolley to get there. I was told that among the mountain of papers my parents had signed before being permitted in the States, there was a particular requirement about me (actually any child of school age) being duly enrolled in a school appropriate for my age group. Ah, the good old days, when you had to follow rules.

Lucky for me (whoopee!), my father landed a new job in Berkeley and we would very soon be leaving the concrete canyons that I considered San Francisco to be and I wouldn't have to ride a trolley to get to my school.

Coming from a small town like Algrange where the tallest building was about five stories high, when I saw Paris, I thought it was huge, even though in 1954, there were no buildings there that would have been considered skyscrapers; though the Eiffel Tower was enormous. And then, when we were driven through the streets of New York City, I actually felt claustrophobic riding along the concrete canyons with the multitude of people making it look like some enormous ant colony.

When we had finally gotten to San Francisco, the ride to Schrader Street was akin to traversing the concrete canyons of New York City, I was what you could call, greatly depressed. I attempted to be thankful and nice to everyone while hoping and praying that I wouldn't have to live there; and I got lucky, thank God!

We lived in the City by the Bay for eight days before moving to Berkeley; the other city by the Bay. Now I can truly enjoy the occasional visit to San Francisco, to go to Fisherman's Wharf, the Orpheum or Curran theaters, the De Young Museum and even an occasional Giants game; although, I'm really an Oakland A's fan.

We are being welcomed by our Hungarian American friends at the San Francisco Ferry Building. Present were: Bert Bartha, Woman in white DK name, Mrs. Penzes-Bert's sponsor, my Mom, Frank Zegrean in back, Me in front, Elisabeth Egry in back, Vikki Egry in front, Vikki's grandmother and my Dad at the end. (Victor Egry took the photo. Author's archives)

A chubbier me with my dad, on Mount Sutro, before the ugly tower –
1957 - (Photo by Victor Egry - Author's archives)

The confirmation class of 1956, from Algrange, without me in the picture (Author's archives)

Victor and Elisabeth Egry, our sponsors in 1956 (Author's archives)

Vikki Egry in 1955 (Author's archives)

30

THE OTHER CITY BY THE BAY

While my father was settling into his new position, my mother was setting up our new home with a lot of well-worn donations of furniture and kitchen utensils and even an old TV set; twenty-one inches of shades of grey and three whole channels until channel 2 from the waterfront in Oakland joined the line-up.

I of course was happy that we were now living in a place from where I could actually see the hills covered with green trees and lots of grass, and I was only one block away from the Cal Berkeley Campus (formally, the University of California, Berkeley) with Strawberry Creek running down the middle of it from Strawberry Canyon up in the Berkeley Hills. With all those large, ancient oak trees and myriad crisscrossing paths, it made me think that I was sort of out in the country, almost.

The church secretary told us where the local junior high school was located and the very next day at Trinity Church, I was escorted by my father to Willard Junior High and promptly enrolled in the 8th grade. The wife of the former church caretaker, Vilma Sandor, who spoke Hungarian as well as fluent English, accompanied us to the school to help us with all the necessary paperwork and translation. We were informed that since I spoke no English whatsoever, well you know, except for hello, goodbye, United States and a couple of dozen other words, certainly not enough to form any recognizable sentence, I would also have to be enrolled in an English course for foreigners. This meant that in addition to Willard, I would have to attend another school for half of the day to learn English. This school happened to actually be located only about five blocks from Trinity Church.

At the time, it bore the name McKinley Adult Education School. It was later torn down and became UC Berkeley student housing. McKinley was where recent emigrants went to learn to speak English, however in addition, this was also where misbehaving and troublemaking students were also sent from their regular schools for some remedial education and attitude adjustment. My father told me that in the old days, back in Hungary, they called these institutions, Reform Schools. We could sure use them today.

At McKinley, I discovered that among my classmates besides my father, were about thirty or so, adult foreign nationals from the four corners of the globe. In 1956, the majority were from Europe and Asia. I made friends with some of the younger Japanese students who taught me a few words in their language, such as *midori*, the color green way before the liquor by that name became popular. They called me *Kioki* which was the closest they could come up with to George. I also picked up some of the common phrases like *Konitchua*, *Moshi-Moshi* and of course *Domo Arrigato* and the reply to that of you're welcome which I never quite got the hang of, so they told me to just say: "Don't touch my mustache" really fast. They laughed, but they said it sounded close enough. While I was expanding my linguistic horizons, I also helped my dad with his English assignments. Did I mention that I was pretty good at picking up foreign languages; and boy did I know it!

In addition to spending a half a day of learning English at McKinley, I had also been signed up for the current English class at Willard, in addition to French, German and Art. They didn't want to overload me the first semester here and have me sour on the American educational system so I got to take courses that wouldn't strain my absorption rate of knowledge.

At Willard, I also met a kid who spoke Dutch and had come over from Holland. His name was Willy Bergmann. He, of course had already learned English as he had arrived a year before me. He told me, he was Dutch-Indonesian. His father, who was a doctor, was on staff at Herrick Memorial Hospital, in Berkeley. Since Willy already spoke reasonably fluent English, he helped with my homework until I got a better grasp of the language myself. We got to be pretty good pals and hung around together at our place or his. He taught me how to ice-skate; so, we spent a lot of time at Berkeley's Iceland, where by the way, they even had minor league hockey league games. He wanted us to join the league but I didn't relish the idea of getting manhandled or get my teeth knocked out over a puck. Our friendship, sadly, was short-lived.

Willy's father had applied for a position at West Point quite some time prior and had finally been asked to interview. He aced the interview and was told that he would be needed around July or August of 1956. We promised to write each other; which lasted a couple months as both of us had discovered the freedom of summer; he in New York State and me in California. West Point is a Census Designated Place (CDP) located in the Town of Highlands in Orange County, New York, located on the western bank of the Hudson River; which I didn't know at the time. So, I was surprised to find out that Willy was going to do some fishing. At the time, I thought that New York was that gigantic stone canyon I had been driven through from New York Harbor to Grand Central Station.

• • •

Thanks to Willy teaching me how to skate, I really got into it and would go down to Iceland on Friday evenings and meet guys from school to race around the rink. We all wore hockey skates because you could go much faster and you didn't have those pesky knurling in the front of the skate like the figure skates had. This meant that you wouldn't accidentally incline your skate forward and crash on your face.

Unfortunately, with hockey skates, you also got to go much faster. This meant that while the talented skaters practiced their moves in the center of the rink, us speed demons got to race around the edges and scare the bejesus out of the smaller kids. Paybacks are a bitch, as they say. On my sixteenth birthday, Mr. Egry took me and little Vikki to do some skating. Vikki tired after a while, so I started racing around with some school buddies. We were passing each other left and right and I was moving along fairly well, when all of a sudden, I got nailed from behind. And that's the last thing I remembered.

I woke up a couple of hours later in a hospital room. I had a bruise on my cheek, where I hit the sideboard of the rink, a scratch on my forehead and my right hand was cut up where someone trying to avoid me, actually got a bit too close. As I looked up, there was Mr. Egry and little Vikki looking down at me with concern in their eyes. They had called my mother from the hospital and told her I was ok. When we finally got home, she started lecturing, but to be honest, she was more scared than angry.

I never did find out who had done the dastardly deed and my 'chicken' little buddies were all afraid to spill the beans.

The next day, a bunch of people showed up for my birthday party. Two girls that showed up, were impressed with my scars and wanted to touch them, to see if it hurt. The guys weren't so sympathetic. They wanted to go find who did it and beat them up. I of course was very happy to just let it go, for the moment anyway.

I thought I knew who had pushed me, but I couldn't prove it, and the rest is history.

• • •

I must segue here briefly forward to the Vietnam War; at about 1966. My daughter Christina was about a year old and daughter number two, Gizella, was on the way. I was sitting in my favorite chair one afternoon, watching the news on KPIX, Channel 5, when the talking head announced that they were cutting over to West Point Military Academy to interview the graduating cadets who of course now, were officers and were to be shipped to Vietnam within the month. I watched and listened as several cadets were being interviewed, when suddenly; a familiar name that I had not heard in almost ten years came to the microphone. "Cadet Willy Bergmann," asked the stone-faced newscaster, "tell us how you feel about having to go over there to that hellhole?"

"I am very proud to go, sir" replied Willy without blinking. "It is my duty."

"Way to go Willy!" I yelled at the 21" black-n-white set. I hadn't heard from him in quite a while, although I knew he had been accepted at West. When he left, I told him I'd like to be there with him. Until my dad passed away, I actually was promised a chance. After his passing, I just couldn't leave my mother alone.

That's the last time I ever heard from Willy Bergmann.

When the World Wide Web materialized, I started looking for Willy. I have tried every combination of his name. To this day, I haven't been able to find him.

• • •

In a little over two months, it was summer vacation time and I spent most of my time running wild around the creek on the UC Campus with the former janitor's son Leslie (Sandor) Jr., or Les as he liked to be called. I goofed off with him during that first summer, however in the fall; he attended another junior high school, on the other side of Berkeley as his folks moved away from Trinity. We scrambled up and down the creek, climbing trees and getting ourselves dirty all the while I was absorbing the idiosyncrasies of the English language. I didn't see Leslie Jr. on a regular basis again until we both graduated from junior high and moved on to Berkeley High School. However, by then, he had his own circle of friends and I sort of didn't fit in with them, the little snobs; just kidding.

Needless to say, all of that running around on the UC campus, all summer, guaranteed that by September, I was reasonably well versed in the English Language, perhaps not all of it proper for classroom usage, still I started to sound like I'd lived here for a while.

Meanwhile when September rolled around, I dutifully returned to my class at McKinley and picked up right where I had left off in June, in terms of class assignment.

"Why exactly are you still here Mister Kapus, in this class?" asked the instructor. I thought he had meant my father. However, he was looking at me, holding my homework paper between his fingers. I had apparently answered all of the questions on grammar and vocabulary, correctly.

"Not senior Mister Kapus, but you, the younger Mister Kapus," he clarified.

"I was told at Willard, that I needed to keep attending this class to expand my knowledge of the English language, for at least a full year," I replied.

"That's what I mean. You go tell the administration at Willard that you don't actually need to attend this class anymore," is what he explained. "Go to your counselor and ask him or her to assign you to classes in the standard curriculum. You have done well here, in fact very well" he said, "now, goodbye and best of luck" he wished me with a handshake and sent me on my way, to my father's and the other adults' amazement.

I blushed a bit as I said *Sayonara* to my classmates and closed the door on McKinley for the last time.

What this meant was that I would be in the 9th grade, in junior high, all day long. It also meant that I would have to add three to four morning classes to my schedule and to start doing real homework. I of course kept the afternoon classes that I had already been assigned; English, French, German and Art and added Math, Geography, History and Physical Education. I now felt like one of the regular kids; no more the special case alien child!

• • •

I must interject here, that around this time, I received an envelope from Pasteur Michel at the Protestant Church in Algrange. It contained an official photograph of the 1956 confirmation class, which by the way was the class I would have been part of had we not left Algrange. All my friends were there, smiling at me from the black and white photo, including Lydia with a new curly hairdo. Gone was the tomboy with the short haircut. I was looking at a pretty young woman. I hadn't had much time to think about them, with the new school, homework, new friends and of course, learning English and all. Holding that black-and-white photo, I imagined myself in the picture, right there, maybe standing behind Lydia. For a brief moment, I felt sad.

A couple weeks later, Emi's brother Ernie and I got confirmed at the First Congregational Church on Dana and Durant in Berkeley, by our new Hungarian Protestant pastor from San Francisco. I wished instead, I could have been back there in Algrange, with my old schoolmates. But, as they say, that boat had sailed.

• • •

The second year at Willard, I discovered a great many things such as, the school had a cafeteria and I could drink as much Coke as I wanted with my lunch, all for about fifteen cents and there were candy bars and cakes as well as Hostess Snow Balls in white and a pink. To this day, whenever and wherever I would see those soft pink and white marshmallow mounds, I would stock up on a handful. Not only that but, on the way home, I could buy ice cream, any day of the week for a dime. I didn't have to wait for Sunday to have a dessert. Unfortunately, I also discovered that all that rich and sugary food led to much larger size wardrobe, all because of my expanding physiognomy.

Interestingly enough, my foreign language classes were populated mostly by girls with only a couple of other boys wearing glasses. Most boys found it to be a sissy endeavor to speak in tongues other than English. In my French class for instance, there were several African-American girls; back then, they called themselves Negroes. As I grew heftier shall we say; they started teasing me, this one young lady in particular.

"Vous avez un grand derriere," she commented one day indicating the size of my caboose while giggling with great relish.

Not knowing what else to say, I said "Merci, however, your derriere is bigger than mine," of course this, in French.

"Humph," she replied with flared nostrils and nose in the air, as she walked away to the giggles of her girlfriends.

Not only had her assessment been correct but so was her French.

"You shouldn't say things like that to a girl; it is not very nice," one of her friends admonished, also in French. Although as she walked away, I could clearly detect some suppressed giggling.

"I'll have to apologize to her, tomorrow," I said to no one in particular. There was still a lot for me to learn in this new world, especially in regards to interacting with members of the female gender.

Nonetheless, round one was still mine. However, I would have to ask my mother to get me better fitting pants and shirts or I would have to lose some of my physical assets. From right about that point forward in my life, I began fighting the battle of the bulges; a never-ending battle as I would learn.

At Willard, I also made my first African-American friend. Not all the black kids were amenable to being friends with white kids, especially one who couldn't even speak common English well enough, unless it had to do with a school activity. This one kid, he of course told me that he was *colored* and also advised me not to hang around with him too much because people didn't care for white kids befriending colored kids; which caught me a bit off guard. I didn't get it at the time.

I discovered I had a lot to learn about all the new cultural nuances I was being exposed to. I still remember his name, Leroy Geuton. He and I went all the way through high school together. We frequently took the same classes and actually shared Home-room. You know, the place where they grouped kids with last names in close proximity one to another alphabetically, for official announcements and to fill out paperwork as well as to do some homework; G was close to K.

At Willard, I was also exposed to some uniquely American sports by of all people a teacher of Japanese descent, Mister Isono. I liked the guy so much that I asked to be in his gym class both se-mesters there. He introduced me to such sports as Handball, Flag Football, Dodge-Ball, Gymnastics and Baseball. I did well in almost all these sports, except in Gymnastics. Then again, I kept slipping off of the steady rings. I tripped on the beam and fell off, even though they had it set at only two feet above the mat. And at first,

I couldn't climb up the rope to save my life. I'm sure some it had to do with the extra luggage I was carrying since I had discovered American junk food.

Baseball was somewhat of a puzzle as well. The big bat, the small ball and that unwieldy giant glove, they all just didn't work for a kid used to kicking a Futbol (soccer ball) around. Later on, I'll tell you how I actually got introduced to baseball, by some friends.

• • •

Soon after enrolling at Willard, my parents decided that I should have a more rounded education which included music. They were introduced to Mrs. Kanyuk and her husband and of course that's how I met their son Leslie. Mrs. Kanyuk also happened to be a piano teacher that had studied at the Ferenc Liszt Academy, which was founded in 1875. How long she had studied there, I don't know since they had escaped Hungary right before WWII had ended and came to the US many years before us. All I know is that she was a wonderful teacher and great pianist in her own right.

I studied with her all through my time at Willard Junior-High School and through Berkeley High, but I eventually quit after my first year of Junior College. I was carrying a rather heavy load and could not concentrate on my piano lessons and practices; to my detriment. Now, sixty some odd years later, I wish I had kept up with it...

• • •

Sometime during the second semester, we had a big assembly where we were told about Polio. There were slides that showed what Polio was and what it did, if you got it. As a matter of fact, we had a boy that walked around with two crutches. Someone told me that he had Polio. Up to that point, I had not been aware of this debilitating disease and I had not known anyone who had had it. After the presentation at the assembly, our parents were asked to sign this form giving the school permission to give us Polio vaccine so that we wouldn't catch the dreaded affliction. This vaccine worked for certain as no more cases of Polio were reported in the whole USA. Until recently, I had not heard of any cases for over fifty years.

• • •

I attended Willard for about a year and a half at the end of which there was a rather nice graduation ceremony that my parents both attended. This was the first time that I had ever graduated from any school, anywhere.

I had finally made it through the Junior High School level of education and with that graduation ceremony and the little piece of rolled-up parchment looking paper with the blue ribbon tied in a bow around it, stating that fact, I was promoted to go on to Berkeley High School.

Many nationalities will be represented at the Hanging o' the Greens Christmas party for YWCA members and their families on Sunday. Among those who will be guests of the YW for their first Christmas in the US are the group above. Seated, left to right are Mrs. George Kapus, holding Carmen Perez, Mr. Kapus, Maria Perez, Mrs. Carlos Perez and son Carlos; back row are Mrs. E. D. Lucas of the YWCA World Fellowship Committee; George Kapus Jr., and Dr. Carlos Perez. Dr. Perez and his family are here from Guatemala, the doctor is studying for his degree in public health at the University of California. The Kapus family are Hungarian refugees.   —Gazette photo

Our picture in the December 20, 1956 issue of the Berkeley Gazette (Author's archives)

My pal Willy Bergman and I on the back steps of Trinity Church, 1956 – my dad took the photo with my Kodak Brownie Hawkeye (my very first ever camera (Author's archives)

A drawing of me at the keyboard in 1956 from an old photo – (GK drawing)

My confirmation photo with Ernie Zegrean, with my parents in the back with Frank and Elisabeth Zegrean as well as Emi Zegrean, Ernie's sister and the old church deacon – the minister took the photo (Author's archives)

Frank and Elizabeth Sipos, friends of my mom and dad from Budapest who just happened to be living in San Mateo, Ca., with me in the middle. My parents hadn't seen them since late 1944 (Author's archives)

UC Berkeley Campus with the Campanile in November 1956 – (GK photo)

31

SIXTEEN DEMANDS

I was enjoying a reasonably cushy life in Berkeley, California in 1956. We'd only gotten here about seven months ago but I was fully ensconced in my new surroundings. My biggest worries were getting to dinner on time and getting my homework done so that I could see Annette Funicello and the rest of the Mouseketeer gang sing "Who's the Leader of Our Club" and then later on watch Jackie Gleason threatening Alice with free trips to the moon on our twenty-inch black and white Philco television set with rabbit ears on top.

I have fond remembrances of Annette looking quite attractive even with that silly black hat with the giant mouse ears firmly planted on top of her head. However, I also started watching the news closely, mostly because it was required by our History teacher, Mr. Johnson, for discussions on Current Events.

One day, much more sinister events were taking over the airwaves, as I discovered when I got home from school, hitting closer to home so to speak. My dad had dropped his mop early and together with my mother, they were intently watching the TV set and trying to make sense of the urgent announcements. They had of course both recognized the images so familiar to them, the streets and buildings, the people with their stoic, defiant expressions; the images originating from Budapest, Hungary.

"What are they doing to my beautiful city, again?" lamented my father.

Now, long forgotten, in October of 1956, Budapest was again being brutalized by the Soviets. What am I saying? The Soviets or if you wish, the Communists, have been brutalizing Hungary and her citizens since the end of World War II. Tiring of the Communist oppression, the government had split and people took to the streets and demanded that their voices be heard.

A committee of Hungarian students had compiled a list of sixteen policy demands to be presented to the Socialist (aka Communist) government.

The document containing these sixteen demands was a de facto declaration of independence and severance from the Soviet Union and covered the following issues:

The removal of all Soviet troops from Hungary.

Party elections via secret ballots.

Creation of a new government under the direction of Imre Nagy.

A people's tribunal to try all those individuals responsible for Hungary's political and economic ruins.

That general election would be held via secret ballot.

That political equivalence with other Eastern bloc countries and a non-interference agreement with them would be negotiated.

The Economic planning and reorganization of Hungary by specialists in Economics and Finance.

Fair foreign trade agreements must be reached, including the inventory and sale of Hungarian Uranium deposits to be returned under the nation's control.

Revision of industry norms and adjustment of salaries according to job classification.

Equal treatment of farms and rational distribution of farm products.

Return and repatriation of all WWII prisoners from the Soviet Union and other foreign   Countries.

Freedom of speech and expression and a free press.

Removal of Stalin's statue and replacement by heroes of the 1848-49 Revolution.

New uniforms for the military as well as return to the old Hungarian national emblems and traditions.

Declaration of solidarity by the Hungarian students for the students of Warsaw, Poland in their fight for their nation's independence.

A national youth parliament to be held on October 27, in Budapest, representing the entire nation's youth.

They organized an anti-Soviet march through the streets of

Budapest with an eventual destination of the city's main radio station. There, they were hoping to be able to present their grievances on the air but were instead rounded up by the security forces (the dreaded ÁVH/AVO – Államvédelmi Hatóság or State Protection Authority) and jailed. Subsequently, when an enormous crowd gathered outside the radio station demanding the release of the detained students, security forces and local police began firing at the unarmed protestors.

Close to a hundred people were killed and many more wounded according to some of the protestors I have met over the years. Needless to say, this act of savagery so enraged the protestors that they vowed to return, this time, armed.

From protestors, they became freedom fighters overnight. They armed themselves with outdated WWII rifles, bb-guns and rocks. They were going to fight back.

Thus began, the 1956 Hungarian Uprising (Sometimes called the Hungarian Revolution or Revolt of 1956).

Imre Nagy, the Premier of Hungary at the time, though a devout Communist party member, actually agreed to a certain extent with the rebels in regards to more autonomy for his country. Unfortunately, his vacillation caused him to be deposed by the Soviets and whisked away to Moscow.

For almost two weeks, the rebels meted out some well-deserved vengeance on the AVO thugs, which were very similar to the Gestapo in power and brutality. This organization was very closely associated with the Soviet KGB, as well as the occupying Soviet troops.

Many of the Hungarian Military which ran somewhat independently of the Soviets actually sided with the rebels, turning over loads of weapons and even tanks. When it all started, most rebels had to rely on old WWII weapons, hunting rifles and even BB-guns. Newly armed by the Hungarian Military, for a while, it looked like the revolution might just succeed. Many in the Hungarian military actually joined the fight on the side of the rebels. The Soviets however, would not have any of that; letting these upstarts succeed might embolden the rest of the Soviet bloc countries and what a mess that would cause for the mighty Soviet Bear!

So, they called in several hundred tanks from their Mongolian divisions who ruthlessly and violently put end to the uprising that might just have succeeded.

By November the fourth, the rebellion had been squashed.

• • •

Cardinal Mindszenty who had been the leader of the Catholic Church in Hungary since October 1945 had been imprisoned by the Communists since 1949. He was imprisoned by the pro-Nazi regime during World War II for his opposition to fascism. After WWII, he was again prosecuted, this time for his opposition to Communism. After he was tortured, he was sentenced to life in prison by the Communist government. The whole world condemned his treatment, even the United Nations passed a resolution, however without much effect.

Resolutions don't scare the Communists. He languished in prison until the 1956 uprising when he was set free by the rebels and granted asylum in the United States embassy in Budapest. He had been offered an opportunity to leave his country, but refused. He basically stated that he would not leave the embassy in Budapest until Hungary was free again. Some may dispute this claim; however, after spending some fifteen years as a guest of the US embassy, in 1971, the Hungarian government relented and allowed him to finally and formally leave. He would eventually die in exile in Vienna Austria, in 1975.

My reason for including the good Cardinal in this chapter on the 1956 Revolt is the fact that I actually had the honor of meeting the man when he came to San Francisco to visit a Hungarian gathering sometime in 1972. Now mind you, not all the people at this gathering were Catholics, including yours truly. All Hungarians showed up and gave him a heartfelt reception at which I was able to take a few photographs of the brave Cardinal.

We all loved and respected the man for the valiant way in which he had withstood his horrific treatment by the Communists and his own countrymen during WWII and his choice of staying at US Embassy in Budapest until his beloved country would be free.

• • •

The final tally for the revolt was, close to twenty-eight-hundred rebels were killed, including some politicians, doctors, nurses and military who had sided with the righteous cause. An estimated thirteen thousand were wounded. By the time it was all over, an estimated 155,000 had fled across the border into Austria, many via a small bridge over a canal by the little town of Andau.

Even Hollywood got into the act by making a movie about it: 'The Bridge at Andau'. The bridge became famous because of all those souls who crossed it, on the way to freedom. A great number of the refugees ended up in the United States. Quite a few made it all the way to the San Francisco Bay Area which already had a reasonably large population of Hungarian immigrants who had been coming here since the turn of the century; the twentieth century that is. At one point, there were close to 10,000 of us emigrants from Hungary in the San Francisco Bay Area.

Interim Prime Minister Imre Nagy, Defense Minister Pal (Paul) Maleter as well as 230 participants in the 1956 uprising, many students, local politicians, media personalities, several doctors and nurses were arrested, put on trial and summarily executed. Notice, none were given prison sentences. I guess the Communists didn't want to create overcrowding in their jails.

The then President Eisenhower of the USA stated "I feel with the Hungarian people." J F Dulles, American Secretary of State, said "To all those suffering under communist slavery, let us say you can count on us."

But America did nothing more.

My father however, never held it against Ike. He felt, the man was looking after the well-being of the country he was in charge of. I didn't quite understand this and was actually very angry about America not stepping in.

• • •

I was not there.

The events I describe were gathered from news broadcast and newspaper articles as well as first-hand accounts by friends I had met over the years who had taken part in the revolt. They fought the stooges of the Communist regime. They were there when justice was meted out on the AVO/AVH and the Soviet invaders. They carried guns and some of their friends died. As a result, many were forced to leave Hungary as they were wanted by the Communist regime which finally and thankfully expired in 1989.

I cannot even imagine how I would have felt had I been living in my city of birth, Budapest at the time. I had just turned fourteen in April of 1956, but I already understood what had become of my country. I wouldn't have hesitated to throw in with the rebels and tossed some Molotov Cocktails at the Soviet T34/85 tanks. I would probably even have helped the rebels hang a few AVO officers. With any luck at all, I might have made it alive and escaped to the West with those 155,000 and crossed into Austria over the Bridge at Andau, but I might just as well have been one of those 2800 hardy souls to die for freedom in the streets of my Budapest. That is probably why, God decided, way back in 1945, to urge us on that circuitous route that would eventually land us San Francisco, California in the spring of 1956.

Doesn't it make you wonder sometimes, why things happen the way they do and why you end up taking a particular path in your life?

My friend Emi Zegrean's brother Ernie who happened to be a couple years older at the time, and I, wanted to sign up to go fight those 'damned Commies'. (He actually used much more colorful language.) Ernie was quite a bit bigger than me, so I believed him when he said "Let's go kick some Commie ass!" Of course, neither of us had a clue as to where we would sign up. Had there been such a place, neither of us really knew how exactly we would have gone about fighting the damned Commies, nor even how we would have gotten over to Hungary; but it made us feel good to beat our chests and show our loathing for the Soviet Socialist Bear.

There was no organized effort to go over there and fight with the rebels and by the time someone would have figured something out, the whole thing was over anyway. The Hungarian community in the San Francisco Bay Area, as well as over the whole country did actually help the newcomers pick up the pieces, so to speak. We collected money and clothing, even at Trinity Methodist Church where I chipped in helping as an interpreter, since no one at the church spoke Hungarian and the newcomers didn't speak a lick of English. That's the best I could do since I didn't have a lot of money myself.

This is really just an all-too-brief synopsis of the events that took place between October and mid-November of 1956. People in the Free world watched in horror and agonized over the events that flickered daily in black and white on all the available Bay Area TV channels. There wasn't much that the free world was willing to do. There wasn't much we, as Hungarian Refugees, could do. We all knew too well that the inevitable was going to happen again: that Budapest was again bloodied and battered and soon the mighty Soviet Empire would be running everything, just like before.

The following may be an urban myth; that Vice President Richard Nixon actually went to the border of Austria with a contingent of the mighty US Military awaiting orders from then President Eisenhower to step in. Unfortunately, just like FDR at Malta, old Ike had apparently made an agreement with Stalin that the USA would keep its nose out of the internal affairs of the USSR.

Fact: Up to this point in history, Hungary had not been part of Russia and neither were the rest of the Eastern Bloc countries. These countries were to be overseen by the Soviet Union but were in fact taken over and occupied. Ike could have done something. Apparently, President Eisenhower had much more pressing issues occupying his interest, like a pesky problem surrounding the Suez Canal.

Then, the media had real concerns about which Hollywood offerings would win Oscars, The Ten Commandments, The King and

I, Anastasia, Forbidden Planet, John Wayne's The Searchers (just kidding), The Invasion of the Body Snatchers (more kidding), Bus Stop with busty Marilyn Monroe or Moby Dick with moping Gregory Peck. Plus, what would the Hollywood elite wear on the red carpet? In other words, other more important things were going on than worrying about freedom being snuffed out in a small, unimportant Central European country.

Since I wasn't there, I couldn't even imagine how my compatriots must have felt. Perhaps the fact that until the very last minute that the rebels' Radio Free Budapest' could be heard imploring the West for help should sum up how the rebels back home and those of us Hungarians already here in the States felt.

"Where are you America? Will you help us? Don't you hear us? Help, Help, Help!"

Then, deadly silence.

See, there's a problem with a revolution; it pretty much just keeps spinning round and around in place and unfortunately without outside help, it comes to a bloody halt when it runs out of momentum. As was the case in Budapest, with 2,800 dead officially and countless others thrown in jail and otherwise punished, parts of Budapest destroyed, there was no victory. The ones who started the whole thing paid the price, many with their lives and freedom while the rest of the world gawked, waiting for something newer and more exciting to happen.

The uprising did, however unintentionally, start a movement to put an end to the chokehold a totalitarian dictatorship like the Soviet Union had over Eastern Europe. That's the beauty of a movement, once it's started; it keeps going forward, however slowly at times until it reaches its goal. It took a while for this movement to get to that point and succeed. But as the United States, in the person of Ronald Reagan finally got behind the movement with his now famous declaration of June 12 1987 in Berlin, when he boldly shouted "Mr. Gorbachev, tear down this wall" and brought about the beginning of the end of the Soviet Empire.

Unfortunately, it took several years more for the USSR to pull its claws out and let Eastern Europe breathe freely again.

I wrote the following Homage to the brave Freedom Fighters who dared to stare the red masters in the face and give them what for; even if it was for only a dozen days.

FREEDOM WAS WITHIN THEIR GRASP
A Ballad of the 1956 Hungarian Revolt

As I was lounging in my favorite chair
Checking out the happenings on the air
When suddenly the babbling talking head
Was handed a piece of paper that he read

The murky black and white TV displayed
Destroyed buildings as people escaped
Tanks were blasting with flashes and booms
Sending peaceful marchers to their doom

A hundred thousand Magyar faces
Singing the Himnusz of the ages
Were trudging forward to the radio station
To present the demands for their nation

Like thunderbolts from an angry God,
Mowed the protestors as they forward pawed
Many were killed and more were maimed
As the red masters' stooges reloaded and aimed

The number of demands was but sixteen
The reply of the red stooges was obscene
The stooges' eyes and ears were closed
The heart within their chest was frozen cold

It all started as a peaceful protest
But soon it turned to bloodshed in Budapest
Marchers came unarmed to the confrontation

They'd now have to cook-up a revolution

For a dozen glorious days they fought and bled
The red star from the Magyar flags was ripped
Generals and soldiers even joined their ranks
The red masters called in Mongolian tanks

The end came very swiftly, so they retreated
No mercy was given to the freedom fighter
As alone stood the Magyar, again defeated
The world applauded it as good theater

Wiping away angry tears, they pleaded
Can you please help us, they repeated
Is anybody listening, help us, they cried
And just like before, the Magyar*died

But for those glorious dozen days
The Russians and AVOs were made to pay
A clear message to the red masters was delivered
Nineteen fifty six, will always be remembered

Hopelessly wiping angry tears away
In desperation they had tried to change
 The world's opinion to their way
But when the radio went silent, nobody came

Freedom had been within their grasp
Always so elusive as in the past
The Freedom Fighters, could almost taste it
With help from the West, they would have made it

Just as it began, so quickly it ended
Thousands had died and hundreds executed
Hundreds of thousands emigrated
There won't be freedom till the Reds are defeated

High up in the sky by the Warriors' trail
God of the Magyar, please do not fail
To remove the yokes and rip away the chains
Do not ever let us be slaves again.

Magyar = Hungarian

• • •

I must segue to the twenty first century, momentarily. In June 2008, on our European trip with my wife, my daughter Christina and her new husband Doug, we spent four days on the Buda side of the Danube River and four days on the Pest side.

Eating dinner one evening, next door to our hotel, we could still see the blemishes of shelling and gunfire on the side of the building across the alley. I asked the waiter why the owner hadn't fixed the damage to the wall from WWII, especially since they had recently installed vinyl windows for the whole building as well as air conditioners. The waiter's reply was a bit surprising: "That damage is not from World War II. This part of the city suffered quite a bit of damage during the October 1956 Uprising. The owner renovated the whole structure on the inside, including the new windows, but he wanted to leave the outside just the way it was to remind everyone that for two weeks in 1956, we stood up against those Communist butchers."

I had to choke back tears; just thinking about the brave populace that had dared to stand up against their unelected Soviet Socialist masters backed by several hundred tanks with the equivalent of bb-guns and bottles filled with gasoline while the rest of the world watched it all on TV like the Roman crowds would watch the Christians against the lions, while stuffing their faces with Nachos. This was a true tale of David and Goliath; except in this case, David was slaughtered.

The protestors hadn't realized that when they decided to challenge the authority of the Soviet Union, they would be entering right into the eye of a red hurricane that would destroy everything in its path.

Just remember, as long as there are dictators like Vladimir Putin and the Brothers Castro, Socialism in one form or another will live on and that's not a reassuring thing for Hungarians, Ukrainians, Cubans, the Chinese, Americans or even Russians.

Peaceful protest turns to bloodshed in Budapest – (my illustration for the book by Irene Tosaky 'The Heroes Will Return Again' – 1996 Ed.)

*Pro-Hungarian Rally poster on the UC Campus
in Berkeley, Ca in November 1956 – (GK photo)*

*Cardinal Mindszenty signing the guest book at the Stephaneum Hungarian Club in San
Francisco in 1972, my old friend Albert Szelle is standing behind him - (GK Photo)*

*Cardinal Mindszenty speaking to the overflowing audience
at the Stephaneum in 1972 - (GK Photo)*

32

SPORTS R-US

Now, let's get back on track to explore my ventures into the sporting life. Let's start with what I discovered was the national pastime, the game of Baseball.

I was actually introduced to this uniquely American sport within a few days of having moved in at Trinity Methodist Church. My parents had organized a gathering of new friends to celebrate our arrival to the USA and also to celebrate my fourteenth birthday. My parents had invited our sponsors, the Egrys, the Zegreans, the former church caretaker Laszlo Sandor and family as well as a couple new Hungarian friends who also happened to have kids right around my age.

The former custodian and his wife brought their son Leslie, my future piano teacher Mrs. Kanyuk and her husband Joseph brought along their son, who also happened to be named Leslie. Emi Zegrean was there as well as the little Bene girl nicknamed Cica (Kitty), a cute little blonde girl who actually attended Willard Junior High at the same time as I and never did quite like me from the get go; don't know why. I was always told I was sweet and adorable, ha, ha, ha…

Anyhow, the two Leslies decided to give their newly arrived, little alien buddy a lesson on how to catch a baseball. The reason I keep calling them Leslie is because they had gotten so totally Americanized that they didn't like to be called Laszlo, which was their given name in Hungarian.

I had no clue as to how this game was played. In Algrange, we had played something akin to stickball in the streets, but we never used anything but an old stick and an old rock or a piece of wood carved into the shape of a torpedo. They of course had brought along these big oversized leather gloves and the small white leather covered ball. They went about tossing the rather small, hardball around and catching it with the big gloves, with great dexterity and ease. In fact, it had looked so easy; I thought I could do it just as well.

"You want to try it?" asked one of the Leslies.

"Sure," I replied.

"OK, put this mitt on your left hand" Leslie Kanyuk instructed. "That's what you catch the ball with and you toss it back with your right hand." I had actually figured that one out.

So, I put on one of the big leather gloves and the other Leslie (Sandor) threw a ball in my direction. Where they had both quite expertly caught the ball in the webbing of the glove, I didn't have the wherewithal or coordination to even getting close to catching the damn ball. I held the glove in the wrong way to catch anything and even when it was pointed correctly, instead of catching it; it bounced off the heel.

"Look," said Leslie Kanyuk. "Position it in front of your face, palm out, like this," he demonstrated. "Through the webbing, you'll see the ball coming at you and you just close the mitt and snag it in the webbing."

It all sounded so easy.

I did as he said. I planted the big glove, palm out, in front of my face, and told Leslie Sandor to go ahead and throw. I figured he would toss me a softy just to try. How could I miss, right?

He let loose a fastball, straight at my open gloved hand. I had no idea on the mechanics of the baseball traveling at about at least fifty miles per hour. Both Leslies were only fourteen, just like me. The ball couldn't have been travelling much faster.

The ball hit the target alright, which was my open gloved hand. However, having no sense of the force and momentum behind the ball, I was too slow in reacting and closing the webbing as in-structed. My wrist gave way and the ball bounced off my left cheekbone, right next to my eye. The result was a nasty welt and a black eye. I still have a snapshot of me with the black eye at my 14th birthday party. Both Leslies were sorry for the 'misunderstanding'. Their snickers didn't help assuage my pain and embarrassment.

The following Monday at Willard, when I explained how the black eye happened, to just about everybody in school, I got no sympathy, just wild laughter.

And, that's how I got introduced to Baseball.

I tried my hand at a number of other sports, one of them being fencing; yes the kind with pointed weapons used to skewer the opponent. In this case however, the weapon being a saber or a foil basically had blunt tips; not quite like the ones the musketeers skewered the cardinal's guards with. More specifically, these sabers had something in size to that of the head of a thumbtack at the tip. This prevented you from actually doing to your opponent what D'Artagnon did to his nemeses, although if you managed to get through their defensive move, you could still leave nasty black and blue welts on unprotected body parts. Which is the reason why, it was highly recommended that you wore a padded jacket to protect your chest and arms, knickers to cover your legs and a mask made of steel mesh with a leather and metal frame surrounding it, even in practice.

Although some of the macho guys actually practiced in T-shirts and jeans. The mask also gave you the appearance of the guy from 'The Man in the Iron Mask' by Alexander Dumas.

Let's just say that I got interested in fencing when one of our dinner guests who had escaped from Hungary after the 1956 revolt, turned out to be a gold medalist fencer on the Hungarian Olympic team.

He was one of the many student athletes who had escaped from Hungary following that unsuccessful attempt, lasting from October 23 until about November 10, 1956. Many of the academics, both students and professors started to arrive in the San Francisco Bay Area, in early 1957 by the hundreds. Again, many participants in the uprising were students of the various universities in Hungary, mostly in Budapest. A number of these students also happened to be some of the top athletes in the country and belonged on the Olympic team.

A number of these young guys found their way to our basement apartment at Trinity Methodist Church for a hot meal and some Hungarian fellowship. My mother was all too happy to feed these young people. She got to cook like she had done in her own restaurant back in Budapest, and instead of struggling in English; she got to converse in her native Hungarian. Initially, they were guests but the young guys appreciated the favor and in turn reciprocated with small contributions to the household budget. It worked out for everybody.

This went on until they got a foothold in the local culture and made their own friends and started their own careers. So, for a couple years at least, as they came for dinner, I got to meet some of best and brightest that Hungary had lost, and the US had gained.

I am proud to say that several Hungarian gold medalists in various sports sat at our humble dinner table. Magyary Miklos (not his real name) was one of them. He had won a dozen gold medals in National, European and Olympic Championships. One day, he looked at me and said "You look like you could be a good saber fencer". I believed him. After all, when I had been a little kid back in Algrange, after every swashbuckler at the local cinema, for days I would run around like a crazed musketeer with a stick in hand, mimicking Errol Flynn, Gene Kelly or Louis Hayward.

I was a natural, I thought. At fifteen, I was still very gullible as well.

So, the next time he came for dinner, he brought along a couple of sabers and face masks. He had previously asked if there was a place where we could practice. In the main building, a big hall in the basement had been painted and furnished as a place for teens to meet for various activities, mostly during weekends. During the week, it sat there empty. This is where I took him for our first session. He gave me a mask he had brought and one of his sabers. Equally attired, he proceeded to demonstrate the basic moves of Parry, Riposte, Remise, Lunge and Beat. There are several other moves of course, but this was the first lesson for me; the basics. Initially, he said I only needed three moves.

I in turn mimicked the moves he showed me. He made me repeat them a few times, and then he engaged me in a little sparring. He obviously wasn't moving at full speed. He and I went at it for almost an hour. He then told me that I had done well and we would do it again when he came over the next time.

Naturally, first chance I had, I went and found a sporting goods store in downtown Oakland that carried fencing equipment. I invested the contents of my piggy bank on a saber and my mom slipped me enough money to buy a mask. Now, back in 1957, fencing sabers cost twenty dollars and the mask, around thirty-five; a bit pricey even then; but you couldn't fence without proper equipment.

The next time Miklos came, I proudly showed him my new acquisitions.

We practiced a couple more times and I was starting to enjoy this sport. I had already told the guy at the sporting goods store that I would soon be back for the knickers and a jacket especially since I was getting whacked on the arm when I didn't defend myself properly. Unfortunately, Miklos got a job offer in Southern California and my fencing instruction came to an abrupt end but not before he told me about a Hungarian fencing club in San Francisco, the Pannonia Club.

When my dad discovered that in order to fence at the club, you had to pay an annual membership of a hundred dollars, plus twenty dollars a month for lessons. I can tell you, today, that would-be chicken feed. Back in 1957/58, it might as well have been a million bucks. We couldn't afford it. That sort of closed the book on my entry into the elite sport of aristocrats, but not before I showed a buddy of mine, Bob, how to use a saber.

Bob was all too happy for me to show him what I had learned. So, one day after school, I took him to the youth center in the church basement. Of course, by this time, upon hearing about my new endeavor, an older friend from the church who had an epee, asked if I wanted it. What the heck, I had two poking sticks. I could show others how to fence; Douglas Fairbanks Jr., that's me.

"Since I'm experienced with the blade," I told Bob, "I'll use the epee and I'll let you use the saber."

"Fine," he said, "Let's do this."

What I have to insert here is the fact that the saber which has a larger hilt and guard, and I had accidentally broken off the protective tip at the end of the blade. You see, one day I decided to practice my moves in the basement by myself and as I lunged at the concrete wall, I got too close and the tip snapped off. The replacement blade would have cost eleven bucks; which I didn't happen to have at the time. As soon as I had saved it up, you know... Not only did I give Bob the weapon with a pointed tip, I also gave him the mask. I figured after four lessons, I was a fencing master.

So here I was with the epee which has a three inch or so little round guard and no mask to protect my face. Without getting too convoluted, epee moves are different than saber moves. So, with the saber, I demonstrated what the moves were. Then, I gave him the saber.

"You do what I showed you," I said. "I'll defend myself with the epee. But if I drop the blade of my epee down and say stop, it means we quit. You understand?"

"Yeah, yeah," he said. "I got it!"

"And remember, your blade has a real point on it, so be careful!"

"Yeah, yeah! I got it."

We crossed swords and began to make the moves we had practiced. The sneaky little jackass, after a while, he went Zorro on me. Instead of sparring as we had agreed, he started slashing and hacking like he'd seen in the movies. I started to get worried. After all, I had no protection and he had whacked me on the arms a couple times already. He seemed to derive great pleasure from inflicting pain on me.

"Hey, I thought you learned how to fence already. Defend yourself. What's the matter?" He teased.

I was starting to worry that he might accidentally poke me in the eye or something. I just kept parrying his slashes until I finally had enough.

"Hey Bob" I yelled. "I want a break!" but he didn't appear to hear me. Maybe the mask was too tight on his head or he was just enjoying himself too much.

"I quit," I yelled. "You win. I give up!"

He just kept slashing away, this way and that. He wouldn't stop. Finally, I jumped out of his way and dropped the epee, indicating that I was surrendering, as we had agreed. He executed something that looked like a Flunge (fencing term: a flying lunge) and struck the broken point of the sword right into my open right palm with my epee dangling from it. All of a sudden, he stopped and pulled back on the point. As the blade slid out of my palm, I dropped my blade.

Blood gushed from my palm.

The point had penetrated the thick meaty part of my right palm, under the thumb. Blood kept on gushing out with other matter following. It was running down my arm. I panicked. I thought that he had actually run the blade clear through. Lucky for me, he hadn't. He pulled the mask off and dropped the saber. He turned white.

"I'm sorry man. I got carried away," he whined. "You gotta go to a doctor."

"Yeah," I said. "I better not let my mom see this. She's going to be really upset or maybe faint or something," although, I had never, ever seen my mother faint.

I wrapped my handkerchief around my hand and took off to my dad's doctor, whose office was located on University Avenue, just below the UC Campus. Obviously, we couldn't tell him that we had been fencing. Neither of us knew what legal implications this whole affair might have had. So naturally we had to cook up a different story, one that would be plausible and believable.

"Doctor Fazekas, me and my friend here were working on this fence in his backyard, you see," I explained, "and there was this great big rusty nail sticking out of this board and I fell on it with my palm."

"Let's take off that handkerchief and have a look see," he said. "And that big nail, you say, was it rusty?"

"Yes doctor," I said. Little did I know the implication of that particular bit of information?

"That means, we'll have to give you a Tetanus shot," the doctor said.

"Oh?" I said.

Why did I have to say the nail was rusty? Why did I let my stupid friend stick a dam sword in my hand? Why had I been stupid enough to give him a damn pointed sword in the first place? How am I going to explain this whole mess to my mother and later on to my father? Those were just some of the questions flooding the space between my ears as I watched the good doctor prepare his surgical tools and the syringe.

Why did he need surgical tools in the first place, should have been utmost on my mind. I thought that he would wipe the wound with some alcohol and put a band-aid on it.

After he had cleaned the wound, I could actually see meaty matter hanging out of the quarter inch hole.

"We'll have to push some of this back in the wound and cut this tip off," he was explaining, as I watched the procedure.

"Now, I got to stitch it all up," he said.

"I need stitches?" I asked. Now I was certain that my parents would notice that something had happened to my hand.

And, even though the safety tip had broken off the sword's point, it was a rather blunt and sharp break, however with a tiny upturn at the end. This almost acted as a meat hook when it penetrated the meaty part of the palm. On the way out, it pulled with it some of the inner stuffing; that's the stuff the good doctor was pushing back in!

After Dr. Fazekas pushed some of the meaty matter back in, he trimmed the rest and put in three or four little stitches and bandaged my hand. Then came the Tetanus shot. "I'll send the bill to your father and you come back and see me in a couple days to see how well your hand is healing," Dr. Fazekas said, "and, you won't be able to practice the piano for a week or two?" That last part was the only good thing that came out of this whole mess.

The rusty nail in the board is the story my mother got. She was sympathetic but also disappointed that I couldn't practice the piano. I had left the fencing gear in the youth center and snuck it back home when my mother had gone grocery shopping and before my dad had gotten back from work.

To this day, I still have a quarter inch scar in the meaty part of my palm, under my right thumb as a reminder of my swashbuckling days, although it has been getting fainter with the passing years. I retired my fencing gear and haven't challenged anyone to a duel, since.

I don't remember what happened to Bob. He pretty much avoided me at school for fear I would sue him...

En guarde – Swashbuckling with my friend John (GK Drawing)

At my 14th birthday party, my left cheek showing where I caught my first fastball (Author's archives)

We switched to Badminton when Baseball didn't work out – From left to right, Leslie Kanyuk, Frank Patty Jr. in the back, Leslie Sandor, kneeling and yours truly holding the other racket (Author's archives)

Gizella B. and Cica Bene along with me and bruised cheek (Author's archives)

33

PUT UP YOUR DUKES!

As if adventure in fencing hadn't thought me a lesson, I almost became a boxer; as I said, almost. One of the many student-athletes who shared one of our meals was an Olympic gold medal boxer.

Almost the minute I was introduced to him, he told me I'd make a good boxer. Sound familiar? By then, my right hand completely healed, except for the little scar. "You're about the right size for a light-middle-light weight and you have hands that look good enough to be a boxer," he said and he had me jab a few times into his open palms and said that I hit pretty good. He then promised that the next time he came by, he would bring some gloves and show me some moves.

"Here I go again," I told myself, "first fencing, now boxing; what next?

He did come for dinner the following Saturday afternoon. He got there early enough that we would have time for a demonstration, right there in our living room. My dad even moved the coffee table out of the way so that we would have plenty of room. I remember all the details. His name was Pali (Pauli).

Pali demonstrated his perfect stance and then proceeded to dance around our living room ever so smoothly, almost like a ballet dancer doing Madame Butterfly, jabbing and punching this way and that, showing me moves I had only seen on the old black and white. Then he said, "Put on the extra set of gloves I brought and let's dance a little", which I thought at the time was a strange expression for what was about to happen.

"Remember how you showed me your jabs the last time I was here," he said. "Do the same moves but try to actually hit me."

So, I tried; tried is the operative word.

Of course, he was able to fend off all my jabs and as I had no experience at all, and I was telegraphing every one of my moves. Now, I was about fifteen and he was way older, around twenty-seven. "Pretty quick for an old guy," I thought.

"You have to be less obvious about what you intend to do next," he said. So, he showed how to feign, to fool your opponent. At first, we were going at it rather slowly. My mother in the kitchen was banging her pots and pans to show disapproval of our little experiment, but we kept at it nonetheless.

"Show me your defense," he said at one point. Then, he started to jab and upper-cut, throwing punches at my defense and told me to counter-punch; which I thought I was doing. We were just warming up and no furniture had been overturned nor damaged to this point. Dad was watching very closely and clapped and cheered at my attempts. This of course caused more cookware clanging in the kitchen.

I was fairing rather well until suddenly I got distracted by something; probably the clanging in the kitchen followed by some unkind words. And even though Pali was obviously holding back, I unfortunately zigged when I should have zagged and his right-hand glove connected with my proboscis; that's nose for youze dat don't know proper English. I saw stars and almost fell on my ki-ester. I just sunk down into an old stuffed chair wiping the trickle of blood emanating from my nose, with my gloved hand.

"I knew something like this would happen," my mother observed rather loudly from the kitchen door.

"Leave it alone Maria," my father said. "He's a big boy. This isn't the last time he'll have a bloody nose"; oh really?

Pauli was very apologetic. I was too proud to cry. Hell, I was embarrassed. We shook hands nonetheless and ate dinner. Pali said he'd be back in a week or so and show me how to avoid getting a bloody nose. When he left, I told my father "I don't think I'm cut out for boxing. I like my nose the way it looks; thank you very much."

Pali came for dinner the following Saturday.

Much earlier, I had left to go to the movies with my buddies.

34

GORGEOUS GEORGE, NOT

In 1960, I took up wrestling, my first year at Oakland Junior College (OJC). The coach's name was Mr. Chapelle. He had been a wrestler himself and for being in his fifties, he still looked to be in tremendous shape.

I now have to backtrack to our old Saturday dinners and the college guys who were our guests. One of them was a gold medal wrestler by the name of Joe Vastag. I was still going to junior high when I had first met him and was still at that underdeveloped stage where I was a bit chubby and my muscle growth was unnoticeable. "When you get a little older," Joe had said, "I'll teach you how to wrestle".

"Yes sir," I had said, "thank you sir." I was still very shy. This happened quite a bit before I got introduced to Boxing. Wrestling might be fun, I thought. I had seen Gorgeous George on the tube dismantling the Crazy Sheik. Maybe I could be the next George of some kind.

Then, Joe stopped coming. We had heard that while he was attending Oakland Junior College, he had been drafted and as a result was unable to compete in the 1960 Olympics, on the US team. It was about three years later that he resurfaced and finally looked us up. By then, you guessed it I was attending OJC. Not only that but I was actually signed up for wrestling.

When I told Joe about it, he said"Chapelle? He was my coach three years ago. He's a good coach and actually, he's still a pretty good wrestler himself."

"We've got some matches coming up against Contra Costa Junior College," I told him.

"That's great! Why don't you come with me to the Olympic

Club in San Francisco? We can practice together. I'll show you some moves your opponents have probably never seen".

By this time of course, I had grown almost six inches and had developed some reasonably good muscle definition. So, naturally I said "yea, why not". I was feeling confident, even a bit cocky. I weighed in at one hundred and seventy-eight pounds, which in those days put me in the Heavy Weight category in college wrestling. The limit was actually a hundred and seventy-six and I could never get under that. That meant that on more than one occasion, the guys I had to wrestle weighed in at over two hundred pounds. I actually wrestled and bested the Oakland City Champion, who was on my team, weighing in at two hundred and fifty pounds. Certainly, I could whip Joe Vastag at one hundred and sixty-four pounds; I was certain.

Joe picked me up in his car and we drove to the Olympic Club in San Francisco where he introduced me to several other amateur wrestlers, several from other countries. We sparred for over an hour. In that time, I couldn't even get him down though he tossed me around like a bag of dirty laundry. I was not able to slip any of his holds though he did complement me on my effort. We did this a couple more times and the only thing I can say is that I learned a lot from Joe. On one occasion, I saw him wrestle one of those professional wrestlers I had only seen on TV. He had muscular bulges all over him. He could even flex his earlobes. He had long blond hair and wore leopard print leotards. I can't remember his name though I can still see his haughty face.

Joe Vastag flipped this guy every which way but loose.

As a result of all these sessions with Joe, I did become a better wrestler and was able to dispatch the two-hundred-and-fifty-pound all-city champion on my junior college team.

I kept on wrestling until I decided that I wanted to play on the football team, in the fall of my second year at Oakland Junior College. This would have been my only chance to play as I would be leaving the following spring.

I had always loved football at OJC. I joined the Rally Committee so that I could attend all the games. My last year there, I talked to the coach and asked if I could join. He told me that I could try out and if I succeeded, I would be on the team. At the end of spring, he and his staff held tryouts. Because this was a JC, most guys were only able to play for two years before moving on to a four-year college or joining the workforce. So, I had a good chance to get on the team.

In the spring semester, we played flag-football after school, of course, there was no contact, unless it was incidental. I had done rather well as a halfback. Way back then, the names of position players hadn't yet evolved to the designations in use today, where just about every position is a unique one and everybody seems to have a specialty. So, I was just one of several plain old halfbacks.

Following the conclusion of flag-football, all the players went back to wrestling, as did I. Not too far down the road, we had a sort of an informal, invitational meet with our sister campus in Downtown Oakland. I beat my opponent by just one point. But hey, a win is a win.

As I said earlier, I desperately tried to get below 176 pounds, so that I could wrestle guys closer to my weight. I asked our family doctor, Dr. Watts to put me on some sort of regimen to help me lose weight. Nothing seemed to work. I just liked food too much.

I was totally at a loss when both my wrestling and football careers came to an end, not at the hands of a much larger guy then me, but one quite a bit smaller. I had become friends with this black kid who wrestled in the 146-pound category. Usually in practice, we tried to match up with someone close to our own weight class. This particular day, due to some absentees, my buddy and me, were the odd men out. So, he and I began to practice our moves and wrestle around. We were rather complimentary of one another's abilities as we managed to elude any serious disadvantages. The big gym was laid out with several large squares of wrestling mats and every two-man tandem got enough time for three three-minute rounds.

Closing in on our third round, my friend locked a figure-four hold around my right knee in an attempted take-down. He had me really good. Under normal circumstances, I could have slipped the hold and toss him like nothing. Unfortunately for me, my right foot got entangled in the mat cover which had gotten loose at the corner and I was unable to pull my foot out of his hold.

He went down, firmly clamping my right knee. I heard a big pop. As a matter of fact, the kids on the next mat heard the big pop. Next thing I know, I'm lying on the mat, writhing in pain. When I finally sat up to look at my knee, it had swollen to the size of a head of cabbage.

Thus, came to an end my chance at wrestling on TV with the likes of Gorgeous George, the Mad Sheik and other greats of Professional Wrestling Dom as well as any chance of running for a touchdown for the 49ers. The Raiders hadn't moved to Oakland, yet.

I was in nowheresville daddy-o!

• • •

To complicate my life even further, my Hungarian friends talked me into joining the Hungarian Folk Dance Club of San Francisco, under the tutelage of Lajos Nemeth, a professional dancer and dance instructor from Hungary. Lajos (Louie to his friends) escaped during the 1956 Hungarian Revolt and organized a rather good dance group in Innsbruck, Austria with a very respectable record of performances. He convinced my mother that it would do me good to join this group.

No mention had been made of my two left feet or the extra weight I was carrying, nor the fact that up to this point, I wasn't crazy about dancing in general. Finally, I gave in. My career lasted only six or seven years as our group performed at various international festivals, in Golden Gate Park, at the Alameda Naval Base, at Napa Valley wineries, at the Berkeley Community Theater, at the UC Berkeley Greek Theater and a number of other venues, with some of our performances actually being shown on Channel Five TV, from San Francisco, to the cheer of thousands...

The reason for bringing up my short career in the world of Hungarian dancing is that, my buddies on the wrestling team found this out and the jokes about tutus never ceased. Now, I obviously didn't wear a tutu, but, I as all of the other male dancers had to wear tight black pants: OK, black tights!

It did take a few performances until I felt comfortable, wearing those black tights. I always thought, they made my caboose look a lot bigger than it really was. Some of the girls said, it made me look slimmer...

In our Hungarian National costumes at the Golden Gate Park Music Concourse for an August 20th celebration. Rose Szanto (my dance partner) is in the middle between Karel Bemelmans on her left and me on her right, following our performance.

At an International Festival in Berkeley, as a member the Hungarian Folk Dance Club of San Francisco, Magdi (Maggie) Szelle and I are dancing a number choreographed by Lajos Nemeth.

35

HIS OWN BOSS

My father was a very determined man. Two days after landing at the Ferry Terminal in San Francisco, he had found work. We stayed with the Egrys, our sponsors for eight days. We had known both Victor and his wife Elisabeth from Schmitzberg Lager back in our refugee days in Austria. Victor had married Elisabeth after we had already moved away to France. Their baby girl Victoria, Vikki to everybody, was born in Austria, I believe. Anyway, we were to stay with them until my father had a permanent job and could afford rent. You see back then, the US government required that a sponsor would be responsible for living quarters and sustenance for their charge guaranteed for at least three months, lest your guests would be returned to their country of origin.

Well, my dad did not want to have to impose on Victor and his family any longer than absolutely necessary.

Like I said, two days after we arrived, he had a job waiting for him around the Port of Oakland, where a Hungarian guy who assembled and repaired wooden shipping pallets, hired him immediately, knowing full well that if a full-time job came along, he would probably leave. Meanwhile, Bert got a job as a mechanic, in Berkeley. He also got a place to live within a week.

Through the Hungarian grapevine, the word reached us that a custodial position would be opening up at the end of the month, at Trinity Methodist Church in Berkeley. The man occupying the position at the time was going to be going into business for himself and needed a replacement. My dad jumped at the opportunity mainly because, he was going to be his own boss, answering only to the church secretary and the minister. Another benefit of the position was that my mother would be able to make some extra cash by working in the kitchen, doing the dishes and cleanup after Sunday socials and other gatherings. Right from the get go, it also got me into the act; translator of all things dietary, including the operation of the monstrous dishwashing machine.

However, the best part of the whole deal was, an apartment came along with the job, right underneath the church; two bedrooms, a small dining area, a rather nicely equipped kitchen and a full bathroom. This space was twice as large as any of the other places we had lived in, anywhere before.

There were some drawbacks. There would be no alcoholic beverage consumption on church property and no smoking. We would also have to refrain from using profane language. Since neither of my parents spoke English, that would not be a problem. And of course, nobody at the church understood Hungarian.

You have to understand, the rule was, no alcohol consumption was permitted under the edicts of the Wesleyan belief. For instance, in communions, Methodists used red grape juice in place of wine. It also meant that all drinking would have to be done discreetly or away from the church, since neither Calvinists nor Catholics were forbidden from imbibing.

So here was my old man; he had been accounting supervisor at a major manufacturer in Budapest, running an accounting office of some twenty employees, who had over the previous several years been forced by circumstances to work in coal mines in Austria and then in France. He had been working at a foundry for the last five years or so of our stay in Algrange and was now going to be the custodian at a church, and yet he loved it.

He thoroughly enjoyed the whole idea of the freedom that this country offered and now he was in charge of his future. All he had to do was get the job done. And, he was the kind of guy who took all challenges head-on.

People at the church loved him because they soon realized that he was obviously an educated and cultured individual and yet was willing to bust butt, doing a menial yet physical job to the best of his ability. I believe what they admired most was that he never complained about this or that being too tough or too much to handle.

He just did it.

• • •

As I mentioned earlier, I was thrilled that we got to live in Berkeley. I got to rampage up and down Strawberry Creek in the middle of the U.C. Campus and to later discover that there actually was a big park with a lake up beyond the Berkeley Hills called Tilden Park, where I got a glimpse of the California Mule Deer, occasional raccoons and even foxes. I was told to be aware of mountain lions, though I never encountered one.

What I hadn't expected was to run into the biggest rat this side of New York City, right there at Trinity Church of all places; right under the stairs which led to a concrete path bisecting two narrow flower beds between the two main buildings.

One early Saturday morning, my father had asked me to help him with some of the yard work that had required us to take the walkway between the buildings to get to the stairs leading to the main courtyard when we saw the brownish gray, furry backside and foot and a half long tail of an enormous rat; in fact, the biggest rat I had ever seen. My father let loose an expletive, luckily in Hungarian, as we were both taken aback.

"My God," he said. "That's the biggest @$#% effing rat I've ever seen!"

"Do you think we should catch it before it bites somebody?" I asked, standing way behind him and hoping he would say no.

"Get a big cardboard box and put on some gloves," dad replied, "and a big broom."

I went and got a big box and a couple brooms from the basement supply room and returned to the stairwell, wearing work gloves. Of course, by then, our pal had firmly squeezed itself in behind some fuchsia bushes and the wall of the stairwell. It was determined not let itself be captured. The more I tried to coax it into the cardboard box with the broom the more it hissed and bared its teeth at me. My father was also wearing heavy work gloves. As he tried to get close enough to the angry creature to grab him from behind the neck. It reared and hissed at his attempt and then bit my dad's gloved finger. My dad finally just backed away.

We left the brooms and the box right there and went up to the church office to ask the secretary, interestingly enough, named Wanda, what to do. And the reason that I used the qualifier 'interestingly enough 'is because one my dad's favorite novels was entitled Wanda. Wanda von Szalras was the heroine of the above titled **Wanda**, the 1883 novel and stage play written by Ouida which was the pseudonym of author Maria Louise Ramé. Sorry, I didn't mean to show off my literary knowledge here and stray from the main topic; well maybe.

In addition, Wanda the church secretary was in fact a rather handsome older woman. Even at fourteen, I could appreciate this…

As my father spoke animatedly, I tried to translate our encounter of a few minutes prior as best as I could, leaving out all of my dad's expletives. We both watched as Wanda's face lit up in a wide grin as she held up her hand in a stop sign and proceeded to give us a brief explanation of what we had actually seen.

"It is not a big rat, please tell your father," she said. "It is called an Opossum. Many times, they cross over Bancroft Street from the U.C. Campus at night and wander into our yard and hide in the bushes. They are mostly harmless unless you get your hands close to their snout; then they are quite capable of biting you."

"Tell her I know that part," my father said, holding up his gloved finger. Luckily, the Possum didn't draw blood, but Wanda wanted to look at my father's finger anyway.

"Next time you see one," Wanda continued, "just leave them alone. They will find their way back to the UC campus and the creek".

And that's how we discovered that although Possums might look like big rats, they are in fact not; and of course, we were also told that in parts of the United States, they are actually eaten. Four years after my dad passed away, Granny Clampett came on, in the

Beverly Hillbillies in a weekly tribute to hillbilly Haute cuisine to tell us how she had the dadgummest, best recipe for Possum stew this side of the Ozarks. It's one of the few recipes I never aspired at trying.

Well there you have it; and that's how I first got introduced to the California Possum over fifty years ago.

My dad, sitting on the back steps of Trinity Methodist Church, in 1957 (GK Photo)

36

KITCHEN MAGICIAN

Anyuka (my mother), Maria Kapus, was born Maria Pelikán on May 18, 1902 in Mezőtúr, Hungary. Over the years, she told me a lot of stories about her early life in Hungary as well. Unfortunately, I was too busy being a teenager in high school. I knew everything there was to know and I didn't listen too well, to my regret. I bet my two daughters (who came along much later) probably know more about their grandmother than maybe even I, as she spent a lot of her time with them.

• • •

There is one thing and this is a very important thing, because it kept me from starving when I was single and that was, my mother was the best cook ever! That's one of her talents that truly stood out. As a matter of fact, it had on occasion gotten me into trouble because when I was a youngster, I had this tendency to compare the cooking of anyone taking care of me, to my mother's; and that didn't sit too well with some of her friends that had occasion to feed me.

"If you want food in your mouth," she would say, "swallow your opinion. Otherwise, you'll stay hungry."

She told me early on about how she had moved from Mezőtúr to Budapest and started working in a cafeteria style restaurant which she eventually became the owner of and ran for a number of years in the thirties and forties. As a result, she was able to cook for four people or four hundred; it also meant that a lot of unattached, refugee guys gravitated to our kitchen and were willing to pay for home cooked meals; in all the locales, we made a stop.

She had a great number of her recipes hand written on scraps of paper that she kept over the years which are now in the possession of my daughters.

I can remember almost every dish she ever cooked, and have had success in recreating many of them over the years. I used to proudly tell my buddies that my mother could cook up beans a hundred different ways. But she could also whip up a multitude of other mouthwatering Hungarian dishes, many times with a meagerness of ingredients. For instance, she would make stuffed cabbage or stuffed bell peppers where the stuffing was made up of ground meat and rice. Many a times, there was very little meat and lot more rice, yet it tasted delicious because of her clever use of spices and herbs. Cream of green beans with ham hock a lot of times was just old hock for flavor and not a lot of ham.

One of my favorite dishes was Sóska Főzelék or creamed sorrel, which was not unlike creamed spinach, except it had a nice tangy flavor and it was free. It grew practically all over the place and at the time, nobody else picked it. You could even eat it raw. Like I said when you were short on Francs, creamed sorrel tasted delicious and you could eat all you wanted…

As things got better, she could fry up a very tasty Wiener schnitzel with sweet and sour red cabbage from an old Budapest recipe of hers; which was probably what got my father to return time after time, after time to her restaurant.

My mother was the 'Kitchen Magician'. Some of her best dishes were: Hungarian Goulash which she could also make into a soup with Csipetke (spaetzli), Stuffed Kohlrabi, Szekely (Szekler) Cabbage, Hungarian Fried Chicken, Stuffed Chicken, Breaded Pork Chops, Wiener Schnitzel (breaded veal cutlets) and Chicken Paprikash. She could also whip up a delicious Dobosh Tort, a delicious twelve-layer cake she sometimes actually made with twelve crepes. She could whip up poppy seed and walnut rolls, bacon Pogácsas, Lángos which was fried bread rubbed with garlic with a sprinkling of salt that my dad and the other old guys playing cards just loved to munch on with a glass of red wine. She just had too many recipes to list here. I could probably write a whole book about her cooking.

Now if you think that all my mother could do was cook, you got another one coming. Back in Refugee Camp days, she not only altered old clothes that were given to us but many times out of what was left over from her alterations, she would sew me shirts and trousers and even dresses for herself. As I mentioned earlier in the book, she would sew curtains from parachutes the military gave us, not only for our unit but for others who didn't know how to use the old Singer sewing machine.

I am not exaggerating when I tell you that my mother was a hard worker, which is why in my eyes she accomplished so much. All those very lean years, she managed to feed us well from practically nothing. When we got to the states and my father passed away, she kept his job as church custodian at the Trinity Methodist Church in Berkeley, until the year before she passed away. Even her final year in the church's employ, she wasn't able to comprehend that they would ask her to step down and retire.

"I am only eighty years old, I don't want to retire," she told the church secretary in the best English she could.

Those years after my father's death, she did her best to keep me on the straight and narrow, and most of the time she succeeded with little help from me. As people often noted, I was a good but often willful child. But that's mostly because they didn't know me really well. I was actually a know-it-all and stubborn; and I couldn't hide it…

I wish I could remember more of those tales of the days before I came along, but hard as I try, the memories are vague and all the photographs both mother and father left behind don't give much details of where and when they were taken and what the occasion was.

When she was much younger, my mother would recount events that happened when I was still too young to make any sense of them. I just wish she could have told me more; or that I would have paid closer attention.

My mother at 13, in 1917 (Author's archives)

My mother from a 1939 Hungarian Government I/D photo (GK drawing)

ADDRESS REPORTS

You are required by law to notify the Attorney General of your current address each year during the month of January, and to furnish notification of change of address within 10 days from the date of such change. A penalty is provided for failure to do so. Forms may be obtained from any post office. Address reports, applications or letters to the Immigration and Naturalization Service, should include the "A" number shown on the other side.

BORDER CROSSING CARD

This card will be honored for border crossing purposes on condition that the rightful holder is returning to the United States from a temporary visit to Canada or Mexico, not exceeding 6 months, and is not subject to exclusion under any provision of the immigration laws.

My mother's Green Card/Photograph side (Author's archives)

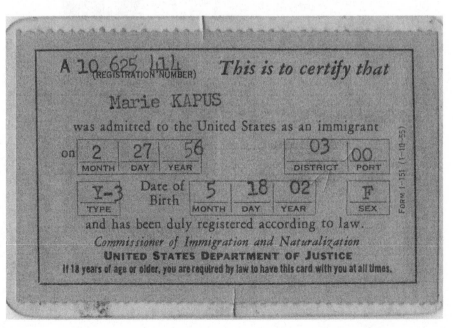

A 10 625 414 (REGISTRATION NUMBER) *This is to certify that*

Marie KAPUS

was admitted to the United States as an immigrant

on	2	27	56		03	00
	MONTH	DAY	YEAR		DISTRICT	PORT

Y-3	Date of Birth	5	18	02		F
TYPE		MONTH	DAY	YEAR		SEX

FORM I-151 (1-10-55)

and has been duly registered according to law.

Commissioner of Immigration and Naturalization

UNITED STATES DEPARTMENT OF JUSTICE

If 18 years of age or older, you are required by law to have this card with you at all times.

My mother's Green Card/Identification side (Author's archives)

My mother in her new kitchen in Berkeley, in 1956 (GK Photo)

37

END OF THE LINE

My dad did this job he loved for about two and a half years, when he suddenly fell ill. That's when everybody started to get worried, including my mother and me. We took him to a physician of Hungarian descent by the name Fazekas, you know, the one who stitched up my fencing injury. After a number of tests, he diagnosed my father having psoriasis of the liver.

The good doctor contacted the U.C. Medical Center in San Francisco and got my father admitted as he knew that they were always working on experimental treatments for a number of diseases. They accepted him for treatment and we were to take him over for admittance within a matter of a few days as soon as a bed would become available.

At his very last meal at home, he had asked my mother for a glass of red wine. She told him the doctor had given her very specific instructions to not give him any alcoholic beverages because it might further exacerbate his condition. It depressed my father to no end. I always had this feeling that he was seeing the road coming to an end.

"What is there left to live for when you can't even have a (expletive) glass of wine?" he cried. A week later he would be dead. His favorite Hungarian saying was: A good pipe, a good Brandy and a good woman make for a happy man.

We visited him at the U.C. Medical Center every chance we had. Unfortunately, we had to depend on Victor (Egry) or Frank (Zegrean) for a ride to get there as we weren't very familiar with buses in San Francisco and neither of us could drive. He had tubes and monitors attached to him and tried to be in good spirits when we came but the doctors told us that there really was no cure for his condition at this late stage and the only thing they could do was to keep him comfortable and pain-free.

On our very last visit a couple days later, just about all his friends were there but he couldn't recognize either my mother or I, or any of them, except this one guy name Joe Ficzere. He had been a graduate of the Franz Liszt Music Academy in Budapest and a concert pianist. He and his parents had escaped during the revolt of 1956 and made it to San Francisco where he became a lounge pianist in one of the big hotels. My dad had liked the whole family and had them over to our house, especially Joe. He had also wanted me to play the piano, just like Joe. Joe had naturally gone to visit my dad a couple times as he lived nearby in the city and at his last conscious moment, apparently, Joe had been the last person he had recognized.

When we finally got home, my mother was totally devastated at the fact that my dad couldn't even recognize her. We both had this very strong feeling that the end was near. We just didn't know when. The end came soon enough. At about midnight, the very same day, we got a telephone call asking to speak to my mother. She asked what they wanted. I was told that they could only speak with a grown up.

"My mother doesn't speak or understand English," I told the caller.

"Then get another adult to translate for her," the voice at the other end of the line told me.

"There is nobody else," I insisted. "It's only the two of us."

"How old are you?" the voice asked.

"Sixteen," I replied.

After some hesitation and what appeared to be some talking in the background, the voice spoke into the phone.

"I am sorry to have to tell you that your father died, just a short while ago," the voice told me. After the phone disconnected, I told my mother. It was the sixteenth of November, 1958.

My mother wept, for days. They had been first loves and for-ever…

• • •

Until a couple weeks before his death, my father did his work at the church without missing a beat. Part of his responsibilities was making the rounds every night around ten o'clock or after all church activities had ceased. He would then secure and lock up all the buildings.

As I said before, he had total autonomy. Occasionally, activities ran a little later, like around holidays or weddings; but every single night, the rounds were made. Flashlight in hand, he usually took about an hour to complete the task.

He walked every inch of the grounds and secured every window and locked every door. On occasion, if my homework was done and I hadn't fallen asleep in front of the television set, I would accompany him on his rounds, especially on weekend nights. It gave us a chance to talk man to man and to bond.

For two and a half years he followed this routine. He never once ran into any problem, never.

When he got really sick, I took over some of his responsibilities on a temporary basis, until he would get better; including making the ten o'clock nightly rounds. When he died, I took over on a more permanent basis.

Actually, the church had seriously considered hiring a new custodian; which would have meant that my mother not only would have been out of work but we would have been out of a place to live. She convinced them that she could do the work, with my help that is. I had to pretty much agree to take care of the more physical tasks such as mowing the lawns, trimming the greenery, doing some of the watering, running the twenty-four-inch floor polisher over all the areas that needed to shine, and of course keep doing the nightly rounds.

My dad's passing left a giant hole in my life; a hole no one else could ever fill.

38

LIVE CHICKEN

It was the spring of 1959, just a few months after my father's death. I had turned sixteen the previous April. I was a big boy. I was brave and tough, I thought. And, I now had a job.

I was going on the nightly rounds I had inherited from my father. It was a Sunday night, somewhere around ten thirty. I had gotten used to doing my rounds pretty much in the dark. I whistled my way through the dark grounds and hallways. I strolled through the pitch-black sanctuary and chapel. I didn't carry a flashlight like my dad had told me. I was sixteen. I wasn't afraid of anything. I knew everything. I didn't need no stinking flashlight, no siree Bob!

I had taken care of the main church building. I had checked all windows, all bathrooms, side rooms and choir room and locked everything up the way it was supposed to be locked up. Next, I had secured the Chapel on the corner of Dana and Bancroft streets.

The Administration Building was next. The courtyard was dark but couple of hall lights had been left on in the big building. I always started at the back end on the first floor. I locked both the back door and the side door and was working my way down the hall checking in all the classrooms for open windows and taking care of that. I went through the auditorium and the fellowship room. The kitchen was last to secure. There was all the silverware and other culinary devices; and silverware in those days meant money. There were some nice serving trays and other accessories, so I had to make sure that all three doors were in fact secured.

I was whistling my way up the stairs with not a worry on my mind. First stop was the library to the left of the stairs. This was an especially critical room because the back door led to the fire escape, which was attached to a metal plate landing that the fire escape was attached to, and the door was a pain in the butt to keep locked. It faced west and when the folks holding meetings in there got hot, they would swing both doors wide open and then leave it like that when they were done. The lock had to be fixed all the time because it kept getting all banged up. When I was finally done wrestling the two doors secure, I started whistling my way down the hall toward the church office about twenty-five feet away, with three separate doors, one of which went directly into the pastor's office.

Did I mention that it was a Sunday night and dark?

I had my hand on the door knob to the main door, ready to turn it when I let go of it to scratch my nose. My mother had told me about an itchy nose and what it meant but at that moment, the meaning had escaped me.

"When your nose itches, something fishy is going on," she had told me.

So, I grabbed the door knob for a second time, twisted it and started pushing it inward when I felt some resistance, like the lock was jammed or, someone was pushing on the other side. So I pushed harder. This should really have been a clue. The first thing I saw was a shiny fifteen-inch butcher knife in the hand of a ugly, nasty looking guy about half a head taller than me and quite a bit wider at the shoulder. He didn't say anything but grunted, like he had been holding on to the door knob and I had made him let go of it.

"Aaaaaaaaahhhhhh," I let out a yell.

Then, I took off running down the hall like a jackrabbit. I flew down the steps two at a time and out the back door that I had already secured, making a right turn on the sidewalk along Bancroft Avenue in the direction of Telegraph Avenue, screaming at anybody if they had seen a cop. College students were still out all over the place. They thought that I had lost my mind and actually jumped out of my way. Finally, at the corner of Bancroft and Telegraph, a Berkeley Police black and white unit came to a stop to ask what all that hollering was all about.

"Big knife, a big, ugly guy," was all I remember saying.

I was out of breath. They had me sit in their car and we drove back to the church. I followed one of them through the Bancroft door; his big police flashlight turned on. Meanwhile, the other officer with his flashlight on, headed for the main entrance from the courtyard which he found mysteriously unlocked; and I say mysteriously because I clearly remembered having secured it after I had entered the building during my rounds. This also meant that in all likelihood, the big ugly guy with long pig-sticker had long since left the premises.

We all converged on the front stairs while I could hear additional officers entering from the Bancroft door and climbing the stairs at the back of the building. We started up the front stairs and met up with the other two uniforms at the office front door. Of course, the perpetrator had long vanished in the night. The officers deduced that the big, ugly guy had pried the door open, probably with the butcher knife that he had most likely removed from the kitchen; which sure made me feel great. This turkey could have ambushed me in the kitchen, with the big knife. Yikes! Then again, he might have observed my routine, hmm?

They also discovered that he had pried open the drawers of several desks, apparently trying to find the cash box with hopefully the Sunday collections. Unbeknownst to this mastermind criminal, even in those days, in 1958, five or six hundred people attended the services and were unusually generous. They would sometimes collect close to a couple thousand dollars. I know this for a fact as I was often asked to usher and participate in the collection. After the service, the money was counted and sealed in bank deposit bags and usually taken home by the head of the financial committee, leaving only about forty to fifty dollars for petty cash. I realized then that church people weren't dumb. Being aware of this fact, I could have saved the big dummy some effort, if only he would have asked. Then again, back then, forty to fifty dollars was worth a lot more money than now.

After they had made the rounds of all the church grounds and filled out the appropriate report, they walked me back to our little apartment underneath the sanctuary. "Call us anytime you have any problems at the church," they told me. I certainly felt reassured by their presence. Back in those days, the majority of Berkeley Cops were either ex-military from the Korean War or ex-football players. The presence of shapely and diminutive female officers with tight braids and tighter uniforms, was rather rare, and thank goodness for that because I would certainly have been totally embarrassed to get walked to my front door by a shapely, diminutive female officer.

As it was, the following Monday in school, anybody and everybody who read the Berkeley Gazette had heard of my exploit. To add insult to injury, the paper had gotten a hold of my statement from the Berkeley Police Department and had published it verbatim, up to and including my famous parting line to the cops.

"I'd rather be a live chicken than a dead duck!"

It took me several weeks to live down the quacking humiliation, although mostly in jest. I was at a point where I wanted to run into this grubby bum so I could have given him what for, yeah!

But I'm glad I didn't...

39

HIGH SCHOOL DAZE

What can I tell you about my high school years? It went by so fast that I almost missed it the day after graduation.

As I walked across the stage of the Big Theater at Berkeley High to pick up my diploma from the hands of Principal J. Elwin LeTendre, it seemed that it had barely been but a few months since I had first stepped onto the quad of what was at the time, one of the best high schools in the country. Berkeley High School had actually just received the 18th Annual Bellamy Flag Award for being the best representative high school in the State of California.

There were just about six hundred and thirty boys and girls in my graduating class; making it the largest class ever to graduate from there. In addition, Principal LeTendre was retiring with this, his last graduating class. He had been principal at Berkeley High since the start of World War II.

Berkeley High was considered such an excellent school at the time, that graduating seniors were accepted at U.C. Berkeley without any extra entrance requirements; with of course the right GPA. I unfortunately didn't have the grades necessary and hence I opted, like I had a lot of options, for Oakland Junior College, now called Merritt College. I hate to have to admit this but I really hadn't seriously thought about going to college and the choice thing kind of snuck up on me; but of course, I wasn't the only one going to J.C...

I also have to admit that I was a pretty average student who occasionally excelled in a couple things such as art and languages, and of course French. My mother naturally wanted me to be a doctor or a lawyer, maybe even an engineer. I wanted to be an artist. And of course, I didn't get a lot of support from her or any of the family friends. Some of the ladies from the Trinity (Methodist Church) Women's Club however encouraged me and had even offered to get me a scholarship to the California College of Arts and Crafts in Oakland, after high school graduation, if I had wanted it. They of course recognized that I did have some talent worth pursuing. I was forced to turn down their generous offer with much regret and many thanks. In retrospect, I wish I hadn't.

(Ever since my high school days, I had done some freelance art work of one sort or another. As a matter of fact, I still do.)

You should be able to decide what to do with your life, unless of course you want to be a hermit and move into some cave on the side of a distant mountain and just meditate.

As I said above, I was a pretty average student in high school. My father dying two years earlier probably had something to do with that. He had been my role model. I took all the classes that I had to, to graduate. My counselor pretty much told me that if I got decent grades, but not good enough to go to Cal Berkeley, I would however be able to attend one of the local junior colleges, which is exactly where I ended up. In retrospect, I have to say that, had my father been alive, his counsel and tight reigns might have encouraged me to aspire toward higher goals. My mother probably understood and although she pushed, I convinced her that after all, I was going to college…

Languages had always been my forte and I of course aced French, and, why wouldn't I? German was a little harder because I had never really attended any full classes in Austria though I spoke it fairly well with the kids; but that didn't get me any good grades. I took Russian, my last year and did sufficiently well to get a C. My father had encouraged me before he died to learn the language of our enemy (Soviet Union) "Because, if you know their language, they can never defeat you," he would say. Thank God, we never had to put his axiom to a test here in the US. Let's just say that speaking foreign languages was my forte; not so much grammar and composition.

I did average work in mathematics. Algebra was a little harder. I actually got a D for the first semester class and had to repeat it;

which I didn't mind since Miss Newhall (Not her real name) was the Algebra teacher. She was all of twenty-three or four when I got into her class and soon discovered that almost the whole class was made up of boys. Everyone of course knew that she was a real looker which was why all the boys rushed to sign up for her classes. We actually competed to see how many of us could sit in the front row. The few girls who did manage to get in our class, all thought that we were all pretty pathetic losers. On the other hand, most of the girls signed up for the class given by a young studdly literature teacher who might have equaled Miss Newhall in terms of watchability...

Needless to say, I was not greatly disappointed when I had to take the class over and then be able to advance to the second semester class; also with Miss Newhall.

Unfortunately, midway that last semester, Miss Newhall announced that she was getting married that summer and become Mrs. Something-or-other. Our love affair with the pretty Algebra teacher was all over with; although some of us conspiracy theorists theorized that she hadn't actually gotten married but was just claiming it to turn the heat down, so to speak...

Back then, having a crush on one of your teachers was not considered a crime or even some social ill like today; because nothing ever came of it.

• • •

At Berkeley High, I also met my lifelong buddy, Karel Bemelmans, who had come over from Holland with his parents. The story of how we met may differ somewhat, depending on which one of us you ask.

My version has to do with me sitting in the cafeteria for lunch with some classmates, when this blonde, curly haired kid came over and asked if I was a foreigner. I was taken aback by the fact that he had the gull to ask me if I was a foreigner when he in fact had a heavy Germanic sounding accent.

"Why would you think I'm a foreigner," I asked, "since you

sound more like you're not from here yourself."

He looked at me kind of puzzled. "Those guys over there," he said indicating some kids on the other side of the cafeteria, "they said you came from somewhere in Europe."

"Yeah," I replied, "we moved over here from France, a few years ago."

"Well, you don't even have any accent," he said, still looking puzzled "it's hard to believe you're from France."

Although somewhat awkwardly, we did get introduced in the tenth grade and we have been friends ever since. Even though, we were enrolled in a somewhat different curriculum, we would get together on occasion; at lunch or for extracurricular soccer. After a while, he simply disappeared and didn't reappear until 1961. I was already attending Oakland Junior College when I found out that he had actually returned to Holland to finish high school there. It's at Oakland Junior College that we actually started hanging out together.

Now if you asked Karel, I am almost certain that he would have a different version of these events.

• • •

There was this really nice girl in one of my study classes in the eleventh grade. I really liked her and asked her if she would go out with me for one of our senior social events; a dance in the cafeteria or something. She was sorry but wouldn't be home that particular weekend but if I'd ask her any time after that, for any other event, she would be more than happy to go with me.

My main reason for bringing up this brief episode of my life is because the girl's last name was Ickes. I didn't find this out until sometime later that she had a rather famous family lineage. She was the granddaughter of Harold L. Ickes.

In case you didn't know as I didn't know at the time, Harold LeClair Ickes served as United States Secretary of the Interior for 13 years, from 1933 to 1946. He was responsible for helping President Franklin D. Roosevelt implement his "New Deal". Of course, being turned down by the young lady, my *new deal* was, asking a different girl to that particular senior shindig. She on the other hand, ended up going to the Senior Picnic with another guy.

I went to the same event with yet another girl. Her name was Helen and she was Chinese-American. We had a great time at the picnic which took place at some lake down past Livermore. We got along so well that I thought I would ask her to our Senior Ball. I saw her in the hall, around school all the time. She liked holding hands and was a very sweet girl. Did I mention that she was a very pretty girl as well and I was surprised that she took so well to me?

Of course, as the saying goes, all good things must come to an end.

This relationship came to an end abruptly. One of my buddies, Mike, advised me that people were not looking kindly on my hanging around with a Chinese chick. He recommended that I break it off with Helen immediately. As inexperienced as I was in the ways of social and cultural mores of the time, I listened to him and after making up all sorts of excuses; I let her down as gently and reasonably as I could. I know that my friend had meant well at the time, but I didn't like the fact that an outside force had interfered with a very personal matter.

I wasn't very happy with myself, my friend and the intolerant boobs that had caused me to react in such a stupid fashion. Bottom line, I wasn't happy with what I had done. Mostly, I didn't understand the intolerance and undercurrent of prejudice that all of a sudden confronted me and interfered with my social pursuits.

This also meant that I was faced with a new conundrum. The Senior Ball was but a couple weeks away and there were no potential dates falling into my lap.

So, another girl that I had met earlier came into the picture. Her name was Gizella B., and she was an acquaintance from the Hungarian community. I had always thought that she was cute and all but she was two whole years younger than me. She had also never really shown much interest in me. Hence the reason why I had not asked her first. I feared rejection.

I finally conjured up enough courage and decided to call her in plenty of time to allow her to make a decision on being my Senior Ball date. While on the phone, I could hear her asking her mother and then saying she'd love to. Did I also mention that her mother really liked me which might have put the dampers on this relationship, however, it did help me seal the deal? I was always considered a reasonably good kid but I wanted to be perceived as having an edge, you know a bad boy side, by the girls anyway. I just could never pull it off very successfully. Anyway, we went to the big affair together with my buddy Robert and his date; mostly because Robert had a car and I didn't, yet.

Not having a car might have been one of the reasons why I struck out with most of the young ladies. They didn't want to have to walk to 'Mel's drive-in' or the movies; which is what I had thought.

After the Senior Ball, I dated Gizella for a while but there didn't seem to have been any mutual interest at the time. Even though, by then, I had gotten my first car. The chemistry just didn't seem to be there until a couple years later when we both came to the realization that it was unfortunately too late. By the time she told me that she had always liked me and all she wanted was for me to be a little more assertive and to put a little more effort into the pursuit, I was already committed to yet another relationship. That boat had sailed and for the longest time, it ate at me.

And now, it would be a great idea to drop this topic altogether right here.

My graduation photo – June 1956 (Author's archives)

Senior Ball at Claremont Hotel in Berkeley, CA, with Gizella B, in June 1960 (Author's archives)

40

AU CLAIRE DE LA LOON

Now my buddy Karel and I had an interestingly contentious relationship throughout the few months I saw him at Berkeley High and for that matter even later on as we hung around in junior college, after he had returned from Holland. We were best of friends, yet we competed for just about anything and everything; like who was the best wrestler or the best runner. Who was the smartest, the cleverest? And of course, who could get the next girl? One girl in particular comes to mind. She was this tall and skinny redhead by the name of well let's just call her Claire; because that was her name. Her red hair was cut rather short, sort of page-boy style. Her eyes were piercing, steel blue-grey. She had freckly pink cheeks and rather nice, red lips, giving her a very high *pucker factor*. As I said, besides those kissable lips, there wasn't much to her, yet for some reason both Karel and I got caught in her web.

We both knew her from Berkeley High where for some reason she was always seen dating guys much shorter than her; maybe because most guys *were* shorter than her, including Karel and yours truly. For a while, she dated this particular kid who considered himself a real tough guy. He was at least a full head shorter than her; maybe even shorter. Their relationship lasted for about a year when for some reason, she broke up with him; maybe the pain in her neck for having to constantly bend down to kiss him on top of his head?

I had all but forgotten about her after graduation until Karel got me a job at Herrick Memorial Hospital sometime in 1961, while we were attending Oakland Junior College. Well actually, Karel's mother helped getting me that job. Soon after I started working there, who but Claire showed up one day, hairnet and all, as the new hire in the Dietary Department; in other words, the kitchen. The three of us, Karel, Claire and I fast became buddies. She would kid around with both of us, sending what I perceived as mixed messages.

"She must like me," I thought. "Maybe I should ask her out." This, even though I was actually a couple of inches shorter than her. Since Karel was an inch taller than me, he was only one inch shorter than her.

"So, Claire" I said one day during our break, "Watcha doing this evening?"

"Karel and I are going to the movies after work", was her surprising reply.

"That weasel," I thought. "He has aced me out again."

"You're welcome to come along," she continued and for some inexplicable reason, I said "sure!"

I'd never watched Karel make out, so I suppose what went on during the movie might have qualified as such. While I was actually trying to focus in on the plot, there was a lot of whispering and giggling going on next to me. Even Claire giggled. I was about to get up and leave the theater but I remembered we were to walk over to Mel's for burgers after the show, so I endured. I put my right hand up next to my face as a blinder so that I wouldn't be distracted by silly activity. I was also hungry.

The next time she asked, I declined with some clever excuse. After that, I wasn't asked any more, thank God.

Then one day, the love birds had a spat and a couple days later as things hadn't gotten worked out, Claire asked if I wanted to go to the movies with her. Naturally, I asked "Is it OK with Karel?"

"We are not speaking at the moment," She replied.

So, I asked Karel for his thoughts on the situation. "I don't really care," was his unemotional response, "Do what you want"

"Very mature," I thought. I also have to say, most of Karel's replies were generally matter of fact. He always treated me as a somewhat mentally challenged little buddy. Oy vey!

Somewhat reluctantly, I agreed to go to the movies with Claire.

I'm certain she thought she was doing me a great, big favor. During the movie, she allowed me to put my arm around her shoulder, you know, to have the appearance of a date. But, there was no smooching; not even much whispering. She mostly told me to be quiet. I wasn't at all certain if she was missing Karel or I'd forgotten to brush my teeth. I was actually bored to tears. What with a movie without John Wayne in it and a girl averse to smooching or even whispering, I was ready to put the kybosh on this less than exciting date.

After our burger and shake at Mel's Drive-in on Shattuck Avenue, she finally granted me a goodnight kiss; by the way, this was the only saliva exchange between Claire and yours truly. She puckered up with two big buck teeth blocking entry to the warmer inner sanctum of her mouth. It was like kissing a blowfish. After that, I avoided dating Claire with one excuse or another and perhaps I had finally discovered why she and Karel had called it quits.

Soon after, Claire moved on to other endeavors and I never, ever saw her again. Karel and I have remained friends to this day.

If you should ask Karel about these events, I am certain he will have a totally different memory of what had transpired.

• • •

During the summer before my last year at Berkeley High, I got involved in assisting this guy named Frank Patty Jr., with his water safety class at the Berkeley High swimming pool. What I didn't realize when he had first asked me was that all the students he was teaching, were from California School for the Deaf and Mute which back in 1959 was located above the U.C. Campus at the foot of the Berkeley Hills.

This is how I got to meet a lot of great kids that I had to learn to communicate with all over again and gained a lot of respect for.

In the process of assisting with the water safety class, I learned a bit of sign language since that was the only way to communicate with these kids. I got to know quite a few of them. At the time, I was living with my mother at Trinity Methodist Church and after school and on weekends, I would be around and about the church property raking leaves or mowing the lawn or trimming the hedges. As the kids would walk up Bancroft and past Trinity Church to get back to the CSD campus on the hill, where many of them also lived, they would always wave and sign hello and I would reply with my limited knowledge in kind.

Unfortunately, when Frank turned in my timecard for assisting him at the BHS Pool, he was told that an assistant had to be eighteen and a US citizen to be employed by the school district. I was seventeen and a green card holding Legal Alien. Frank gave me my fifteen-dollar paycheck and reluctantly released me from my contract. This put an end to my plans for earning extra summer money. But the CSD kids never forgot that I had been there to help, even if, just for a while.

For some reason, I had decided that I would take up running in high school. I ran the mile in the fall and cross-country in the spring. I wasn't very fast but I was determined. Our team participated in a North Bay Cross-Country meet at De Anza High in Richmond, California. There were about a hundred and fifteen boys participating in the event. I came in at number 11. I didn't get a medal or even a ribbon; but I didn't feel too bad as I watched the ninety some odd kids crossing the finish line after me. Needless to say, I didn't get a letter in this event. The question of getting a letter did come up in track the following spring.

Our coach, Mr. Dickies had promised that if I came in no worse than third in at least three meets, he would get me my letter. Since this happened in my senior year, there wouldn't be a next year. I would either get it in the spring of 1960 or never. Up to this point I had come in third in two races. In the rest of the meets I came in fourth; not good enough for a letter.

Our last meet would take place at CSD. I was in the Mile race; that's four laps around the track. I did well on my first lap, but after that I slowed down a bit. That's when I heard it; the kids in the stands were actually starting to cheer me on. You've probably never heard anything like it unless you've been in a similar situation. Their cheering got me going. I caught up with the pack and got in a position to possibly win. I actually came in, in third place. The kids I had known from my pool days were in the stands and came to congratulate me. It was only a third-place finish but their cheers (yes, some of deaf kids could actually cheer and even whistle) had meant more than if I had won the whole enchilada. I had my three third place finishes; enough for a BHS letter.

Mr. Dickies told me when all the letters were being handed out that the last meet hadn't really counted in the scheme of things because it was an invitational and not a league meet. It was par for the course! At least I didn't have to buy a letter jacket; that would have been a red jacket with yellow leather sleeves and BHS on the front and your name. Back then, they cost twenty-five dollars and I didn't have enough dough in Mr. Piggy-Bank anyway.

Daddy-O, I really wanted that jacket. So far in my life, nothing had come to me easily.

After all this, I concentrated on my grades. If nothing else, I wanted to graduate. I didn't want to have to repeat any more classes and have to stay in high school when all my buddies were moving on.

On June 14th, 1960, along with six hundred and thirty of my contemporaries, I walked across the stage of the Big Theater at Berkeley High School and proudly picked up my high school diploma and walked out into the real world.

I had finally made it!

• • •

On a side note, Mr. Le Tendre who had been the principal at Berkeley High School since World War II had decided to retire with our class. He said he'd been at it for a long time and it was time to do some travelling.

41

AND THEN, THERE WAS TANGO

I remember this event as clearly as if it had happened just a week ago. It was one of those events when fate plucks you out from among the mere mortals, or a bunch of average, ordinary losers and turns you into a supreme being: A Cool Cat or as they might say today, a Stud or at least a Bacon; a Kevin Bacon, that is.

While attending Oakland Junior College, my friend Emi Zegrean was going to school in the city; that's San Francisco for you all not from the Bay Area. Somewhere along the way, she decided to get married. She was my age, so I asked why now? I was still a teenager, in other words, a big kid in fact. Marriage hadn't even entered my mind. I wouldn't be twenty until the following year and I felt as I was just on my way to adulthood. Notice how I said: on my way to adulthood, because I knew that I hadn't gotten there just yet. Well, like my mother always told me, girls mature faster than boys. She was right.

I chose this episode as the final chapter of my growing up phase because at this time, I was still only a legal resident of the United States. In other words, I still had to show my Green Card on a number of occasions; especially while seeking employment. I had actually been turned down for several jobs, all of which required US citizenship. However, as of October 1st 1963, I would no longer be Displaced and considered an Emigrant. I would be turning in my Green Card; well I actually kept it as a souvenir, and picking up my citizenship certificate. This story is not only about Emi's wedding but also about falling in love; oh, and also about learning to Tango.

Her name was Darlene.

I hadn't thought about her for almost fifty years, until one day while I was rummaging through our garage, looking for something. I got somewhat sidetracked and started to go through some old moving boxes from long ago cluttering the shelves, to see if I could find anything worth saving or to just toss their contents. This has been an ongoing process for the past several years; without much success, I must admit. That's when I came across an envelope addressed to me at that old address from long ago. Its paper now faded had originally been light purple or puce in color. It was hand addressed and contained a four-page handwritten letter on the same color paper. The postal cancellation on the envelope read Lodi, California, April 25, 1961. On the back of the envelope, it just said Dar with her old address. It hit me. The letter was from Darlene Watson (not her real last name).

Four personal-note-size light purple pages recounted the events at a wedding reception, some two weeks prior and Darlene's hope that I would not wait too long in calling on her and in the meantime, to send her a photograph. And, if I remember correctly, I did end up sending her one of my high school graduation photos, the one in the suit and tie, not the one with the cap and gown, which made me look like a dork with my rather prominent proboscis and oversized ears; my vain opinion.

You see, this whole affair had started as I stated earlier, with my school friend Emilia, Emi to her friends decided to get married to a fellow named Rico, a couple years her senior that she had met while attending college in San Francisco. My mother and I had been invited as her family and mine had both immigrated to the States from Eastern Europe, Hungary specifically, though through somewhat different and more circuitous route in the mid-1950s, some four to five years apart. Naturally, our families had fast become friends and remained so even after the passing of my dad in 1958.

This was going to be an old fashion Hungarian style wedding bash with an American twist. There would be lots and lots of old people and tons of screaming little kids. I thought, whoopee! That was exactly why I desperately tried every which way I could to come up with any excuse good enough to keep me from having to attend at least the reception part if not the whole affair, by claiming that I had insurmountable studying to do for some tests. In those days, that was a darn good excuse and usually worked for getting out of just about any social situation deemed unpleasant.

I of course had already decided that I would buy the newly-weds a nice gift that of course I could afford on my part-time job, but I just couldn't bear the thought of having to suffer through the reception. As a late bloomer, I didn't enjoy social gatherings all that much. It wasn't until much later that I really got into partying. So I had presented my case on several occasions prior, that I would most certainly attend the ceremony but I'd have to leave right after due to the aforementioned heavy homework load. At some point, I became certain that I had given a rather convincing argument for my case and it appeared that I might have succeeded and would be free to disappear before the reception started; phew!

I had been so wrong!

Emi however persisted, and very convincingly so, that I might just have a very good time with all the family and friends and lots of food. Now food would normally have captured my interest. I loved to eat and unfortunately it showed. However, I was going through a period of shall we say, life style adjustment. OK, I had decided that it was time to shed a few pounds because ever since I could remember, I had always considered myself fat, since we had relocated to the States that is. Friends always said I was cute and cuddly. Notice, they didn't say good looking? Even our family doctor got into the act by telling me on several occasions that I was just big boned. "You're a healthy young man," he would reassure me. "With that big healthy frame on you, you'll never be like one of those thin, beanpoles. Who'd want to be that skinny anyway?"

How about moi? Besides, who liked to be called chubby?

I wanted to be skinny. Well, maybe not that skinny but decid-edly skinnier than what I was. My mind had been made up. The food argument was not going to work this time!

"There will be lots of young women your age at the reception" Emi said. "You might meet somebody you like. And, you'll miss all the fun if you don't come". Of course, she was talking about the same girls I already knew; some who liked me and I didn't, and the ones I liked that weren't crazy about me. "Nah, way too much homework," I persisted.

Then, with the sweetest pout, she pulled out her trump card, "You're really going to hurt my feelings".

OK, that did it.

I was a softy at heart. Under no circumstances would I have ever wanted to hurt her feelings, and two, she sort-of threw into the mix "you haven't even met any of my bridesmaids. They're my friends from college and they're really cute, you know?"

"OK, I'll bite!" I thought.

Up to that point in my life, my luck with the female persuasion had not been very successful, to put it mildly. Let's say I was striking out a lot. To put it another way, with that batting average I'd have been on my way to the instructional league. Now don't get me wrong, I had on rare occasion dated some very nice girls like Gizella, in a casual sort of way, but in most cases I had the advantage of their mothers and sometimes even their fathers, liking me. That was like putting the kibosh on any relationship from the get-go in those days.

I wanted the fairer sex to want to date me because I was exiting, good looking, and athletic; know what I mean? Not because their mama and papa liked me. I was just about to complete my first year of junior college and thought I already knew almost everything there was to know about everything, except of course, women.

Then again, what guy can say they know everything about women anyway? Nuff said!

I had kept my nose to the grindstone and carried thirteen units those first two semesters, and burned a lot of midnight oil just to keep me above C-level. My mother had also advised me that if my grades would not improve, I'd be looking for a full-time job; I believe that was just a scare tactic on her part. Still, my grades did go up a notch.

After considerable deliberation, I decided that maybe attending the reception would not be such a bad idea; mostly you know, to appease my mother and shift her attention from that job finding threat. Besides, she insisted that I might meet a nice girl. By nice, I knew exactly what she meant, some sweet little plain Jane she approved of. Oh mama!

As far as weddings go, Emi's was a great event in the Hungarian community with lots of pretty bridesmaids as Emi had promised. There were of course the 'Cool Cat' grooms, lots of flowers, sentimental blessings, a ton of people and a rock 'n' roll band of all things. I had expected violins and a cimbalom (a Hungarian musical instrument). Family and lots of friends showed up, especially a slew of Emi's new college girlfriends as well as some of her high school buddies. Most of them were in my age group, but acted as though they were so much more grown-up and sophisticated; lade-da! In other words, my dreams of romantic conquest were soon shattered and my ego deflated; but certainly not my appetite.

Truth be told, that whole weight thing reared its ugly head, in my mind anyway. In addition, I had a civilized 'mama's boy' haircut and even in those days, girls were more attracted by healthy crops of filamentous skull covering; you know lots of hair. So, the tall, skinny guys with the puffy Brylcreem (a little dab'll do ya) pompadours were naturally the primary recipients of the fairest maidens' attention. And the bad boys ha-ha'd and teased while the chickees ooh'd and aah'd and giggled. That left a few of the, shall we say mere mortals or ordinary girls that hadn't made the cheerleading squad, or been invited to join the hottie cliques, to socialize with.

I was dressed in my Sunday best, three-piece combination of dark blue pants with a grey vest and suit coat and a white shirt with a nice tie from my father's collection, which by the way, I had learned to tie in a full-Winsor at a very early age. If you're going to go through the trouble of buying a tie, you might as well learn to do a full-Windsor. But, I digress!

After a wonderful church ceremony, we all caravanned over to the reception hall.

All the hip cats had converged at the bar, where drinks were free, and were entertaining all the future Miss Americas in a haze of cigarette smoke and exploding Champagne bubbles, while the band was only just tuning up.

As the band began to play their first tune, you could see the young women tapping their feet and snapping their fingers while very noticeably, swaying to the beat. The guys with all the hair and the attitude were too busy impressing the chickies with their egos to realize that the young ladies in fact desperately wanted to dance. All the bad boys seemed oblivious to the girls' desires or were it that they possibly didn't know how to dance, to this or any other kind of music anyway. For you see, this wedding was an old fashion wedding, even with the rock-n-roll band and all. The people in attendance were a mix of old and new Americans mostly of Hungarian origin and everyone else in between. They didn't all yet fully appreciate the immeasurable nuances of Rock 'n' Roll, so the band was resigned to playing waltzes and polkas and a czardas here and there with occasional guitar riffs of course.

The more the young women whined and tried in vain to coax the boys out onto the dance floor, the more the boys resisted, desperately gripping the bar. With drinks in hand, cigarettes dangling from their lips they simply didn't want to make fools of themselves. They all retreated ever further to a secure corner of the bar, for you see, all of a sudden, the band began playing a Tango.

I had just turned nineteen. The mother of one of the girls I had liked, Gizella, the one I had taken to the Senior Ball, had showed me some basic dance steps including the tango. She had told me that my chances not only with her daughter, but any eligible young lady would greatly increase if I turned some of my attention to this most graceful of pursuits. She had whispered with a wink "Women simply adore a man who can Tango." This was 1961. What'd I know? Besides, this was a mother talking. I listened respectfully.

I learned!

Naturally as the music played, I danced with some of the girls I had been chatting with. A couple of buddies, who had struck out with the cheerleaders, did likewise. I was being nice. The girls liked the attention, and they all liked to dance. As it turned out, Emi hadn't lied. There were more young ladies there then young men. I was enjoying myself, although I had not yet fallen in love.

Having finished a few dances and in bad need of refreshment, I sat down to have a soda and was chatting with no one in particular around the table when this young woman walked up to me. I had noticed her before, sitting with a group at another table. She introduced herself and explained that she was an acquaintance of Emi's and then asked if I would dance with her. I was somewhat taken aback. After all, at that point in my life, no strange woman had ever walked up to me and asked me to dance before at such an event, actually at any event. Let me rephrase that, a woman like that was usually seen on the arm of a more mature man with a gold watch, Armani suit and Italian shoes. I owned none of those.

"I didn't come with a date," she explained "and would really like to dance a Tango."

"I'm not a very good dancer," I stuttered as I felt perspiration trickling down my forehead, along my sideburns and down my neck. And I didn't usually stutter. I ran my finger inside my collar so that I could gulp in some air more comfortably.

"I only just learned the T- T-Tango...j- just really recently." I mumbled.

I was really getting nervous and when I got nervous, I had this stupid habit of scratching the back of my head and mumbling, which made me look like a rather confused dork. All the heads at the table were suddenly turned in my direction like I had just trans mutated into the Creature from the Planet-X.

In those days, a lady simply didn't ask a man to dance. This got me to staring into space, somewhere past and above the young woman's head. I felt a rush of red slowly rising out of my collar. Part of me wanted her to just disappear while the other couldn't help looking at her. She was so elegantly attired and ah, so demure. The old ladies around the table were whispering to each other. "Pss, pss, pss," they went. Oh boy, did I feel really stupid? She looked sincerely disappointed but smiled, very sweetly as she turned to walk away.

As I watched her leaving, I finally took a good look at the

auburn haired, older young woman, conservatively dressed in the white blouse under the simple grey suit. She looked very elegant and the whole ensemble was far from hanging shapelessly over her svelte frame. She was about my height, in her black heels. She didn't look any older than me. She had a sophisticated air about her though not at all conceited. I also noticed disappointment and sadness in her demeanor as though she really hadn't wanted to be here in the first place, but had done so as a favor to her younger friend who had just gotten married. Does that last part sound familiar; guilted? After she took a couple steps, she turned.

"If you should change your mind, I'll be sitting over there," she pointed to the empty chair at the table from whence she had come. Before she could take another step, the band started up again.

"Pa-rump-pa-rump, pa-rump pump pum!"

"Go on and dance with her," said one of the old ladies at the table. "Do you really want to sit here and listen to us gossip? Do it before one of those greasers (in 1950s, guys with greasy hairdos) grabs her."

Oh boy was I ever stuck on the horns of a dilemma.

Somewhat reluctantly, I got up and after a couple steps, reached out to tap her on the shoulder. "Would you like to dance?" I asked very awkwardly, and felt my blush level again rise towards my forehead. Awkward would have been an understatement.

"Why, I'd love to," she replied with a smile that melted right through my sorry facade. What a beautiful smile, I thought. Her veil of sadness appeared to slowly lift. Her eyes twinkled and my embarrassment evaporated. She reached for my hand and pulled me to the center of the dance floor. Her hands were warm, irresistibly warm. As a nineteen-year-old, I had not felt this kind of warmth coming from any woman before. Mind you, this was probably my very first experience being this close to a real woman. And I mean a woman older than the girls I had associated with to this point and the mothers that liked me, for associating with their daughters. You also have to remember, this was, 1961! Society wasn't as loosie goosy as it is today. Things were done more properly.

Slowly we began dancing and she introduced herself.

"My name is Darlene," she said, "and what's yours?" I had half expected miss or missus so and so.

"George," I barely got out.

As we started to slowly glide around the dance floor, she told me her story. She was twenty-one years old, two whole years older than me. She was definitely an *older* woman. I didn't volunteer my age. I figured, leave well enough alone! Even though behind that beautiful smile I could tell she had it all figured out? My buddies at Oakland Junior College would never believe this story, I told myself.

"I just recently went through a nasty divorce," she was saying.

OK, so she was not only older than me, she was already a divorcee, making her a social pariah of sorts. She might as well have been ten years my senior and swung from the chandeliers. Gulp! It was too late. As we moved around awkwardly at first, we were trying to get our steps in synch. It took most of that first dance. It took me quite a bit longer to consider the repercussions of my action.

"The man I was married to wasn't very nice," she continued. "The whole experience of the divorce really upset me; the things he said and the lies. I wasn't even going to attend this reception, and had actually called Emi and floated excuse after excuse trying to get out of this invitation. I offered my apologies, but she would have none of it. She said it would be good for me to get out and be around people, and besides she'd have her feelings hurt if I didn't show up. So, here I am. Sorry, I didn't mean to dump my dirty laundry in your lap."

"Well, I'm really sorry to hear about your divorce," I said "and I'm really glad you made it. I wasn't sure I'd be here either, you know studying for some big tests and stuff." She smiled in acknowledgement.

"I had attended college for a while myself," she said. "I understand about studying."

So far, the band had played a rather soft version of tango and I didn't know why it just didn't feel right. Then suddenly, I not only heard, but felt what made the tango, a Tango! One of the guys in the band had apparently arrived late but when he let it rip with the accordion, the dance suddenly caught fire. What's a tango without an accordion, right? It's just another dance. The staccato emanating from the squeeze box revved up the whole dance floor. We started to move more in unison, as though we had danced together like that forever. Already I could see that she danced better than any girl I had ever danced with before. Then again, she was no girl. She was a real woman.

"You're a pretty good dancer, for a beginner." She teased. "You probably tell that story about you being a novice, just to get a rise out of the young ladies. Then, you knock'em dead, right?"

"No, I really did just learn some steps…" I sputtered, "Very recently".

She put a slender fingertip to my lips and shushed me. Her fingernails were painted red which was the only bright color on her, except of course for her pretty red lips. We twirled around and around. After a couple of dances, I thought she would get bored with me or just tire and would want to return to her table, but she stayed with me right there on the dance floor, anticipating the next number. She almost wanted the band to hurry, lest I would decide to quit and I, well I wasn't going to, no siree Roberto. Are you kidding me? I couldn't have planned this any better. We held each other's hand for fear of the whole thing ending in a big poof, like the whole thing had been no more than a dream.

No one at her table seemed to miss her too much. I later found out that being by herself she had simply been assigned to that particular table by default. Everyone appeared to be enjoying deep champagne induced conversations, and laughing at almost every word uttered. We just danced on. By the third or fourth dance, she did something unexpected; unexpected that is in my nineteen-year-old reality. What can I say? I had always been rather slow catching on about the fairer sex. Up to this point, we had been whirling about, at a polite distance, the way you had been taught to at these social events.

Suddenly she pulled me in close, very close. Not the way a guy would try to nuzzle up to an Angora sweater clad high school girl at a sock hop. No, this was different. When she moved in tight, I could feel every curve of her body against mine.

"This is the way you really tango!" She whispered.

We whirled and high stepped as one. I felt like a chubby Rudy Valentino. To this point, I had been leading, however awkwardly, but all of a sudden, I was no longer certain, who in fact was leading whom. I wasn't even certain I knew some of those steps I was taking. We had practically taken over the middle of the dance floor, and people seemed happy enough to clear the way. Some of them even clapped, mostly the ladies. Even Emi, who had been busy doing her newlywed duties, turned to look and gave an approving wink. The macho cool-cats snickered making silly gestures and I heard one of them say: "look at the fat kid go!"

"Fat kid," I wanted to say "can any of you cool daddio's do this?"

I was slowly beginning to feel some of my hormones moving in unison as the rhythmic bending and heaving went on. I could barely feel her left leg guiding my right leg, and her right thigh pushing against my left, guiding my every move through the bends and swirls. In fact, I felt totally melded together with her as part of a four-legged whirling dervish-Valentino.

I would not have believed at that place in time that any two people could move that way. Jittering and hopping to rock-n-roll back then was considered 'Dirty Dancing', but not this. After all, this was Tango and it was beautiful!

I could feel her heart purring against my chest, as I am sure she could feel mine thumping. My excitement did not make her back away as a prudish school girl would have done, instead she held on even tighter, as though she never wanted to let go. No words passed between us. The rhythm and our eyes did all of the talking. I can't remember now, but I am certain that I had been smiling, the whole time. We stayed on the dance floor together like this until the very last dance.

When she finally got up to leave, she came over and whispered in my ear, "Call me!"

Back at her table, she had written her telephone number on one of the wedding napkins, and slipped it into my jacket pocket, as she softly planted the sweetest kiss on my cheek. She squeezed my hand, gently. I watched her walk out the door, in her tight gray skirt and white blouse accentuating her slender, perfectly proportioned (in my nineteen-year-old mind) body.

As I stood there, in the middle of the room, hands in my pocket and perspiration running down my forehead, I could barely hear the excited chatter of the people around. I realized that I had become the subject of some of their chatter. Some were teasingly commenting on my technique. A group of little girls stood to one side giggling and one of them commented "I didn't think you could make moves like that!" The much older girls just looked at me and whispered. I could only wonder what was being said. The best part was I didn't give a hoot...

It took a while, but finally, I even noticed signs of approval turned to admiration, from the Brylcreem greaser brigade; they raised their Vodka tonics in my direction in salutation.

I had accomplished something that none of them had even attempted; I had danced with the pretty divorcee; the untouchable, back in those days anyway. Our dancing had lasted almost three hours, and I was not even a bit tired. I felt exhilarated. I wanted to pound my chest and let out one of my Tarzan yells, which of course would have been immature. Well, I actually did it in the car on the way home. I remember my mother looking at me with big, rounded eyes, like I had completely lost my senses.

On the way back to my table, the old lady who had urged me on to dance with Darlene, motioned for me to come over and whispered very softly, "When I was in my prime, many, many years ago, I danced the Tango just like her" and she gave me a quick little wink.

Mind you, when my sweet wife Bonnie and my daughters Christina and Gizella get to read about this little episode that took place in my nineteenth year on this planet, I hope they realize that back then, I wasn't yet a husband or a daddy. The idea of matrimony and children had not even been seriously considered. They will have to consider the context of my story; about growing up and all.

At that very moment, the only thing I was praying for was to finish out my spring semester in junior college with decent enough grades so that I wouldn't have to go find a full-time job just yet, and I was really looking forward to my summer vacation. Until that point in time, romance hadn't even been picked up on my radar.

I must also add that after those few hours of gliding around the dance floor, I had felt like I had experienced this most total and wonderful relationship with a real woman that I had ever had, and would not have for a long time. We had met as strangers. We had talked about life. We had danced the Tango. We had developed feelings for one another. When she finally had to leave, she planted a warm kiss on my cheek and whispered to not forget to call her. At that moment, there was an anticipation of a further warm relationship with perhaps more kisses to come.

Unfortunately, it was not to be...

I also forgot to mention that, sitting with some of the older folks off to one side of the hall, was my mother. On the way home, I got a hefty lecturing from her regarding appearances and dancing too close and associating with strange divorced women of questionable reputation. I suppose, back then being divorced was not considered virtuous. She also repeated her warnings on dating redheads specifically. Considering that Darlene had auburn hair, I didn't get the connection. OK, so my mom was old-fashioned. You were supposed to dance with girls of your own age, preferably with curly brown hair, and at a very respectable distance. Most of all, you never, ever danced with a divorced woman, no matter whose friend she was. Somehow though, I had this tiniest inkling of an idea that deep inside, she might have been impressed by my newly acquired Tango moves.

"I don't even want you to think of ever seeing that woman and most especially of dating her. She's much too old and experienced for you! Blah, blah, blah..."

It all went in one ear and out the other.

OK, maybe that thing about her admiration of my tango moves

might just have been the imaginings of my less-than-fully-developed thinking. The rest of her lecture, well I honestly can't recall. I was too busy thinking about Darlene. And of course, I did do my Tarzan yell...

That night and for many nights to come, I dreamed of Darlene.

After the wedding reception, Emi had entrusted in my care, her black and white 1956 Ford Fairlane convertible, while she and her new husband honeymooned on one of the Caribbean islands I believe. I was to return it to her, intact, two weeks later at their new apartment, where they were to have a small gathering for some close friends and members of the wedding. Up to this point, I had not had the courage to call Darlene. Like I said, I was slow to react in these situations.

Emi however, reassured me that she would be there. As they said back then, I put on my glad rags and got to the party on time. At this point I was also under the weird delusion that I actually looked really good because I had, I believed, lost some weight; based on what angle I read the bathroom scale. As soon as I arrived, I scanned to room but I didn't find the person I was looking for. Emi had noticed my obvious disappointment and called me aside. Darlene wasn't coming. "She went back to Arkansas to visit her parents and more than likely won't be back. I'm really sorry about that," she added "I could tell you liked her."

Talk about an understatement.

Hey, I was nineteen. Up to that point in my life, she had been the hottest woman I had ever met, had a good time with and lost, all in one day. So maybe, just maybe, it is time to get rid of the light purple note in the light purple envelope with a hint of her perfume still lingering. Or is that also just my imagination?

By the way, this story really happened just as I wrote it. However, if I had to swear to the veracity of every minute detail, I must admit to some fuzziness.

But Darlene, she was very real. And the reception, it really took place just as I have described it. Ask Emi. I never did lay eyes on Darlene ever again. That letter I received must have been mailed by her just a couple days before she finally decided to return home.

When I finally had gotten up the nerve to call her a week later, I had been too late. I was told that she had in fact moved away without leaving a forwarding address.

I of course had pretty much all but forgotten about the wedding and the reception afterwards, until I came upon Darlene's purple note, because it had reminded me of that day in 1961, when I really learned to Tango.

I even wrote this short ballad commemorating this event...
I was just nineteen,
She was twenty-one
She'd done many things
I hadn't done

A bad marriage
Made her a divorcee
Everyone told me
I should stay away

She came and asked me
To dance with her
And reluctantly
I followed her

She pulled me in closer
And I heard her whisper
Come on let us go
I'll show you how to Tango

Pa-rum, pa-rum, par-rum pump pum
Pa-rum, pa-rum, par-rum pump pum
Pa-rum, pa-rum, par-rum pump pum
Hey, hey, she showed me how to Tango!

Just a final note on this episode, in the letter, Darlene wrote that as soon as she got some photographs developed, she would send me one of herself. She never did. So, Darlene and our tango together will forever be just a click away in my photographic memory.

As Orson Wells once quipped "If you want a happy ending, you have to know when to end your story."

This is a good spot!

Darlene, she showed me how to tango (GK drawing)

42

FULL CIRCLE

The older I get, the more I contemplate where I started out, where I have been, and what I have accomplished. Of course, this story deals with my early years, which is why I decided to end my tale with a slice from my nineteenth year on this planet. I remember with fondness those earlier times that at the time I didn't realize how exiting they really were. My daughters Christina and Gizella, friends and even strangers had to tell me. To me, it was simply the life I lived.

As I wrote in my introduction, in 2008, I had the opportunity to revisit some of those old places I had walked in, way back when I was a kid. That whole trip to Europe had been a total quirk of fate. Had my daughter Christina no wanted to get married over in Europe, I might not ever have made the journey. For various reasons, over the years, I either had not the means or desire to revisit that past. It has been one of my greatest regrets. Bottom line, I'm glad I did it and now I could write about it.

My wife Bonnie and I weren't able to visit every single place that I had lived in before immigrating to the US, but I did get to revisit a few of them: Budapest, Paris and Algrange and even Strasbourg. Had I been able to go to Austria, I know the fences around Schmitzberg Lager had been torn down a long time ago and even the camp might no longer exist; so there wouldn't have been anything left to see except the new housing developments. Now Cavillargues in Southern France has changed considerably. The mines are long gone and the little village has turned into a retirement community centered on a 19th century church with an old 12th-16th century castle to explore, nearby.

After a fourteen-hour trans-Atlantic flight, with a two-hour stopover in Houston, we landed at Charles De Gaulle Airport, about 25 kilometers or 15 miles northeast of Paris. What can I say? This airport was huge. To get from there to downtown Paris, you had the choice of taking a bus, limo or a train similar to BART. We listened to some people *in the know* and they convinced us to take the train.

"It's that way. You take a left turn and go downstairs," a helpful fellow passenger advised us. The long and short of it: it was about a mile walk just to get to the escalator which took us three levels below the airport proper to the train station. Since this had been our first trip overseas (since I came to the United States in 1956), we naturally over-packed. Bonnie's and my suitcase tipped the scale just right at or slightly above the limit. They were heavy! Dragging one of them, I lost five pounds...

The irony of this was that when we immigrated to the US, our three suitcases didn't weigh as much as we were taking in just one of our suitcases for our trip.

As I said, this Metro train system was similar to our own Bay Area Rapid Transit. The ride was comfortable enough and took about an hour to downtown Paris with all the stops in between. I also noticed some changes from the last time I had been in France, over fifty years ago. From my window seat, I was mesmerized by the passing scene, so strange yet so familiar. I could of course read all the signage and advertisements which weren't that different from what you see over here except of course they were in French. The other thing that was also all too familiar was graffiti. When I was a kid in France, we occasionally absconded with some chalk from the classroom and wrote silly stuff on building walls. If the teacher ever caught us, we had to clean it off. If on the other hand, one of the local gendarmes nabbed us, we were lectured and scolded, and we had to clean it up, sometimes with threats of being taken to jail. They took it very seriously even though chalk was easily erasable.

The graffiti we saw while the train rumbled toward Paris would have put to shame anything I'd seen in New York or our own Bay Area. These images were eight to ten feet high and several feet wide and done in permanent paints. They covered the sides of industrial buildings, signs and advertisements. I guess the artists wanted to make sure that travelers wouldn't have any difficulty in seeing their chef-d'oevres (masterpieces).

My second surprise came when we arrived at the **Latin Quarter** Metro station, which happened to be three levels below the street. We also discovered that the elevators were under repair that day and the escalator was only working in the Down direction. This meant that we had to drag two pieces of luggage totaling almost a hundred pounds, up three sets of stairs, about forty to forty-five steps, each. We were both pleasantly surprised when a young woman offered to help Bonnie with her suitcase. That pleasant surprise carried all the way through our four-day stay in Paris.

When we had ridden to Paris to the American Consulate, back in 1954, the train personnel were grumpy, the cab drivers were sultry, the concierge at our hotel was surly, the waiters were insufferable and the rest of the inhabitants we had contact with, were just plain unfriendly. My father had wanted to go to the Notre-Dame since we would probably never be able to return to Paris again.

It was a Sunday and we went inside just as a mass was about to finish but just in time for the collection. A surly looking rail-thin monk was passing a basket at the end of a ten-foot pole, up and down each row. If someone didn't drop a donation in the big basket, he would shake it in front of their nose until the penitent broke down and contributed. When he got to our row, you could hear the clinking, rattling basket approaching. Apparently, not everyone was able to donate bills. When it had made in front of my father's nose, the surly friar kept shaking it until my father got some coins from his pocket and dropped them into the basket. Apparently, friar Surly didn't think the donation sufficient and kept on shaking the basket until my father pulled out a hundred Frank bill and tossed it in the basket. Looking sideways, I could see my dad's face turning beet red. "Let's get out and get some fresh air," he grumbled between gritted teeth. We got up and went outside before the mass had ended.

"That nasty friar just irritated me to no end," he told us. "They literally charge you to pray. I wonder what God has to say about it?"

In 2008, I went to visit the Notre-Dame with Bonnie. Everyone seemed friendly. No one shook collection baskets under our noses. We purchased some postcards. We burned a candle for my mom and dad. I left a donation in one of the collection boxes. It had been a heartwarming experience. My guess was that all the greedy friars were doing penance somewhere in Purgatory.

In 1954, we also went to visit the Eiffel Tower. Unfortunately, due to financial constraints, we could only afford to go to the first level. We only did this so we could say that we'd gone up the famous landmark.

In 2008, Bonnie and I visited the Eiffel Tower, a first for her. We of course went all the way to the top; meaning, we rode the elevator up to the third level and actually climbed up to the observation deck. We even sat in the second level lounge and had a drink.

At our hotel in the Latin Quarter, the concierge was very pleasant and helpful and even endured my attempts at communicating with her in her native Lingua Franca. I must admit, it took me a couple days to feel comfortable in French even though, for seven and a half years that we had lived there, it had been my everyday language. It wasn't so much the speaking part I had trouble with; it was trying to understand what they were saying because they spoke so fast that my ears (maybe more like my brain) couldn't keep up with them.

To sum it up, the attitude of the people we dealt with in 2008 was such an improvement over that of the people we had encountered in 1954 Paris. Concierge, cabbies, tour guides, store clerks, Starbucks baristas (yes, they have Starbucks), they were all helpful and pleasant. Only one thing hadn't changed, but then I would have really been disappointed; waiters. They were a bunch of surly, know-it-all, brusque, ill-tempered, and disagreeable and in general, crabby. But then again, if I couldn't have counted on Parisian waiters to be the way I had fondly remembered them, my whole world view would have been shattered. After a four-day fun-filled adventure in Paris where we visited the Louvre, the aforementioned Eiffel Tower and the Notre Dame, as well as a side-trip to Versailles, we packed it in for our next destination.

As I have said, our concierge was a very gracious and helpful woman. In fact, contrary to our helpful flying mates who had suggested the Metro to Paris as being the cheapest mode of transportation to get there, they were wrong. She recommended a limo. To which I replied "C'est very expensive, non?"

"It is actually the same price as a bus ride and even the Metro," she replied.

She'd been right. She got us a Mercedes limo, driven by of all people, a young Chinese gentleman who spoke perfect French and English. This is how we rode back in class to Charles De Gaulle for the next leg of our adventure: Naples.

That's one place I had never been to.

We flew to Naples where another limo picked us up for a two-hour drive to Praiano. The reason it took two hours is because the direct route which included an eleven-mile tunnel to the coast had to be closed due to a deadly car crash. As a result, we got to see some smaller sites that we would not have seen, had we gone through the tunnel. We stayed in Praiano on the Amalfi Coast for six days and celebrated our daughter's nuptials to Doug Messer. The ceremony in Praiano was presided over by the deputy mayor. We celebrated the event with a dinner in Positano; the very same restaurant that can be seen in the movie **Under the Tuscan Sun**.

We explored the damage done by Mt. Vesuvius to the towns of Pompeii and Herculaneum. This, I recommend to everyone who goes to Italy go and visit.

From Naples, we rode TGV or ITALO in Italy (Train Grande Vitesse or Bullet Train) to Roma where we stayed for three days. The 177 kilometers, or 110-mile ride took only about one hour and ten minutes; in the comfort, you get on a 737.

In Rome, we explored the Coliseum, naturally. As we were having dinner at the Piazza de Navona, we discovered that they were shooting a scene from 'Angels and Demons, just on the other side of the Piazza. And wouldn't you know it; we got to see Tom Hanks reshoot about a half a dozen takes of the same scene that we actually saw in the movie. I stopped the movie to see if I could spot us standing behind the barricades. Of course, it was too dark to see. Not only that but we also got to toss '3 Coins in the Trevi Fountain'. It doesn't take much to get us exited. Our Italian sojourn was most enjoyable and fun-filled, but could probably fill a few chapters in a book on travel. We flew to our next destination from Rome.

In keeping with the theme of my story and working on the full-circle aspect, our next stop was Budapest, where my whole adventure started way back on April 12, 1942. As opposed to Paris, I had nothing to rely on to compare with a previous experience. Since I was just a couple months shy of three years of age when we left my city of birth, my memories were limited to what was handed down to me by my parents and those occasional trips I have taken in my dreams; oh, except for that one brief scene where my mother is tossing us a bag lunch from the fourth story balcony.

I had landed in a place that felt so familiar to me, yet foreign, like it would have been to any tourist coming from another country; except that they all spoke my language. It was an eerily strange feeling, hearing people speak a language I only understood, not Bonnie. Most of my adult life everyone on the street spoke English. The TV and radio, spoke English. Business was conducted in English. To say the least, it was sort of a culture shock although a pleasant one, when I woke up the second day and the waitress in the coffee shop at the hotel didn't ask me for my order in English.

Bonnie and I did all the touristy things expected of foreign visitors. I did however greatly need to get back to my roots, if you will. Our first four days in Budapest, we stayed at the Hotel Victoria on the Buda side of the Danube. As it turned out, the hotel we moved to on the Pest side, happened to be within about a mile from the neighborhood where I was born. So you understand what I'm talking about, here's a brief explanation.

Buda or Óbuda was built on the hilly or western side of the Danube River, and Pest sprung up on the very flat eastern side of the river. Buda and Pest became a single city, Budapest, with the unification of the two independent cities, on November 17, 1873.

As we walked to my old neighborhood on a rather hot June

morning, I made certain that I documented every step, well almost every step. Our address had been number 20, Nap Utca (Sun Street), in the seventh district or precinct of Budapest. We made it to my old neighborhood and found the old address. I took some photos with my trusty digital camera, although there was nothing left of the building I had lived in but a pile of rubble.

As I wrote in the early part of my story, the old four-story condominium complex with the balconies looking down on the courtyard, had been leveled by one of many Allied or Soviet aerial attacks and was never restored or rebuilt. Instead, it had been replaced by an ugly 1960s two-story concrete, Soviet Block multiple-family housing structure. Rubble from the old building was still piled up ten to twelve feet high, on the other side of the property and was fortunately covered in a mantle of tall weeds. The entrance to the newer structure had the old number twenty affixed to it. As we were leaving, I wondered if somewhere underneath that pile of rubble, some remnant of our former life there might be hiding, to be discovered some day by whoever would eventually come along to clean up the mess.

"This is not my old house," I complained to Bonnie. "It's my old neighborhood, my old street, our old number, but it's not our old house."

I had half expected to be able to walk into the old courtyard and look up to the fourth story balcony and watch my mom throw down the paper sack containing the sandwiches. Alas, the old balcony was but a memory.

As we started to walk back to our hotel, I couldn't help but notice that almost all of the buildings on Nap Utca were still pockmarked from WWII as well as by some blemishes of the 1956 Revolt. All of those blemishes were however covered by the signs of a new disease: esoteric graffiti by new age taggers. I was momentarily transported back to inner-city USA. Even stranger was the fact that the former socialist government had not seen it fit to repair any of the war-damaged structures; yet in recent years, brand new vinyl windows and window-mounted air-conditioners had been tacked on to the outer facades.

On our return walk, we stopped by the outer gates to the children's hospital where I was born. It was literally within a couple hundred steps from our old flat. Across the street from there was the park where my dad would pull me in the big red (MATEOSZ) truck. It had gone to the dogs, literally. It was now a canine park. I didn't bother to cross the street to take a closer look. I was letting my memories fill in the gaps.

Bonnie and I walked up and down ***Váci Utca***, the Rodeo Drive of Budapest. I tried in vain to figure out where my mother's restaurant might have stood, to no avail. We ate at a number of great Hungarian restaurants and the famous ***Gerbeaud*** pastry shop. Every bite I ate seemed so familiar like my mother had cooked or baked it. I bought some trinkets for Bonnie, t-shirts for the family and a Budapest baseball cap. And therein lies a sign of times: baseball in Budapest? Get out!

After eight great days in my city of birth, we flew to Eindhoven in the Netherlands to meet up with my old school chum from Berkeley High School days, Karel Bemelmans. He picked us up in his Mercedes E320 and after a four-star dinner at an airport restaurant, yes 4-star at the airport, we started our road trip through the Benelux countries on our way to Algrange.

Before we got to Algrange, we did stop off at Strasbourg to meet up with Karel's lovely wife Marie-Louise who at the time was a senator from the Netherlands, representing her country at the Council of Europe whose charter includes: Defending Human Rights, Raising consciousness about cultural identities, Social and Medical Issues, Helping new rising European Democracies implement political and constitutional changes and so on. We got a grand tour of the architecturally fascinating Council building and actually got to attend a full council in session from the upstairs gallery. Just so that we would feel right at home, we got treated to a full-scale demonstration with loudspeakers and protest signs by citizens of one of the former Soviet Republics...

Following a superb dinner at one of Strasbourg's finest restaurants, we had a good night's sleep in a 4-star hotel, courtesy of Marie-Louise. She did make us feel like royalty!

The following morning, we took off from Strasbourg and headed north-east toward Metz and eventually to Algrange. As I have stated a couple times at least, this whole European journey had to include Algrange. Only second to Budapest, this was where most of my early childhood memories originated. I just had to get back there and see if things were as I remembered, as I had so often dreamed about or had the passage of time imposed some serious changes to the images in my memory banks?

Let's just say that Algrange seemed a lot smaller than when we had left in 1956. The main street didn't seem as long as I remembered. And of course, I didn't run into Lydia or any of my buddies from way back when. Not only that, but when I asked if anybody recognized any of the names I asked about; they hadn't heard of any of them. I thought I had come home for a moment and realized that I was nothing more than a stranger, a tourist. I was back in a different timeline, an alternate universe…

Gone were the rows of old three-story mine housing buildings. The hillsides had been full of them in the 1950s. They had all been replaced by single-family homes. The old mine shop buildings have been renovated and turned into artist studios. The mine's administration building has been turned into a shi-shi hotel. One of the buildings at our old address at number 6 Rue de Londres had been turned into some sort of social club, the one we had lived in, had been torn down for extra parking, as everyone in town, seemed to now own a car or two.

All the storefronts on the main street had been spruced up and painted with new signage. Ecole Mixte, my old school, had been renovated and flower beds surrounded the perimeter. As we stopped to take some pictures and walk the grounds, the cheery twitter of small voices emanated from the schoolhouse. Summer school was in session.

The Gendarmerie/Hotel de Ville next door had become la Mairie. There were no longer any gendarmes. They were now Police. They no longer wore Kepi style pillbox looking hats but baseball caps, just like American cops. Oh yes, and instead of bicycles, they rode around in smallish European police cruisers. Ah, and finally, back in the old days of the 1950s, we could kick a soccer ball around in the middle of the street, in the middle of the day because you could see any vehicle coming a mile up and down the street. At the time of our visit, vehicles of all makes and models lined the spaces next to the sidewalks on both sides of the street.

Algrange had turned into a yuppie suburb; a bedroom community and the old Miner's Fork Restaurant was now just as shi-shi as the guests frequenting it.

As I said earlier, I got to visit my old address on Rue de Londres, walk up and down some of the old streets, visit my old school, walk up the steps of the Catholic Church and go into the pastry shop that used to be Monsieur Schmouk's and buy three Baba-Rums. I was also surprised to find that two movie theaters, the Eden and Sax had been closed down. Where Eden once stood, there was a big new sign indicating Video rentals. You would now have to drive a couple towns over to see a movie on the big screen; of course, now it was easy, everybody has a car.

My visit to Algrange wouldn't have been complete had I not had the opportunity to go up to the Plateau and revisit the place where in 1954, my friend Lucien and I had our encounter of the UFO kind. I was certain that there would still be a thirty-five-foot diameter ring of wilted vegetation, right there where I saw it way back then. In the back of his mind, my friend Karel was hoping that he could prove to me once and for all that no such things as UFOs exist. He desperately wanted to find something that would indicate that he had been right all along. Of course, we were both disappointed. There was no evidence to show that a flying saucer had or had not landed on the Plateau way back in 1954.

Shrinks, they want to help you by trying to convince you that you didn't really see what you saw; yet they have no alternative. Oh hell, they mean well!

The street we followed to get to the top, didn't actually go all the way. We had to climb almost a half a mile on a dirt road to get there. Did I mention that it was about 96 degrees that day, a temperature that would have been unheard of in 1954? The Plateau looked pretty much the same; extending a mile plus in each direction from our point of ascent. However, a landing strip which was not there in 1954 had been roughly carved out in the middle of the grassy field and a limp wind sock on a crooked pole hung there in silent testament to the change. The leveling of the landing strip might also have been the reason that the 10 to 12-foot-high mound that the UFO was hovering next to had been removed, like an old pimple. No wonder I couldn't locate the exact landing spot.

There was also a non-descript thirty-foot-long by half that wide, sheet-metal building with a securely locked door at one end of the landing strip, to add to the puzzle. Further down from that structure, a small herd of goats lazily grazed the tall ground cover around a tall windmill, without much apparent success and without any dogs or human supervision.

My thoughts on this setup: cover for UFO research by French Black Ops in cooperation with the US Military. My buddy Karel's theory: horticultural research, as evidenced by the sadly wilting patch of a variety of garden flowers. Then why the secured door and blacked out windows on the rather large metal building? And why would you need an airstrip; to fly in seed packets, hum? You know I'm just kidding. But what if I'm right?

Karel drove us back through the Benelux region via a different route than the one we had driven on the way down from Eindhoven. We stayed a few days in a wonderful little inn, right on the canal by Miller's Bridge called 'S Molenaarsbrug Hotel Restaurant. It was quaint, friendly and very pleasant and comfortable. The meals were excellent and the staff and management bent over backwards to make our stay a unique one. Both Bonnie and I wished we could have spent a few more days there just lying around or sipping some cocktails on the veranda, watching the water fowl floating lazily along the canal. Unfortunately, our time was up and our return to reality and California were inevitable. Thirty days and a few thousand dollars later, we were ready to board our jet at Schiphol Airport in Amsterdam, for our return flight to the US.

Here, I must inject a caveat: there are numerous details from our trip of 2008 that I did not elaborate on because they were not relevant to my story. Someday perhaps, if time permits, I'll write a more extensive tale of our experiences.

Our flight back took over fourteen hours due to some glitches caused by inclement weather in Houston. We felt it had taken an eternity, when we finally arrived home. Then again, I thought about it: compared to my original voyage to the United States which had taken seven plus days, way back in 1956, we had really made it back in a flash.

In my mind, I had come full circle; well almost. I had retraced some of my steps from long ago and managed to touch some of those places from my memory closest to my heart, perhaps for the last time; although I do hope I can make a more leisurely return sojourn someday and see if I had missed anything.

So, for now, Goodbye, Ciao, Arrivederci, Auf Wiedersehen, Au Revoir and Viszontlatasra!

My wife Bonnie on a Double Decker tour bus going around the Arc de Triomphe in Paris, in June 2008 (GK Photo)

That's me at the entrance to Eglise Saint Severin in Paris, in June 2008 (Photo by Bonnie Kapus)

My wife Bonnie inside the Coliseum in Rome, in June 2008 (GK Photo)

One of my best shots of an arch in Pompeii, Italy, in June 2008 (GK Photo)

That's me sipping beer at a festival in a Budapest square, in June 2008 (Photo by my daughter Christina)

The corner of Nap Utca (Sun Street) as it looked in June of 2008. The pockmarks, chipped masonry are the remnants of WWII, which the Communist government did not deem essential to rehabilitate. Since then, the newly elected Conservative government has started to slowly erase the damages of WWII.

View from the Royal Palace on top of Buda Hill, looking down on Adam Clark Plaza, the Chain Bridge, Built by Adam Clark and a view of Pest on the opposite side of the Danube River with the Parliament building at center left top of picture, June 2008. (GK photo)

That's me in one of the balconies of the Royal Palace in Budapest, Hungary, June 2008 (Photo by Bonnie Kapus)

My wife Bonnie in front of the entrance to the Royal Palace on the Buda Hilltop, June 2008 (GK Photo)

My wife Bonnie with Marie-Louise and Karel Bemelmans inside the Council of Europe building in Strasbourg, France, June 2008. (GK Photo)

That's me on the steps of the old Catholic Church in Algrange, Moselle, France, June 2008. (Photo by Bonnie Kapus)

Bonnie in front of my old school in Algrange, June 2008. (GK Photo)

My old buddy Karel Bemelmans and I on the steps of the old Catholic Church in Algrange, Moselle, France, June 2008. (Photo by Bonnie Kapus)

SOME AFTERTHOUGHTS

S oon after graduating from Berkeley High School, my mother helped me buy my first car. Like every other kid, I wanted something cool; what could be called a chick-magnet, today. Instead, I got something 'practical' 1952 lime-green, 4-door, Plymouth Cambridge, for $200.00.

A year later, I sold it to my friend Karel's dad, for $200.00. I turned around and bought a car that was definitely cooler, a white, 1951 Chevy 2-door, for $200.00. This was one of those cars that mechanically inclined teenagers would soup-up with dual carburetors and glass-packs (Loud mufflers), and of course a groovy paint job and pin striping. I was going to do all that, but decided to not follow through with my customizing plans; instead I started saving for my next car. I sold the Chevy back to the guy I had bought it from, a couple years later for $150.00.

By then, I had been working and was able to save up enough money to buy my friend Eugene's girlfriend's car, a 1957 Plymouth Fury. I paid her $500.00 for her car which had reasonably low mileage and was in excellent condition. I wish I would have kept it because this car would be worth a fortune today. The 1957 was 3-inches longer and 5.5 inches lower than the 1956. It had white and gold side trim with anodized gold wheel covers and gold grille bars.

Power came from a 318ci V8. It produced 290hp with dual four-barrel carburetors, special camshaft, high compression engine heads, heavy-duty valve springs and free-flowing dual exhausts. This model had the now famous Torque Flite transmission which you controlled via a 5 push-button, shifter. Only 7,438 Furys were produced when the car cost $2,925 and I had one of them. I kept this car for several years because it was a chick-magnet.

Unfortunately, one evening, on the way home from a party, I got egged on into a little race on I-80 which had not yet been completed past Richmond. These four kids in a red and white 1958 Ford Sunliner Convertible, challenged me to a little race. They were yelling things like "That thing can't keep up with this baby" and "Show us what you got under the hood". "I'll show them," I thought, so I said "OK, let's do this!"

They took off like a bat outta-hell. I punched the 1-button or low gear and soon I was even with the Ford. So, for a while we rolled head-to-head, until I punched the 2-button which was middle range, but they still kept up with me. Finally, I hit D-button or drive and the fury took off like a rocket. When I looked at the speedometer, it read 105 MPH and the Ford was several hundred feet behind me. There was an off-ramp because the freeway ended. So, I got off, made a left to go over the freeway and was merging onto the opposite lanes just as the Ford was being pulled over by a CHP (California Highway Patrol) car.

I loved that car, but eventually, I messed up the engine with all the high-speed racing. I also had failed to check the oil level and these big engines needed close attention. At some point, it needed a valve job and I couldn't afford it. So, I ended up selling it to an auto dismantler who 'took-it-off' my hands for $50.00. I believe, I got snookered, but I learned to take better care of my car.

• • •

Let's switch topics here, for a moment: I wanted to say a few words about my art. My folks told me that early on people predicted that I would become an artist. There is even a photograph of me taken at about a year and a half of age where I am sitting in this high chair, a piece of paper spread in front of me and a pencil firmly in my grip.

I can attest to the fact that scribbling pictures of one sort or another was what had kept me out of trouble since I could walk. I could sit at the old kitchen table and doodle for hours, stopping only to ask my father to put a point back on the pencil. Since there was no TV in our lives until we landed in the United States, I could doodle while listening to the radio broadcast or my own humming.

In 1954, when the regional federation of schools in Moselle (county) held an art contest, I decided to enter it. The theme was 'A Wedding Celebration'. It was to be done in pen and ink, water colors or color pencils. Because I couldn't make up my mind on which medium to use, I went with a combo of all the above. Of course, I picked a Hungarian wedding, making my task a little harder. When it was all done, I was rather proud of my master-piece. I took it to school and our teacher packaged all the entries and sent them off to contest headquarters. It took a couple months to evaluate all the entries and when it was all done, I was awarded 4th Prize; a very nice book. I thought my illustrative rendering was better than fourth prize, but my father said I had won something that many other kids hadn't. I still have the book. I wish we could have had a photograph taken of my masterpiece...

I can safely state that I have drawn and painted literally hun-dreds of pictures since those early days. Many have been very good according to some of the beholders; some not so great. Some were even masterpieces, to me anyway. None are hanging in gal-leries, not yet anyway; but maybe someday, just maybe...

The following illustrations were done for a book by an author who has since passed away. The title of the book was 'The Heroes Will Return Again'. It was an epic poem about the history and leg-end of the Hungarian people. I actually translated the book for the author, from Hungarian into English and the translation appeared back-to-back with the original Hungarian.

I was asked to do eighteen (18) illustrations in pen and ink as well as front and back covers in color and the book layout. As I was still working at my regular job as a Computing Systems Engineer which was nothing more than a glorified computing tech, it took me the whole summer of 1995 to execute the illustrations and the cover art. I spent a lot of late nights working on this project with little sleep, but was greatly rewarded when I finally saw the fin-ished product.

I also discovered to my dismay that after having delivered the completed layout and illustration package, the author asked the printer to insert additional material which I had not deemed worthwhile to include. Then again, she was the author and making changes was her prerogative, however bad the idea might have been.

Swallowing my pride, I was still rewarded by seeing my art in print for which I received a number of compliments as I joined her for a couple of book signings. It was nice to know that people appreciated the work that had gone into not only illustrating but translating the book and finally seeing it in print.

Some of those illustrations are interspersed throughout this book.

My mom stepping out of my 1957 Plymouth Fury, in 1961 (GK Photo)

Imagination – One of the many mazes I have created – Was used on the cover of the LBL Computer Center Newsletter back in 1982 - (GK drawing)

ABOOKS

ALIVE Book Publishing and ALIVE Publishing Group
are imprints of Advanced Publishing LLC,
3200 A Danville Blvd., Suite 204, Alamo, California 94507

Telephone: 925.837.7303 Fax: 925.837.6951
www.alivebookpublishing.com

CPSIA information can be obtained
at www.ICGtesting.com
Printed in the USA
BVOW06s2347050218
507355BV00002B/21/P

9 781631 320439